Mozart in the Jungle

Mozart in the Jungle

Sex, Drugs, and Classical Music

Blair Tindall

Atlantic Monthly Press
New York

All events in *Mozart in the Jungle* are true, and all characters are real. However, the following names have been changed: Sydney, Jayson, Percy, Betty, Mr. Geizhals, Maria, Jean, Frank, Donald, José, Peter Huffine, Jimmy, and "Basically Baroque."

Published simultaneously in Canada
Printed in the United States of America

FIRST EDITION

Library of Congress Cataloging-in-Publication Data
Tindall, Blair.
    Mozart in the jungle : sex, drugs, and classical music / Blair Tindall.
    p. cm.
    ISBN 0-87113-890-5
    1. Tindall, Blair.   2. Oboe players—United States—Biography.
I. Title.
ML419.T48A3 2005
781.6'8'0973090511—dc22   2005041105

Atlantic Monthly Press
an imprint of Grove/Atlantic, Inc.
841 Broadway
New York, NY 10003

05 06 07 08 09   10 9 8 7 6 5 4 3 2 1

For my parents,

Carliss Blossom McGarrity Tindall and George Brown Tindall

You ask my opinion about taking the young Salzburg musician into your service. I do not know where you can place him, since I feel that you do not require a composer or other useless people. . . . It gives one's service a bad name when such types run around like beggars; besides, he has a large family.

> —Letter from Archduke Ferdinand's mother,
> upon learning of his interest in Mozart,
> 1771

CONTENTS

Third Movement:
Symphonic Metamorphoses

Prelude

JANET DIRECTED THE taxi driver to stop just past the Manhattan School of Music on 122nd Street, where I heard students practicing violin scales, trumpet études, and clarinet melodies in the inexpensive apartments nearby. The cab stopped halfway down Claremont Avenue, on a somewhat seedy block bordering Harlem, and I followed Janet inside the foyer of a narrow tenement. The front door buzzed open; we passed into a hall's murky light, then out a fire escape exit to a barren airshaft. A bulb lit up an old paint-blistered door. Music was throbbing from behind it.

"It's just me, Donald!" Janet shouted, punching the mechanical doorbell. One, two, three deadbolts unlocked. The door creaked open and music blasted out.

A window shot open up above. "Jesus fucking Christ, will you shut the fuck up?" A Gristede's bag sailed out the window over our heads, just missing me but spraying coffee grounds everywhere else.

A scruffy man in a stained yellow T-shirt pulled us inside, barricading the door with a five-foot pole lock anchored to the floor. Two Virgin Mary candles from a local bodega flickered in the darkness to the beat of music pulsing from huge old Klipsch speakers. I could smell, faintly, gas leaking from somewhere and mildew creeping across the gray walls. Through the metal accordion grate on the windows, mountains of garbage accumulated in the shaft. My heart started beating faster.

How did classical music ever bring me to this place?

Three men I knew howled with laughter on the frayed brown sofa. "Dude, I'll never get over him fucking his sister." Stan choked on his words. "It's so out."

1

Donald just shrugged and pulled on the fat joint that was making its rounds.

"Yeah, I know. Now their kid's fucking his aunt," Milton chimed in, pushing his stringy blond bangs aside to see the knobs on a large vacuum-tube amplifier. "Listen to this riff. Man, you're not gonna believe." The record blared, and they were silent for a moment.

Stan sighed during a lull in the music. "Those cats could really play."

I watched Janet bend over the desk to snort cocaine through a straw. I'd never done coke, but I was feeling pressured to try Donald's stash too. Donald drummed his fingers on the table, regarding me suspiciously. Suddenly, his attention shifted to Milton, who sprang back to the couch to roll a crisp $100 bill into a tube.

"Miltie's chasing the dragon, man," Billy, the third one, sputtered. "He's totally chasing that shit." He doubled over with laughter, gasping for breath. Confused, Janet looked at Milton and cocked her head, the straw dangling between her fingers.

"You know how it is, man: trying to stay up, get the buzz back, you gotta do more blow. Gotta chase the dragon," said Milton almost defensively, cutting two lines of coke on the coffee table. He leaned over with his $100 tube, and the lines disappeared.

"No, man, I meant the real dragon." Billy chortled, knocking a tin of Szechuan noodles onto the rug. "The one in the opera. It's *Siegfried*, man. The giant turns into a dragon. Guards the trolls' gold. Shit. People think *Star Wars* invented this fucking stuff." An operatic bass wailed through the record's pops and scratches.

"Goddam, sounds like he's coming," said Milton, sneezing violently. "Wagner's so out. What's with those Valkyries?" The words tumbled out, and he choked on his own laughter. "Pointy, dude. Torpedo tits."

Billy got up and switched records, carefully slipping the first one into its faded jacket. He dropped the needle, and brass instruments played a religious tune. "Valhalla, man." He sighed, folding his hands reverentially. "Castle of the gods. Power. Power and glory, man." The windows vibrated as the music rose and fell.

Milton took a long swig of Beck's. "What kind of Wagner tubas they playing, Paxman? Alexander? It's Vienna Phil: Solti, right? Damn, they're nailing it." He was shouting over the din. He wiped his nose and then smeared back a cowlick in a seamless motion.

These guys had fire in their bellies, I thought. I watched Janet hand Donald $250 and tuck a Baggie of coke into her purse. Young and inexperienced, I wanted this in-crowd of classical musicians to accept me so I would be asked to play with them in the city's hottest orchestras and chamber music groups. I'd already started playing oboe as a substitute in the New York Philharmonic, even though I was still in school. At twenty-two I was too scared to do coke, though, so I tried to appear nonchalant by propping my black alligator sandals on the coffee table.

"Oooh, nice shoes, Blair. What'd you play at the Phil tonight? No, wait wait wait." Milton was ogling my feet. With a toothpick, he arranged a cocaine flower pattern on my toenail and snorted through the bill. Everyone exploded in laughter.

"I need more blow, Donald. I got stage band rehearsal tomorrow," said Stan. "C'mon, how much? Gimme a break. *Meistersinger*, dude. Six hours long, man!" The intercom buzzed and Donald walked to answer it.

"Billy, you got *Götterdämmerung*?" Billy nodded, pulling a box of LPs from a ripped Associated Supermarkets paper bag.

"Twilight of the gods. The end, man. Redemption. Oh, man. Beautiful. Gold. Oh, yeah, magic fire."

I wiggled my toes, admiring the expensive shoes bought with one of my New York Philharmonic paychecks.

"The gods go up in flames," bubbled Milton. Billy dropped the needle, and everyone listened hard. As the music grew to its climax, he screamed over the finale.

"Nothing like it!" he shouted. "Don't you love it when Valhalla finally crashes down?"

First Movement
Appassionata Sonata

Looking southeast over New York City, from the Allendale Apartments at Ninety-ninth Street and West End Avenue.

The Magic Flute

WHEN I WAS seven years old, I wanted a magic dress. Our family had just moved to Vienna, Austria, by way of a summer's voyage across the Atlantic, and every corner of my strange and wonderful new world was filled with fantastic stories, beautiful music, and paintings about real kings and queens.

Fairy-princess clothes, like nothing I'd seen back home in North Carolina, were everywhere. The native garb of the Austrian provinces was adorned with pleats and flounces. Museums displayed golden robes from the Hapsburg Empire. Ballerinas at the opera house twirled on point in pink satin shoes and fluffy tulle skirts. Even ordinary girls wore pretty dirndl dresses that looked like costumes.

I'd looked at pictures of Europe in my grandparents' stash of *National Geographic*s, and now it all came to life. I'd never seen huge old churches, cobblestone streets, or snow-capped mountains at home. The world's tallest Ferris wheel and the real blue Danube made Vienna into a child's wonderland.

Europe also cast its spell on my parents, who had almost never traveled abroad. Both born in 1921, they were the first in their families with college degrees, and our year in Vienna immersed them in the culture, history, and arts they'd come to love.

My father had just been appointed a visiting lecturer in American history at the University of Vienna. Like many World War II vets, Dad was educated under the GI Bill after returning from duty, in his case earning a PhD in the history of the American South. By 1958, he had settled into a suburban professor's position in Chapel Hill, North Carolina, which aside from the university was a quiet spot. There were occasional concerts, and the Varsity showed first-run films uptown. Dinner out meant the S & W Cafeteria over in Durham.

Before the trip, my mother had exercised her wry humor by naming our toy boats after our ship, the SS *Atlantic,* then sinking them at bath time. She showed me pictures of the vessel, the pier, and the "women and children first" emergency drills, which turned out to be true. Nothing she said could have prepared me for the glamour on board, however.

It was 1967, and people traveling on ocean liners took dressing for dinner seriously. A string trio played as my brother, Bruce, and I checked out the grown-ups in their long gowns and dinner jackets; there was even a top hat like the ones in *New Yorker* cartoons. The captain could have been a movie star in his epauletted whites. As an enormous tuxedoed Arab twirled his cigar, I could not look away from an exotic darkness and blue-black hair I'd never before seen.

On the seventh day, land rose from the horizon. Casablanca! Mosques and minarets. Ancient buildings, fountains, paving stones. I smelled strange things—spices, maybe—and heard bleating goats and shouts from food stalls. Since my idea of good eating meant processed lunchmeat, I gawked at entire animals roasting. Beside a vat of turtle soup, a man wailed like a grieving widow, blowing tunes through his Moroccan *rhieta,* a sort of snake charmer's reed instrument. Men raced by in white cotton djellabas, tassels bobbing on their red fezzes.

We sailed to Mallorca, Nice, and Genoa. In each strange city, I slung my shoulder bag diagonally across my plain jumper dress for security. At the last port, we transferred to an overnight train bound for Vienna. There, amid loud sirens and clanging trolleys, our sprawling apartment overlooked the cupola of an old wooden food market, which literally sat in the middle of a busy intersection.

Dad soon traveled to Munich, bringing back a white Volkswagen bug he had bought there. In it, we bounced down the autobahn to weekends in Bucharest, Belgrade, and Budapest. In Thessaloniki, I remember the Aegean's aquamarine sea, white stucco houses, and ancient ruins. In Capri, the surf had carved the Blue Grotto, a natural vaulted cave accessible only by a tiny opening for boats. On the Hungarian border, I set a toe onto Communist soil and tried to understand the meaning of "Iron Curtain."

The sixties were a tumultuous period of change around the world, but none of it touched Vienna, which felt locked in the past. We immersed ourselves in Austrian treats, sampling schnitzel at the Augustinerkeller, sugary cream horns at Konditorei, and apricot Sacher torte and cocoa smothered in whipped cream. On Kärntnerstrasse, a string quartet played Beethoven for ten-schilling coins pedestrians threw into an open violin case.

Classical music was everywhere in Vienna. Franz Lehar's operetta *The Merry Widow* played near our apartment at the Volksopera—the People's Opera—whose music filled Vienna's streets. During shopping expeditions at the nineteenth-century market hall on our street, light streamed in from windows far above our heads, and the building's walls sealed us into everyday local life. The butcher sang arias off-key as he wrapped *Die Presse* around our meat. The old woman who sold us milk clotted with butter hummed a familiar *Merry Widow* tune.

Even the white Lipizzaner stallions at the Spanish Riding School danced to classical music, as they had since 1572. Their arena looked just like a ballroom or concert hall, with chandeliers hanging above riders wearing bicorne hats and tailcoats, guiding their horses through routines of synchronized prancing.

We met other Americans, gathering for parties in the American Embassy and private dinners at home. At Thanksgiving, I played with our hostess's Christmas doll, Krampus, an Austrian archenemy of St. Nick, and listened to a pretty first-grade schoolteacher from Chicago. She said she'd won a singing contest, and the prize had brought her to Vienna. She only knew two songs and didn't speak German, but the Vienna State Opera had heard her voice and begged her to sing Mozart's opera *The Magic Flute*. Her name was Arleen Auger.

My parents talked to Arleen about music, since they both played the piano and listened to symphonies on the radio at home. My grandmother had played the organ at church, and my grandfather said he played a little violin during World War I. Even though my brother, Bruce, was only eleven, he could already perform some pieces by Mozart on the piano.

I knew a little about Mozart too, after visiting his house in Salzburg. His parents had trotted him around Europe as something of a curiosity.

He could play several different instruments and repeat a piece of music blindfolded after hearing it only once. His *Magic Flute*, written just before he died at age thirty-five, captured the composer's childlike imagination in a story of sorceresses and enchanted animals. Music itself was almost a character in the opera, as Prince Tamino could pass through fire and water with the power of his magic flute.

We went to hear Arleen in *The Magic Flute* at the State Opera, an ornate temple to music built in 1869. Busts of conductors who had performed here lined the lobby: Gustav Mahler, Richard Strauss, Herbert von Karajan. I was glad we weren't going to the Musikverein, where I'd already sat through three or four boring concerts. The old men there played symphonies for hours without telling any story at all, leaving me to stare at the naked gold ladies holding up the balcony.

I'd already been to the opera house to see *Swan Lake*. I imitated ballerina Margot Fonteyn's boneless arms and imagined myself wearing her jeweled white tutu and sparkly tiara. Tonight's story would be different. As we walked through the opera house lobby, my mother traced out scenes from *The Magic Flute* that were woven into the foyer's huge tapestries. There was Papageno, dressed like a bird, his lips padlocked by the Queen's ladies-in-waiting. Then Pamina, the sun-cult priestess, in the temple of Isis. And finally Arleen's character, the evil Queen of the Night.

As the usher seated us, I smoothed the skirt of the Austrian dirndl my mother had bought me. It was pink and chocolate-brown, with a lace-up bodice, puffy underblouse, patterned skirt, and fringed scarf that tucked into the neckline. It was the first time I'd worn it, and the dress made me look like an Austrian girl.

I fidgeted during the overture music, but at last our schoolteacher friend came onstage. In her embroidered velvet costume and towering headdress, Arleen had been transformed into something very special. She began ordering Pamina to murder the priest of Isis:

Hell's revenge cooks in my heart,
Death and despair flame about me!
If you do not kill Sarastro
You will be my daughter nevermore.

Suddenly, my dirndl felt ordinary, something that everyone wore. If only I could snap my fingers and become Queen of the Night like Arleen, with all these people watching! I wanted all that attention. I wanted to be a queen onstage, like her. I wanted that magic dress!

Soprano Arleen Auger in her "magic dress," as Constanze in Mozart's Abduction from the Seraglio, Vienna State Opera, 1970. (Photo reproduced by permission of the Arleen Auger Memorial Fund)

* * *

One year later, in 1968, we sailed home on the SS *Michelangelo*. New York's skyline had changed; construction had started on the World Trade Center at the tip of Manhattan. The city felt somewhat European, with French and Italian restaurants crowding side streets near the Taft Hotel, where we were staying. International travelers came and went from the West Side piers. Uptown, fancy cars and fancier people streamed by the white plaza of Lincoln Center—a shopping mall for the arts, bigger and newer than anything in Vienna.

North Carolina had changed too. I was eight now, and my old classmates had grown into third-graders. They asked where I'd gone during second grade. "Austria! Did you see kangaroos?" My classmates bopped along to Beatles songs I didn't know, so I secretly hummed the *Magic Flute* tunes that reminded me of Arleen's magic transformation.

Vienna started fading from my memory as I moved back into my old pink bedroom. Mom tried to re-create our European life and its sophistication by spreading out books full of paintings from Austrian museums—she hung up a Dürer print that I liked—and tuning in to Metropolitan Opera broadcasts every Saturday. She found marzipan bunnies and Konditorei pastries at a little shop on Franklin Street, owned by Hungarian Jews who'd fled Austria in 1939 to escape the Nazi occupation.

There was home-grown culture too. The North Carolina Symphony soldiered from Manteo to Murphy on a rattletrap bus with its mission of music education. Founded in 1933 as a Works Progress Administration project, the state's Horn-Tootin' Bill of 1945 had funded it ever since. My third-grade class rode the bus with the rest of the elementary school to one of their concerts. First we listened to them play Prokofiev's *Peter and the Wolf;* then we made a horrible cacophony by tweeting along on plastic tonettes the school provided.

My parents enjoyed playing piano for fun and encouraged me to start piano lessons too. After a few months, I found that scales and easy melodies were boring. I wanted to learn the loud dramatic Brahms and Beethoven pieces my now-thirteen-year-old brother could play. I didn't realize how much work he put into learning them.

Sometimes my family drove thirty miles on two-lane roads to see the Philadelphia Orchestra or pianist Arthur Rubinstein in Raleigh's cavernous Reynolds Coliseum. Just one stop on a nationwide "community concert" circuit started in the 1920s, Raleigh brought in culture by selling subscriptions in advance, offering arts managements the fees up front and eliminating middlemen. Over three hundred towns in America had formed these civic music clubs, bidding on whatever artists they could afford. By filling the vast basketball arena's fourteen hundred seats, our series could sell seven concerts for seven bucks.

Even though I knew the concerts were considered a cultural resource since we lived so far from a big city, I found them dull. In addition, the barnlike sports arena couldn't compare to Vienna's elegant State Opera House. The huge stadium's boomy acoustics made it hard to hear the instruments or see performers on the faraway stage. My mind would wander to places I'd rather be: watching tadpoles in the creek near our house, riding my bike to the swimming pool, or canoeing past rhododendrons on the Neuse River.

All through elementary school, my parents urged me to keep taking piano lessons. I hated practicing and wasn't particularly interested in piano, but by sixth grade I had finally advanced enough to play in a local group recital. My mother rewarded me with a fairy princess dress with candy-pink chiffon pleats and a satin ribbon around the waist. I loved walking out in front of the audience in it. Once the applause died, though, I suffered an attack of stage fright. Sitting at the nine-foot Steinway, my hands shook. I had a memory slip and stopped, then started again. I wanted to disappear or run offstage, but I managed to finish my halting performance. Only when I walked away from the keyboard was I transformed back into the fairy princess.

That year, 1971, someone from the music store brought trumpets, flutes, saxophones, and trombones to Estes Elementary. First, the bandleader gave us a music test: Is this note higher or lower? Softer or louder? I got all the questions right. So did Johnny Edwards, a black kid who lived in a house with a dirt floor and an outhouse in rural Orange County.

Afterward, Johnny wandered outside while I stayed behind with other budding musicians. Our schools had been racially integrated for six years, but renting a trumpet for thirty bucks a month would have been a challenge for Johnny's parents.

The bandleader started handing out instruments alphabetically by our last names. Finally I'd get my magic flute! I watched impatiently as Miketa got the last trumpet, Osborne the trombone, and Smith, the last flute. By the time he got to Tindall, my options had narrowed to two unfamiliar instruments, oboe and bassoon. (Anyone named Zebulon was destined for a kazoo.)

"I'll take the little one," I said, pointing at a dull black tube scattered with metal keys. I sure wasn't wrangling the bedpost-sized bassoon.

If only I'd stayed awake during *Peter and the Wolf*! In Prokofiev's tale, the sinuous cat slithers around a clarinet, wolves sneak through the forest to the sound of French horns, and a silver flute pipes sweet birdsong. The oboe plays a goofy waddling duck that is devoured by the wolf and left to quack plaintively from his belly.

Trotting home with my consolation prize, I put the plastic Selmer oboe together, stuck its reed mouthpiece in the top, and blew. Nothing. My mother sprang into action, paying for oboe lessons. My new teacher demonstrated how difficult the oboe was compared to other instruments by inviting Dad to blow on a flute just like he did a Coke bottle. Then he tried the oboe.

Blat! Squawk! The vibrating reed tickled his lips.

She pointed out that good oboists were a hot commodity and dispatched us for store-bought reeds and various accessories. Mom even braved a black-lit head shop for cigarette papers to mop up spit under the keys. Fully equipped, I marched off to band practice.

I was already bookish, so no one would confuse me with the angelic cheerleaders who all played the flute. My nerd factor spun off the charts. I turned scarlet from blowing through the tiny reed; veins popped out on my forehead. Since no one picked the bassoon, I became band bozo by default.

The instrument didn't play itself. Even the best commercial reeds, handmade one at a time from bamboo, barely made a sound. Since the fragile mouthpieces had to be crafted to individual players and instruments, there was little choice: I had to learn to make my own reeds.

With a bad reed, my oboe could be a beastly instrument honking and squeaking as if it had a mind of its own. When my reeds were working, though, I learned that making a sound spoke my emotions more directly than my own voice.

The pleasure of making music was not the oboe's only attraction, however. My teacher had been right; the oboe did come with rewards. Composers wrote juicy solos for oboes that sent band directors into ecstasy. Teachers excused me for band competitions, a trip to All-State Orchestra in the mountains, and, finally, the university wind ensemble's week-long tour.

At fourteen, I checked into a Pinehurst motel with fifty college students and within an hour was sipping a twenty-year-old drummer's beer while he stroked my ego. The ensemble's director—something of a local celebrity, having played French horn on the original recording of the *Captain Kangaroo* theme music in the 1950s—also fawned over his little oboe player.

That summer of 1974, I attended the Transylvania Music Camp, which was part of the larger Brevard Music Center near Asheville, North Carolina. There, I studied with oboists from the Dallas and Atlanta symphonies. Since I was advanced for my age, I was also placed in the Music Center's Repertory Training Program, where I played through most of the Beethoven and Brahms symphonies with high school and college music students.

Upon returning from Brevard I took a summer job at the mall music store, a position I landed from a manager who liked my wholesome appearance. Before long I was sneaking drinks with the piano salesman and breaking for loading-dock tokes with Guitarman Ray. My parents and teachers didn't say anything. I doubt if they suspected a junior high school classical music student could get into such trouble.

Back at school, I noticed that my classmates toiled harder over their textbooks than I did over my oboe, yet they didn't receive the same special attention. I'd found my magic dress. If I played the oboe reasonably well, I was rewarded without having to do the difficult academic work required of everyone else.

There was only one hitch. I needed to spend hours making reeds, or my oboe would make no sound at all. Reed-making became the conduit to my elevated status. I didn't visit my secret creekside spot anymore, or canoe, or even read much. I certainly didn't study.

My adolescence had boiled down to swamp grass. *Arundo donax* is the bamboo used for wicker furniture, paper pulp, cellulose for rayon fabric, and reeds for the oboe, bassoon, clarinet, saxophone, and bagpipes. In my case, two pieces of the cane are tied together in a bundle and scraped until they vibrate, making a sound when the oboist blows through the reed's opening.

A brown paper bag arrived from Antibes, France, every few months, packed with cane tubes that clinked like wind chimes. After measuring their diameter, I sliced lengths from the tubes, cutting them to uniform length and shoving a special gouging machine's carriage back and forth to scoop out a U-shaped channel. Next, I bent the resulting cane strip in half, paring it to a tapered shape before tying it to the cork-covered silver tube. This step involved manual dexterity, twanging fishing twine, and a finished product that sometimes gaped where the cane didn't quite meet, a problem remedied by pasting slimy so-called fishskin (a specialty item used by goldsmiths) over the space. I tried to forget the membrane actually came from ox gut.

Only then did I start scraping, thinning the cane enough to vibrate. My knife tore the reed's ragged tip. I blew on the reed to test it. Nothing. I kept scraping, finally getting a loud honk, more like the primitive *rhieta* I heard in Morocco. Time to start over.

The mess soon blossomed in my pink bedroom—three different lubricant oils, steel filings, and mountains of bamboo shavings. The process took hours, only to be repeated when the reed wore out, which was almost daily.

Not surprisingly, my next report card featured a D-plus in French, almost balancing the D-minus in algebra. I managed to hide it from my parents. What musician needs math? I had become isolated from everything at school, considering myself in a superior class: a musician. My only friends played instruments too; we were a proud bunch of geeks.

I was the girl chosen last for kickball teams. My classmates in the locker room huddled away from me with talk of hairstyles, makeup, and training bras I thought was silly. My music crowd wouldn't have been caught dead at school dances or football games. Instead of the platform shoes and hip-hugger jeans that were popular in 1974, we wore piano scarves and music-note earrings. I was especially proud of the OBOE POWER T-shirt I'd had custom-printed.

The local music clique ranged in age from twelve to eighteen. Dedicated and diligent stay-at-home moms like mine drove us in carpools to band competitions, piano recitals, and youth orchestra practice. I chose a pianist named Forrest for my boyfriend. I was fourteen, he was eighteen, and his disowned brother was the national head of the American Nazi Party. I couldn't get enough of Forrest, smoking pot in the tobacco fields behind his family's farmhouse and swooning over his compositions. When he applied to college at the North Carolina School of the Arts (NCSA), I auditioned for their high school division.

My parents had offered to send me to private school, hoping I'd attend Exeter, the New Hampshire prep school where my brother had gone to study four years earlier among sons of Supreme Court justices and presidential advisers. My grades weren't promising, but because of Bruce's performance they had said I could come. At Exeter, I'd get a fine education, study with a Boston Symphony oboist, and bargain my way into an Ivy League college with a music scholarship.

My parents tried to help me make the right decision. Exeter sounded like a sure path to success, but NCSA's oboe teacher, Joseph Robinson, wooed me with a flattering personal letter. Maybe he was something special, since a chorus director at the Transylvania Music Camp had already urged me to seek him out. Mom and Dad were careful not to discourage me, in case I turned out to be a colossal talent. Times had changed. In the 1970s, unprecedented arts funding might also make a career as a professional classical musician possible for someone of my generation, where it would have been considered absurd in my parents' day.

They left the decision to me. I was scared, and too embarrassed by my bad grades to talk about the options with them openly. At fourteen, I couldn't see myself as a professional anything, especially since I knew very few southern working women in the 1970s, except for schoolteachers. I was a teenager and could only see a few months into the future.

My music friends were confused by similar decisions too, since few parents and teachers were equipped to offer them guidance. Perhaps the adults felt discomfort about their unfamiliarity with classical music, fearing they would be labeled as ignorant. There was a sense that we possessed a divine gift they could never understand.

I considered my choices. NCSA, a boarding school about eighty miles away where Forrest was headed, was known for its loose academic standards and rowdy campus environment. There was drinking. There were drugs and high school pregnancies, which meant high school sex. It sounded very adult. It also sounded familiar, since I would be around other kids who were praised for being creative, wacky, and playful, even if they didn't accomplish much.

On the other hand, if I went seven hundred miles north to New Hampshire, Forrest would break up with me. On top of that, Exeter had strict rules and tough academic standards. I'd already gotten a sense that I was good at music and nothing else. Surely I was too stupid and undisciplined to make it at Exeter. I couldn't imagine passing the difficult courses that Bruce had aced.

My teenage mind reviewed what information I had. At fourteen, I had no idea how people eventually became doctors, lawyers, or professors. I didn't particularly want to become a professional musician, but at least I could survive that way for the next few years, enjoy even more attention, and see what happened. This vague, unguided process was how many of my young friends ended up in musical careers before they were old enough to decide their life's work.

My parents didn't look happy, but they accepted my decision to attend NCSA. I felt that my life had already hit a dead end, but Mom and Dad said they believed in me, no matter what.

Cunning Little Vixen

2

BRUCE DROVE ME the eighty miles to Winston-Salem, passing shanty-towns, abandoned industrial buildings, and rusty trailers. Ragged curtains hung in the window of Spoon's bar, just before we turned right at the Mack Truck dispatch into NCSA's gates. A high fence circled the grounds, separating students from the slums outside.

It was a modest campus: a few scattered dorms, a student commons, a main building, a geodesic dome, and an old gym converted into a black box theater. Now part of the state university system, NCSA offered students from across America and abroad specialized training in classical music, ballet, modern dance, acting, stagecraft, and visual arts from seventh grade through college. Its precollege division was the country's only state-supported live-in high school for the arts. My tuition cost $17 per year, with room and board totaling $1,400 in 1975 dollars.

Because the school provided one of the nation's only training programs for high school-age performers, its alumni already included a handful of success stories after only ten years of operation. Flutist Renee Siebert and violist Dawn Hannay had joined the New York Philharmonic, baritone John Cheek sang at the Metropolitan Opera, pianist Margo Garrett was teaching at Juilliard, and others had launched solo careers, like cellist Sharon Robinson and flutist Ransom Wilson. The school had attracted excellent instructors like violinist Elaine Lee Richey, who had won the 1958 Naumburg Prize, and the entire Clarion Woodwind Quintet, which had transplanted itself from New York City.

I thought I glimpsed Forrest as we got out of the car. I didn't want to see him; he had dumped me over the summer. Bruce and I turned away and waded through a sea of tiny girls in black leotards to the student commons. At the registration desk there, a sweet old lady squinted at her typewriter. She was just the sort of volunteer whom arts groups often credit as helping them stay afloat. Like many women of her era who were interested in culture, she probably didn't work and believed her involvement could help her husband's business networking when they attended concerts and fund-raising events with other local supporters.

"Birth date, dear?" she asked.

Suddenly, here was a practical application for math. "Two /two / fifty-seven," I said calmly, changing my age from fifteen to eighteen. Bruce's eyes widened, but he didn't say anything. At his prep school, students were forbidden even to ride in a car. Here at NCSA I'd be buying beer before I could drive. My heart thumped in the silence, but the grandma pecked away at the yellow ID card and fed it into a laminating machine.

The high school dorms swarmed with new arrivals. An abundance of ballerinas skewed the gender ratio three to one in favor of girls. I knew several of them from my hometown, along with a bassoonist named Audrey. Beautiful and talented, Audrey had found solace in music since her family recently lost their home.

I met my dorm mother, Sarah, a type of arts groupie I already recognized. Flummoxed by our talent, she would forget we were just kids. Greeting each student, Sarah looked nervously at the floor, as if meeting famous musicians backstage, and moments later changed character, squealing with delight to introduce us to one another.

Meeting my new classmates over freshly baked cookies, I was struck by two things. First, many of the girls looked fragile, like translucent china. Second, I sensed something mature and guarded in nearly everyone— something I never felt in my classmates at home. These young people shared an ability to take care of themselves, as if they'd been on their own forever. There was a determination to perform, and reinvent themselves onstage, that I knew as well.

Now that I'd left home, perhaps I'd undergo a metamorphosis. I was weird: a bit chubby, wore glasses, and spoke with a southern accent. I hoped that by the end of three years, I'd have turned into a beautiful swan, performing for my adoring audience. I wasn't sure how this happened to people, but I remembered how Arleen had been instantaneously transformed from a plain schoolteacher into the powerful Queen of the Night.

Sarah introduced me to a blond boy about my age whom I'd seen unloading a long rectangular instrument case from his lime-green Datsun station wagon. I'd assumed he was someone's brother, since his preppy appearance looked out of place among students more flamboyantly dressed, but I quickly learned not to judge my classmates too quickly.

Geoffrey's button-down shirts betrayed his blue-blood lineage; his famous segregationist family and his bassoon completed the picture. His sad tale went beyond his unwanted heritage; Geoffrey's father had died recently in a plane crash. His mother, a painter, suspected he was gay and sent him to NCSA instead of to the military school Geoffrey had considered. Geoffrey had only played for a few months, and he hadn't decided if he wanted a musical career.

Then there were the Treticks: Clifford, Noelle, and Drew. They were all under three years of age when their violinist father died and they were separated to live with various relatives. Reunited for the first time, the three made music fiercely in memory of a father they knew only from recordings.

Clifford, the oldest and a talented flutist, filled a paternal role not only for his siblings but also for all of NCSA. He ran the film series, had a master key to the campus, and could start any car in the parking lot with his lock picks. He was glad to be rid of last year's roommate, a messy Arkansas ballet dancer named Patrick Bissell, who'd swilled beer and blasted rock music night and day. In Patrick's place was a brooding violinist whose wealthy father ran a midwestern juice drink empire.

Noelle was enrolled as a ballet major, though she also played her father's eighteenth-century Italian violin. She drew me into the dancers' circle in our dorm, a secret world filled with little girls living out ballerina fantasies. They came from small towns across America to study with the well-known ballet masters at NCSA, hoping to sign with scouts from big-city dance troupes. In the ten years NCSA had operated, it had become known for one of the finest ballet programs for young dancers.

Noelle's roommate, Elizabeth, came from Lubbock, Texas, where her parents had settled to teach after finishing European operatic careers. Elizabeth needed to leave home young. If ballerinas weren't hired by a major dance company by eighteen, they'd never make it professionally. Her mother let her go to NCSA but feared she risked Elizabeth's academic education in the process.

Next door to me was Kristin. She'd brought her French horn from a Montana town of 250, where, at best, girls returned home to a husband and farm after attending a local college. One snowy night, pianist Lili Kraus had played eighty miles away in Great Falls, the only big town between Billings and Calgary. Kristin was a little girl, then; she had barely noticed the music for staring at Kraus's sequined ball gown. A princess had come to the prairie. In that moment, Kristin decided she would find a dress just like that to transport her to a better place.

Opening in 1965, NCSA was conceived as a college music conservatory to keep southern talent at home. Until that time, students of music were lured away to Juilliard or even Europe, because appropriate training was unavailable locally. A high school was later added, as were dance, drama, and art departments.

The project was politically contentious. Politicians ridiculed using public money to finance a place to "learn people tippy-toe dancin'," but governor Terry Sanford prevailed, a triumph for a state ranked forty-fifth in education spending. Funds trickled in, starting with a telethon in which the Ford Foundation matched donations dollar for dollar to raise a total of $1 million in twenty-four hours. North Carolina's tobacco, furniture, and textile wealth provided additional support to train performers, artists who were expected to fill the arts centers that America's tycoons were just starting to build.

Spending big money on a school for the performing arts in the mid-sixties required a high degree of faith in the rapid growth of American culture and the employment it might provide. At the time, few classical music jobs existed outside of education. Symphony players worked day jobs to survive, since their orchestras played only partial seasons. In 1961, only nine of America's top twenty-six orchestras worked more than thirty weeks a year, with only four of the nine providing hospitalization insurance.

Despite this lack of practical application, the number of university arts degrees ballooned. "Anyone who can play the scales is rushed off to

Vienna to study music," said playwright Thornton Wilder, as the 1960s culture boom intensified. The number of theater majors tripled between 1960 and 1967, with dance, music, and art departments showing similar growth. Arts academies became popular; professors argued in favor of specialized institutions like NCSA, complaining that dilettantes were diluting college arts departments.

"These programs," wrote Alice Goldfarb Marquis in *Art Lessons,* a 1995 history of public arts funding, "grew without regard for how the arts sector could support such vastly increased numbers of certified arts graduates."[1]

Navigating uncharted waters, NCSA found few students at first. It recruited beginning ballerinas, banjo pickers, and an Appalachian girl playing a bent flute. These students had never heard a symphony orchestra, yet administrators insisted they would want to join one. "Will there be jobs for that many?" one Raleigh women's club member wondered, pointing out that New York already overflowed with aspiring performers who worked at menial positions outside the arts to make ends meet.

By focusing on professional training, the school created a boundary between amateurs (the arts' most loyal supporters) and freshly minted virtuosos with uncertain futures. NCSA additionally snubbed regional arts, even the rich Moravian music that had been played in Winston-Salem's Czech community for two hundred years, its epicenter a mile away in the restored eighteenth-century village of Old Salem.

Novelist John Ehle, one of the school's first advisers, was inspired to design its narrow curriculum by a speech Robert Frost delivered shortly before he died. Frost had argued that artists, like successful athletes, must develop their talent early and in the company of others like them. In his address, the eighty-six-year-old Frost said that a young artist's "passionate preference" must not be wasted on a comprehensive education. In the spirit of the day, Ehle's plan promised to cloister students in a creative laboratory, removed from society's influence.

The noble intentions of NCSA encapsulated what would later plague classical music in America: explosive growth without a realistic mission, few accessible resources, and the simultaneous isolation and elevation of a foreign art form above the comprehension of those who were expected to support it.

The school succeeded in providing spectacular artistic training and was truly a gem for young students who were certain they wanted a career in the arts and possessed the talent to achieve it. However, many high school students were undecided, and NCSA provided minimal academic preparation. The school slighted general studies, gambling teenagers' basic education against an uncertain future in the arts. Its students, some as young as twelve, learned little about history, social studies, business, math, and science. In this loose unstructured environment, literally fenced in and removed from outside oversight or regulation, many students celebrated Frost's "passionate preference" through sex, drugs, and alcohol.

Joseph Robinson, my new oboe teacher, had parlayed a Fulbright scholarship to study German arts funding into a summer of lessons with French oboist Marcel Tabuteau, winning a job with the Mobile (Alabama) Symphony in 1966 and moving on to the Atlanta Symphony before landing at NCSA. Thirty-five years old, Robinson also had degrees in English, economics, and public affairs from Davidson College and Princeton University.

In his studio, Robinson closed the door tightly, starting our first hour alone in a windowless basement room. I was eager to show him what I could do, to demonstrate the finger technique and sight-reading skills that translated easily to the oboe from seven years of weekly piano lessons. I placed the Mozart Oboe Quartet on the music stand, but Robinson was more interested in my reeds and tone. Dressed in polyester golf slacks and two-tone shoes, he sat at his Formica-topped desk, making crowing sounds on my reeds. Then he shook his head pitifully.

"First, you'll learn to breathe properly. Play a D like this." The room rang with a sound so beautiful, it was pure tone. As I imitated him, Robinson gazed at my torso.

"Guess your little lungs are still developing." He chortled, rising for a closer look at my developing breasts. Next, he guided my hand to his abdomen, demonstrating how his belly expanded when he inhaled. "Right below the belt," he said, to illustrate proper breathing technique. This didn't feel right, but I figured it must be what private lessons were all about. At least he gave me two of his reeds, which worked perfectly.

After my lesson, I found Audrey practicing in her cubicle. I told her about my lesson, and how the physical contact made me squirm. She said her own teacher, Mark Popkin, demonstrated the breathing technique without touching her at all. She also thought my assignment sounded dull—one note, this way, that way—when she was getting to learn Johann Nepomuk Hummel's Bassoon Concerto.

Audrey and I walked down the hall to check the orchestra seating, which had been posted on a bulletin board. Although I was only fifteen, my playing was more advanced than some of the older of the ten oboe majors, so I had been assigned to play English horn—a larger, lower version of the oboe—on Samuel Barber's overture to *The School for Scandal.*

Since NCSA was also a college, its orchestra was more mature than any I'd yet played in. The musicians' average age was somewhere in the early twenties, and their playing sounded strong and confident. Marian, the college-age first oboist, gave the tuning note, A, as oboists traditionally do, because their sound is focused and easy to hear. Hungarian conductor Nicholas Harsányi tapped his music stand to get our attention, and the orchestra's group tuning session quieted.

Harsányi, a former violist turned orchestra leader, gave the downbeat with his baton. He wasn't the greatest conductor and had partly relied on the connections of his wife Janice Harsányi, a widely respected soprano, to climb the career ladder. Despite some unclear motions on his part, the orchestra responded and I became part of the most spectacular sound I'd ever heard. The melodies being played all around me reverberated through the hall but also created a physical sensation that I'd never felt while sitting in the audience; it was as if I were standing before a thundering stereo speaker. Unlike listening to music from afar, sitting in the center of a live performance was even more exciting than the vertical plunge of the roller coaster. This was thrilling!

My initial adrenaline rush of excitement quickly grew into uncontrollable nervousness as I realized that I would soon be called upon to play a solo in the piece. I wasn't having fun anymore. I became even more terrified and could barely breathe, as the musical score called for fewer instruments to play as my big moment approached. My hands were trembling as if I was freezing, and Harsányi had a nasty expression on his face that challenged me to mess up. He was not conducting very clearly, either, and held up his hand to signal softer and softer dynamics (a musical term for degrees of loudness), preparing for the dreaded moment when I'd have to play this borrowed English horn, alone in front of college-age musicians. Because of his imprecise flailing, I wasn't even sure where we were in the music. Little spots of music swam on the page. My heart thumped when Harsányi pointed to cue me, as if to say, "There —her.... Look, everyone!" I gasped in a breath of air and as I started playing, my D-major arpeggio wavered.

"Stop, stop!" Harsányi scowled as fifty pairs of eyes stared at me. "Louder. Don't rush. Why you rush? How old you are?" I'd had stage fright before, but my pounding heart and quivering body were worse than ever now. I felt like a firecracker with its fuse spitting and jumping, about to rocket to the ceiling, explode, and shower ashes everywhere. I gulped, feeling faint.

"Fifteen," I squeaked. Harsányi snorted. I noticed John, the concertmaster, trying to catch my eye.

"Again. Letter E." This time, I played, but I was too nervous to remember anything about my eight-bar solo.

Rehearsal ended, and Harsányi clumped off the podium. Heading backstage, he groped through the string section toward Noelle, who was packing up faster than a jackrabbit. On the way, he elbowed me in the boobs, pausing to let his forearm luxuriate on my left breast. Kristin scurried behind the tuba and Audrey ran for the basses, the bassoon case across her chest as a battle shield.

Older girls had already warned me to take the maulings if I wanted any more orchestra parts. I was learning about the subjective nature of music and how our superiors—counting on bewildered outsiders not to interfere—could twist creative issues to control us. Musicality was subjective, and a lack of cooperation with a teacher, whether sexual, academic, or interpersonal, could be described as bad intonation, boring phrasing, or even weak talent to an administrator with no knowledge of music. Problem students weren't invited back the following year, allowing faculty broad "artistic freedom."

John, the concertmaster, lingered onstage. I blushed as he leaned over my stand, smiling intimately. "Nice job," he said, inviting me to the college dorms after lunch. I accepted, even though high school rules forbade it.

"People call me José," he said, switching on Bugs Bunny cartoons in his dorm's TV lounge. "Tequila?"

I glanced at my watch. Music theory class had started five minutes ago. My insides warmed from the alcohol as José talked.

A Juilliard dropout, José had freelanced in New York until NCSA offered him a scholarship. His life in the big city sounded thrilling. He'd played with several different orchestras at places like Carnegie Hall, and he'd recorded some soundtracks for movies and television shows. It was glamorous, he said, but he'd come here because he needed to finish his college degree. He could always go back to New York.

As a talented boy, José had risen quickly after the first violin lessons, hungry for the attention he never got from his alcoholic parents. He never fit in because of his mixed Latino–black–Russian background. The neighborhood kids rejected his music as white, and he'd hardly ever seen another black classical musician. Everyone told him violin was his ticket out of the ghetto. José forged ahead to Juilliard but dropped out after a suicide attempt.

José was the most exotic person I had ever met, and I returned to drink tequila with him every afternoon. After a week, we moved the party into his room to smoke dope. He lit incense and showed me his violin, made in the eighteenth century by France's finest luthier. I peered through the F-holes, where he showed me the label that Nicholas Lupot had pasted there in 1795 before gluing the spruce top in place. Worth $170,000, the violin had been passed down and played by generations of musicians before a wealthy collector donated it to José.

By violin standards, José's fiddle was modest. The finest cello, made in 1730 by Italian luthier Antonio Stradivari, fetched $4 million; a 1735 violin by Guarnerius del Gesu cost $3.5 million. Even bows could cost more than fifty oboes; the best nineteenth-century French model, made of dense Brazilian Pernambuco wood and horsehair, brought over $100,000. Because rarity and age price these instruments beyond the means of most musicians, they rely like José on collectors to lend or donate them. José slid the case beside his only other pair of shoes.

I kept returning to José's room in the afternoon until he finally invited me over after dinner. In his room, I took a long draft of rum and another hit from the bong as José shuffled through records. First we listened to a Brahms symphony. Then Arnold Schoenberg's *Transfigured Night* crackled loudly from the stereo. Swooning, I slumped against him as he stroked my hair; I hadn't seen a classroom in weeks now. Passion fueled music for me—not theory, solfège (a sight-singing subject), or high school English—and I was in love.

José took off the same black turtleneck and dashiki he wore every day, the odor of his unwashed body mixing with cheap musk. We kissed, embracing as the climax of Brahms's G-minor quintet washed over us. José peeled away my top gently, caressing my shoulders, nuzzling my neck and pulling back the covers. I could see another woman's menstrual blood smeared on the bottom sheet, but I let him push me back on the bedding. When he thrust himself into me for the first time, it didn't hurt too badly.

"Thank you," I murmured dramatically. José froze.

"Oh, come on, you're not a virgin," he said scornfully.

My head throbbed when I woke at noon, and I trundled down to the infirmary to ask about birth control pills. The nurse gave me a parental consent form for a prescription that would cost four hundred dollars for a year's supply. I couldn't ask my parents to sign it; they would yank me out of school if they knew I was having sex, and I'd go back to being half outcast, and half star in public school. My parents were also generous with my $40 monthly allowance, but it wasn't enough to cover such an expense. Instead, I found the city health clinic, weaving through Winston-Salem's ghettos on a series of city buses. With no birth control counseling at NCSA, I could see why the high school girls kept a kitty for emergency abortions.

Tucking the free pills in my oboe case, I mapped my after-curfew escape route from my dorm room to visit José. Since one resident assistant always tipped us off to surprise checks, the staff never found anyone missing, which further preserved our cherubic image. Just in case, I stuffed my bed, covering a small pillow with a brown silk blouse so it would look like my head and adding a fake rubber hand that just peeked from under the covers.

The front door would have set off sirens, so I slid through an open window, shinning down vines to the sidewalk and skirting the campus fence. I was caught twice. A third meant mandatory suspension, but it would never have been enforced. The school did expel a few problem students, but I was safe. The music department needed every oboist for performances.

After I got caught breaking curfew, José started disappearing for days on end. I went to hear him play a master class (an instrument lesson in front of an audience that observes the instruction) with his teacher, Vartan Manoogian. It was a stressful situation for José, who, as the orchestra concertmaster, was expected to set a good example for the other violinists. Hung over, José slouched and his intonation faltered, his thin tone wavering on Bach's virtuosic *Chaconne*. After his third memory slip, José stopped, dangling the Lupot violin and bow from his left hand. Manoogian's watch ticked in the horrible silence.

"I . . . I'm sorry," he muttered, and stormed out of the room. His open violin case lay orphaned as he ran to a basement cul-de-sac outside another teacher's studio. He swung the fiddle overhead, arcing against the cinder blocks; varnished spruce splintered and the dense ebony fingerboard, tailpiece, and bridge exploded in a spectacular encore. Amid the broken strings, the instrument's guts were exposed for the first time in two centuries.

José surfaced after a few days, looking rougher than I'd ever seen him. "Whore," he snarled at me, and positioned himself at my practice room window. There he kissed his new love, a smug brunette violinist in her mid-twenties named Teresa, who gloated over a sixteen-year-old who'd squandered her virginity.

The couple exploded in laughter as I left my oboe behind and stumbled out back to the abandoned train tracks, landing in a tangle of damp kudzu. Closing my eyes, I leaned against a fat oak trunk. An owl hooted through the humid air and honeysuckle.

Gradually, I calmed down and tried to think about my future. I was halfway through the eleventh grade and had no idea what I would do when I graduated. Parts of playing music were intoxicating, almost addictive. However, most of it was dull and didn't look like it could lead anywhere, except in the case of a few exceptionally driven students.

I had joined the musicians' union at fourteen, in case someone offered me a gig. With my membership, I received the American Federation of Musicians' monthly newspaper. Scouring the help-wanted ads in the back, I saw only four or five oboe jobs advertised in a year, and most of them were in places like Wichita, Kansas, or Grand Rapids, Michigan, and provided so little salary that the musician would have to work a day job to survive. Was I the only person who noticed the lack of employment for students like us?

I looked at the College Music Society's newsletter too, which advertised university jobs. Most of them required a doctorate. The music professor's career looked like part of an endless cycle to me, as musicians without performing gigs taught more and more music majors who wouldn't be able to find performing work either.

My brother was about to graduate from the University of North Carolina in math, Phi Beta Kappa. He excelled in all subjects and had developed a deep understanding of the university's huge mainframe computer, to which his teachers and professors had given him special access ever since elementary school. His options for the future were broad. He might go to law school. In the late 1970s, he would certainly be in demand for a computer job.

I, on the other hand, felt like my future had disappeared. I loved music but had come to hate the oboe, especially because I couldn't make reeds well. I wanted to talk to my parents about it, but I was ashamed that I'd chosen to attend high school at NCSA instead of Exeter. With my poor academic record at NCSA, I couldn't transfer to Exeter now. I wondered if any college at all would take me.

It was nearly dinnertime. I drew a long breath and straightened my clothes. I would have to pretend, just like everyone else here, that we were all headed somewhere special.

"My boyfriend dumped me." I sniffled, standing in Mr. Dunigan's doorway after woodwind ensemble.

Philip, as I soon called him, pulled me inside the studio and locked the door. He was forty-three, recently separated from the young flute student he'd married. With his reputation as the campus Casanova, I knew he wouldn't reject me like José had. I was sixteen, the age of consent in North Carolina, and NCSA didn't prohibit faculty-student liaisons even with high school students.

Philip told me I was beautiful and to stay away from José. In his bachelor flat, he lit a candle and turned on the stereo, preset to the "Liebestod" from Wagner's *Tristan und Isolde*. The opera's couple drink a love potion, dying together in order to seek pure love in the afterlife. "I can translate," whispered Philip, pushing a strand of hair off my face:

The sun concealed
itself in our bosom;
the stars of bliss
gleam, laughing.

Heart on your heart,
mouth on mouth,
the single bond
of a single breath.

Philip slid both arms under me and carried me to the bedroom as Isolde sang her final paean to divine love. He opened my dress and sighed contentedly. The scene felt a little weird, since Philip was old enough to be my father. At least he was good to me, unlike José.

As the weeks went on, he taught me how to make love and enjoy my own body. He also made me do my homework and gave me a copy of *Lolita*. Afternoons we'd cut through cotton fields on his BMW motorcycle, roaring up to my dorm just before curfew. We cooked together in his little kitchen. Afterward, he played Brahms for me, then Bach and Puccini. We lay on his living room floor, listening to all of *Tristan*, following a score checked out of the library.

That summer I toured Italy with the student orchestra, and Philip served as chaperone. In Assisi, we walked the through the Basilica and followed Giotto's frescoes. Candles flickered from wall sconces as we embraced in the crypt of St. Francis before a concert.

Settling in Spoleto, Philip and I ate with the other musicians in a restaurant where the old men played bocci under a trellis. Lamb roasted on an outdoor fire. Each day, we feasted on linguine with truffles from the winter harvest, drinking young red Montefalco from crude water glasses. Fat and sleepy, we climbed to an olive grove during the city's afternoon nap. As the late sun streaked through Roman aqueducts, I straddled Philip, my hair tangled with crushed leaves, my skirt stained with fruit. The sky turned slate and we sipped Vecchia Romagna straight from the bottle as Philip combed twigs from my long hair with his fingers.

The trip was romantic, but when we tried to resume our relationship in the autumn of my senior year, it felt dirty. Maybe I wanted someone like Philip to take care of me, a father figure. We tried to make love, but I recoiled from someone who suddenly looked like an old man. Philip was so much more interested in sex than I, our lovemaking almost felt like a violation. He sadly let me go. For the rest of the year, he treated me with kindness and respect. I returned to dorm life and new adventures.

For the 1977 fall homecoming, NCSA played Winston-Salem State, a teachers' college first established as a Negro university in 1892. As always, homecoming was our only football game of the year. Our male dancers' muscles rippled as they stretched at a portable ballet barre, wearing NCSA PICKLES jerseys and pink tutus. NCSA's mostly homosexual team of male ballet dancers with graceful posture lined up opposite a crew of burly African-American men. The head cheerleader's falsies slipped precariously as he egged them on. With so many gay men around willing to don skirts, only a few women managed to land on the cheerleading team.

While the tutus pummeled their opponents, I wandered up to DeMille Theater to prepare for a photo shoot to be used in the school's annual brochure. On the set of the drama department's *Midsummer Night's Dream* production, I held my oboe and tried to smile, wearing my high-collared black jacket and floor-length skirt. The group included twenty-seven other students: ballerinas, a visual artist, actors in costume, and modern dancers. None of us looked happy. "You kids seem so old," lamented the photographer.

Across the drive, our dorm mother, Sarah, joined other staff in decorating the gym for the dance that night in the outrageous Beaux Arts theme they'd dreamed up for their wacky little charges. It was dawning on me that our high school memory book was not something I'd reminisce over. Girls weren't eligible for homecoming queen, or even a date, since a large percentage of the male student body was gay. A college actor in loincloth, draped in tire chains, ascended the throne, while clusters of teenage ballerinas danced, watching boys bump and grind on the other side of the gym.

For the first time, I sold some dime bags of pot that night for ten bucks each, the weed bought from Guitarman Ray in Chapel Hill. Though a friend of my brother's had recently been arrested for selling dope, I had figured out that my chances of being caught or punished were slim, as long as it happened inside NCSA's gated community. My endeavor was part of a tradition noted in 1969 by the school's president. "We have . . . a little problem with drugs," Robert Ward admitted to his trustees. In 1970, Ward noted that narcs busted twelve students and also mentioned "a small number of male faculty members" pursuing students sexually. The solution? Providing an on-campus coffeehouse for entertainment, plus instructions to the students to police themselves.

Applications had boomed.

The administration was just as clueless in 1977, when I was peddling pot. "A few years ago, we were getting the students who figured they'd come here and spend a few years finding themselves. That led to suspicions of long-haired dope smokers," our admissions director told the Associated Press. Although the director didn't mention it, student-faculty sex hadn't waned either.

Our English teacher, Mr. Ballard, one of the few adults on campus who was widely trusted, warned my classmate Geoffrey against dance instructors Richard Kuch and Richard Gain. The two, who were a couple, had earned the nickname Crotch and Groin for their special interest in young male dancers. Male high school dance majors said that the pair, after adjusting their students' form with physical contact in the studio, sometimes befriended homesick boys and invited them to their home for the weekend.

As a music major, Geoffrey could easily avoid them, but at seventeen, he wasn't safe from his academic adviser. At his "appointment" in the adviser's home, Geoffrey sipped the wine he'd been offered and woke up to find himself pinned him to the floor. He wriggled free, running back to campus and keeping mum until graduation day to avoid expulsion for "artistic" reasons.

Unlike Geoffrey, I volunteered for extra faculty attention. Signing out to visit my parents, I boarded the Southern Crescent to New York with my piano teacher instead. The trip started out romantically. As I sipped a cocktail on the tufted seats of the Southern Railway bar car, tasseled lampshades swung like a scene out of an Agatha Christie novel.

From the moment we reached New York, I tasted the excitement José had described: musicians dashing around town, crowds beneath Carnegie Hall's marquee, études spilling from apartment windows. We even attended the funeral of my teacher's teacher, Irwin Freundlich, surrounded by famous musicians as the Juilliard Quartet performed a final tribute at Riverside Memorial Chapel.

On the train ride home, we made love on our coach seats, hiding beneath our coats. The sexual relationship lasted for a couple of weeks more, which created a tense atmosphere in my hour-long private lessons, before he moved on to another student. I began fantasizing about life as a musician in the big city.

I learned this was a popular dream for dancers too when I began hanging out with Noelle and her ballerina friends. They were nervously preparing to be examined by scouts from the New York City Ballet, who lined up the girls like cattle, measuring length between elbow and hip, evaluating turnout and proportion. Only the skinniest had a chance in George Balanchine's company, filling out the master's choreography with their emaciated bodies.

"I got a pink slip," one girl moaned at Friday lunch, holding her summons for private "fat conference" with the dance faculty. Girls were told to lose weight or go home for good. There was always a way to get just a little thinner.

In the cafeteria, pods of ballerinas swarmed over desserts, cheese, and pastries, flitting to the restroom and wiping their mouths a few minutes later, and then repeating the feast. Raiding the bagel table, they created a favorite dish: two parts peanut butter, one part honey, and one part bran, rolled into balls that looked like baby porcupines. Some nibbled vegetables or scraped the skin off fried chicken, blotting it dry; one spooned up low-fat chocolate milk in slow motion, visualizing ice cream in its place.

They waddled off for the last class of the week, where Crotch and Groin let the girls hide their little bellies under sweaters while they concentrated on the boys. Afterward, weekend frenzy started in earnest. A bun-headed army of sylphs stormed Mickey's convenience store, a few blocks off campus, for Twinkies, Snickers, Moon Pies, and quarts of Breyer's, bribing me to buy them Boone's Farm Strawberry Hill Wine with my fake ID.

On Saturday, they wolfed down French toast in time to catch NCSA's blue school bus to Hanes Mall, buying new leotards at Capezio, buttery sugar-bread at the Moravian bakery, and cheese at Mr. Dunderbak's deli. At Eckerd's, they stocked up on peanut butter, Ritz crackers, cigarettes, Ex-Lax, and throat lozenges, finishing with a stop at Dunkin' Donuts.

As the other ballerinas prepared to pig out, Maria, a stunning Latina, whispered into the pay phone that she forbade anyone else to use. Tonight, like every Saturday, a stretch limo would pick her up at seven, gliding back just before curfew. Maria had more clothes and money than anyone else; she appeared to be keeping company with the wealthy tobacco executives of Winston-Salem.

The rest of us stayed in the dorm playing cards, with jelly and cream-filled doughnuts spread out around us. Awash in candy wrappers, the little swans sat on the floor whacking point shoes to break them in, ripping their new leotards to personalize them, and babbling about food. Remember to mark your puke with orange Cheetos so you know when to stop. Peanut butter's delicious but painful to throw up; nachos, pineapple, and fries are even worse. Ice cream goes down clean and comes up smooth, so eat all you want. Cafeteria white rolls, macaroni and cheese, cereal, and pudding work great too.

Partying wound down on Sunday, hours before Monday's leotard inspection. The dorm bathroom was a war zone, spattered with watery puke and feces. The timing and dosage of laxatives was imperative: no explosions, just gentle all-day diarrhea. Consuming only water, dancers sucked on lozenges for throats hoarse from vomiting. Bones ached and moods turned bitchy. Some fasted all week, repeating the binge again on Friday.

I joined the wispy dancers in their feasts. Since I did not throw up, my weight went up thirty pounds. Even though Noelle gained a little, she was still stick-thin. When she was finally pink-slipped for being five pounds overweight, she drank tomato juice until she weighed ninety-five pounds, her tongue turned black, and she felt faint in dance class. "Faster," scolded her instructor, as Noelle's five-foot-eight-inch frame pirouetted sluggishly.

Noelle's roommate, Elizabeth, had already left NCSA to join the Atlanta Ballet. Only sixteen, she lived in an apartment all by herself. Elizabeth couldn't find a high school to accommodate her touring schedule, until she found the one institution that would have her, which otherwise instructed juvenile delinquents and truants.

I missed her as the rest of us lined up on the sofa for our monthly dorm meetings. A male painter from Hickory spat tobacco in a clear glass, absently flipping a ballerina's blond ponytail back and forth as the smell of freshly baked cookies wafted down the hall. Our dorm mother bustled about, hanging decorations.

"Now then," she chirped, setting down her glitter glue stick, "how *is* everyone?" She cocked her head, and her voice grew syrupy. "Whoooooo's homesick?"

"You kids will do well," called our chaperone from the bus seat ahead of me, clapping her hands cheerily. "Musicians are *so* good at math."

"Where are we going?" Noelle whispered.

NCSA's high school division provided no preparation for the SAT and required only two years of English, one in social studies, and a semester of biology and math. Physical education meant saying that you'd gone to the pool, or skated, or performed some other solitary sport. Physics and math beyond geometry weren't offered at all.

Most students were too young to be alarmed about their limited education. A 1969 high school violin alum, Lucy Stoltzman, wrote, in materials prepared for a 2003 Chicago conference for the Consortium for the Liberal Education of Artists, which addressed humanities education for performers:

> I was brought up as a violinist and had a traditional music education, forgoing academic subjects in favor of music beginning in tenth grade at NCSA. The most complicated thing I did in my chemistry class at NCSA was to boil water with and without salt in it . . . a friend told me I'd have a brain the size of a pea by the time I graduated.

Douglas Calloway, in 1977 an eighteen-year-old dance major from West Virginia, told the Associated Press he simply wanted to "drop the whole classroom thing."

Parents of NCSA students didn't express much more concern over the future of their children. The mother of one 1981 drama graduate told the Raleigh *News and Observer* that she "never thought a son of mine would live that way. But he's dedicated. He'll make it." The budding actor had just moved into a third-floor Brooklyn walk-up and worked part-time for a polling firm. Another mother told the same reporter that her daughter "may end up selling pencils on Forty-second Street, but she plans to make it a career!"

I wasn't feeling optimistic about my chances either. At eighteen, after three years of arts education, I didn't know what started the Civil War; I'd never heard of the periodic table of elements; and I couldn't calculate a percentage. I fiddled with the SAT answer sheet, filling in random bubbles like abstract art.

Afterward, the chaperone herded us back on the bus. "I love the sound of the oboe," the old lady said, after asking about my major. I wondered why the school had chosen this innocent event to supply a chaperone. "You're too young to know, dear, but Danny Kaye—he's a comedian, you see—he always said, "'The oboe's an ill wind that no one blows good.'" She looked at me hopefully. "Ill wind . . . Shakespeare?" She settled in her seat, pursing her lips.

Ill wind? We never read any Shakespeare.

A ballerina behind me whispered, "Why was that test called SAT, because it's Saturday?"

A few months later, we streamed across the stage at commencement, and then went in separate directions. "It's like they sent us off on a speeding train, and now it's breaking down in the desert," Geoffrey said quietly. I felt the same, but I had a plan—to keep studying with Joe Robinson in New York. He'd just won the New York Philharmonic's principal oboe position.

I wasn't that thrilled about continuing my relationship with Robinson. He never stopped putting his hands on me. He'd given me a big red F on one of my juries (the final examination for performance majors), soon after my mouth had been injured in a car accident. And although he clearly ranked me as one of his better students, he regarded my misbehavior scornfully, instead of asking what was wrong or speaking with my parents. I'd been accepted at both Juilliard and the Manhattan School of Music. I chose Manhattan, since Joe was teaching there exclusively.

As my parents hugged me at commencement, I felt like I'd gotten away with murder. I couldn't admit to them how tenuous I felt, after insisting on coming here instead of attending Exeter.

Anne Epperson, one of my other teachers who was a former Juilliard staff accompanist, overheard us talking about finding a New York apartment and scribbled something on a scrap of paper. Pushing it into my hand, Anne said, "It's the address of a building on West Ninety-ninth Street, where the landlord likes renting to classical musicians." She told me to give the building agent, Rudy Rudolph, three hundred dollars cash and mention her name.

"It's called the Allendale."

To celebrate graduation, I bought tickets with my dope profits to hear violinist Itzhak Perlman, who was playing with the pianist Samuel Sanders. I was terrified to approach Perlman backstage afterward, since he was so very famous. He was also mobbed by women members of the concert series' volunteer committee. Sanders looked much friendlier. Except for his luxurious head of curly brown hair, he looked like a younger, cuter version of Woody Allen, right down to the prominent nose. Since Sanders had taught my piano teacher during his Juilliard days, I almost felt I knew him.

The concert had taken place in Greenboro in an old university auditorium with a utilitarian backstage area. I waited until Sanders had gathered up his hairbrush, address book, wristwatch, and a vial of some kind of pills, which had been perfectly lined up on the dressing room's plywood counter. He checked the spot three more times, as if some object could have magically appeared.

"Mr. Sanders," I said, and mentioned my piano teacher. He began looking at the shelf a fourth time. Wondering what Sanders would think of me, I was too intimidated to compliment his playing or mention the concert at all. He was the most famous musician I'd ever met, and I wanted him to approve of me. Sanders scanned my plastic glasses, polyester dress, and drugstore pantyhose bagging at the knees.

"So what?" he spat, and whirled back to the society ladies who were clustered around Perlman.

3

The Prodigy

MOLLIE SANDERS COULDN'T understand why her son Samuel wasn't growing faster. Born a chubby baby in 1937, he weighed only eighteen pounds one year later and gasped for air whenever she or his father, Irving, gave him a bottle. When he was old enough to walk, he would stop to squat every thirty feet or so, panting through blue lips as his brother, Martin, bounded down the sidewalk.

Doctors diagnosed a hole between the left and right ventricles in Samuel's heart, a congenital defect called tetralogy of Fallot, that reduces the oxygen in the bloodstream. Surgeons were pioneering cardiac surgery at the time, but rarely for children. Like some two thousand other blue babies born annually in the United States, Samuel was expected to die before his teens.

Without health insurance, medical care drained his family's finances. Irving's wholesale meat business thrived, though, and he had bought a two-family brick house by 1941, with a bedroom for each of the boys and one for their older half sister, Marjorie. As Samuel grew older, the Bronx schools tucked him away with other children who didn't look right, the crippled, twitching, and wheezing students of all ages who didn't fit in anywhere else.

Even though he couldn't play sports, Samuel wanted a baseball glove, just like the Yankees used. Instead, he got a used upright piano and lessons with Hedwig Rosenthal. The matron terrified him, her frizzy hair standing on end, eyes bulging and scarlet nails rapping as Samuel played Czerny beneath a portrait of a stern man. He unleashed his wrath on

Pianist Samuel Sanders at around age ten, with his teacher Hedwig Rosenthal. (Ashley Studios, Hotel Great Northern, New York. Courtesy of the Juilliard School archives.)

the keyboard, banging with fingers clubbed from bad circulation, drilling each phrase to perfection in a corner of his parents' living room.

Sam grew weaker. Then, when he was nine, his mother heard about a new surgery at Johns Hopkins Hospital in Baltimore. As the family drove across the George Washington Bridge, Samuel looked back toward Manhattan's lights, twinkling across the Hudson, and yearned to be a part of all the exciting things that happened there. For Samuel, the bridge represented the pathway to a more normal life.

Two doctors at Johns Hopkins examined him, Helen Taussig and Alfred Blalock. The team had first operated on a fifteen-month-old blue baby in 1944, building a duct to carry blood directly to the girl's lungs. Samuel became the 298th child to receive the procedure, which increased the oxygen saturation level in his blood by about 50 percent. No one knew how long he might survive.

A surgical complication caused a curvature of the spine. For a time, one leg felt numb and then grew slightly shorter. Samuel and his mother stayed in Baltimore for nine months for physical therapy, while Irving watched Martin in the Bronx. Once Samuel returned home he started practicing again, even though he didn't much like lessons and recitals.

Only two years later, Samuel went public with Chopin's difficult F-minor Concerto at age eleven, his story printed in the *New York Times.* Transformed from misfit to star, he was finally allowed to enroll in a regular class at Taft High School.

For Samuel, 1950 was a watershed year. His bar mitzvah brought a Steinway grand; he won a brand-new competition called Concert Artists Guild, which paid ten dollars for a Town Hall debut recital and management with Arthur Judson's prestigious Columbia Artists; and the *Times* called him "bright with promise." Basking in the limelight, Samuel won a $500 wardrobe for his mother by competing on *The Big Payoff*, a CBS television quiz show, and then appeared on Arthur Godfrey's *Talent Scouts* and CBS television's *Prize Performance.*

Martin was talented as well, studying violin at New York's High School of Music and Art. But he joined the army and then headed for college. After graduation he launched a successful real estate business, begun years earlier when he bought, with his own bar mitzvah gift, land in Brooklyn the city would later purchase for the new Verrazano Narrows Bridge to Staten Island.

Their half sister, Marjorie, had married a physicist and moved to Oak Ridge, Tennessee, in 1945. The Oak Ridge National Laboratory was only two years old, a facility for plutonium production associated with the Manhattan Project. Marjorie organized a music committee, just as many communities across America were doing, raising money to pay recital fees for visiting musicians and a local part-time orchestra. In 1954, Marjorie brought in her sixteen-year old brother Samuel, who entertained the local scientists by playing Maurice Ravel's *Jeux d'Eau.*

Samuel's reputation as a child prodigy grew. After winning WQXR radio's Musical Talent in Our Schools competition, he stepped onstage at Carnegie Hall to play Rachmaninoff's Concerto no. 2 with the New York Philharmonic. A solo career looked inevitable, but Samuel grew restless and enrolled at Hunter College instead.

Teachers assigned him to accompany an Irish Catholic student tenor at Hunter, a singer who'd already finished a career as a child star. From age six, Little Bobby White had sung on radio shows from Fred Allen to Kay Kyser, bantering with Bing Crosby and other celebrities of the era. Since the emergence of television, White was searching for a new image as he worked toward his bachelor's degree.

At their first rehearsal in a Hunter College practice room, Sam nervously fiddled with the sheet music, apologizing in advance. Bobby cursed the music department for sending him an incompetent pianist and handed Sam the music to an aria from J. S. Bach's *Magnificat.* "It's not in A major. It's F-sharp minor," Bobby enunciated slowly, since both keys had the same three sharps, and this boy was clearly an idiot.

"Uh, okay," stuttered Sam. "Um, I'll try."

Sam played the aria perfectly. The two performed together again and again and became close friends, even though Bobby was gay and Catholic, Sam a straight Jew. Taking his new friend home to the Bronx, Sam introduced Bobby to his parents, and Mollie served up not one but three pork chops to her son's new friend, who watched her cook in a kitchen lined wall-to-wall with white butcher paper, immaculate as her son's musicianship.

What's not to like? thought Bobby. The food's great, there's a Cadillac downstairs, and the kid can sight-read!

The pair earned fifty bucks a performance at communion breakfasts, where they also developed a deadpan comedy routine. "I have to move, the neighborhood is changing so," one lock-jawed Catholic lady droned. "Up here in Fordham Hill, we're taken over, you know, by the *noses,*" she whispered, putting fist to forehead, her elbow mimicking an enormous Jewish schnoz. Sam rubbed his beak and looked her slowly up and down. "Bobby, can you imagine? The noses."

Sam went on to study at Juilliard with Sergius Kagen and Irwin Freundlich. He married a singer and moved across from Yankee Stadium on Gerard Avenue, where the couple could count Roger Maris's home runs by the roars from the stadium.

He started to earn real money playing piano, but like most classical musicians in the early 1960s he did whatever paid the rent, artistic or not. At Carnegie Recital Hall, he played one concert accompanying singer Carolyn Raney, another with blind violinist Ruben Varga, and a third with a concertina soloist who fainted onstage, canceling the performance. For extra cash, he recorded a project with "the singing lady," Irene Wicker, who was married to the brother of energy tycoon Armand Hammer. Wicker's disc was packaged with a picture book aimed at parents of "the pre-nursery precocious," with Sam repeating "Twinkle, Twinkle, Little Star" for each letter and number.

He joined Juilliard's faculty at its granite fortress above Columbia University, demanding new recognition for accompanists, who were generally underpaid and unrecognized at the time. But just as Sam tasted success, his marriage and his health fell apart.

Sam moved to an eighty-dollar-a-month five-room apartment (bathtub in the kitchen) in a building at 56th and Tenth owned by his brother, Martin. Bobby moved in upstairs, sometimes missing his rent payments. Since money was scarce, Sam began developing the powerful circle of artists, patrons, and journalists that would embrace him for many years, providing networking, employment, and financial support.

Sam's heart started giving him trouble again in 1965, as he dragged himself through coachings, rehearsals, and concerts. Frightened, he sought medical attention. Doctors hooked him up to diagnostic devices, carefully choosing classical music to soothe him during the tests. Sam grew restless and at one point exploded, "That's all wrong!" Machines were shut down and tubes pulled out until the team realized he wasn't in pain, at least not physical pain, but was instead critiquing the Dvorak Cello Concerto that was playing on the Muzak.

New technology provided a solution for Sam's latest heart complication: "total correction" that would close the hole between his ventricles, usually the final operation needed by a former blue baby. Mollie sold her diamond ring to help pay for the surgery, while Martin guaranteed the balance of the $30,000. When he woke from surgery in Columbia-Presbyterian Hospital and heard Lawrence Welk's "Champagne Music" theme drifting from the intensive care unit's TV, the tune convinced Sam he'd died and was not necessarily in heaven.

Released from the hospital on November 9, Sam decided he really *was* dying as he rode down FDR Drive in a taxi with his mother and the lights of his beautiful city flickered and went dark. Mollie and the cabbie saw it too, as the blackout of 1965 plunged the entire Northeast into darkness. Since his parents lived on the eleventh floor of an elevator building now rendered a walk-up by the power outage, Sam struggled up five flights to Martin's Sutton Place apartment to recover.

A few months later, Sam married painter Rhoda Ross in the Hastings-on-Hudson home of cellist Leonard Rose and launched a busy travel schedule of community concerts. He'd become first choice for such classical music stars as Jacqueline du Pre, Leonard Rose, Itzhak Perlman, Mstislav Rostropovich, Yo-Yo Ma, Jaime Laredo, Jessye Norman, and Beverly Sills; played debut recitals for cellists Lynn Harrell and Robert Sylvester and flutist Paula Robison; and accompanied silver medalist Stephen Kates at the 1966 Tchaikovsky Competition in Moscow. Playing two hundred concerts a year, he zipped between different artists, cities, and repertoires.

When Juilliard moved from Claremont Avenue to Lincoln Center in 1969, Sam shifted his teaching to a plush modern studio. Unfortunately, the school, along with the rest of Lincoln Center (and its new high-rolling arts budget), couldn't afford to pay its faculty adequately or provide them health insurance.

"Every institution at Lincoln Center is broke . . . and Juilliard will be when it gets there," said Juilliard's chairman, John Drye, as the school opened. With the move, Juilliard's maintenance expense quadrupled, and the stagehands' union demands threatened to shut down its theater altogether. A *New York Times* article noted that Juilliard relied on massive subsidy by prestige-chasing faculty who could make better money elsewhere.

By 1972, Bobby White had landed enough teaching gigs to move out of Martin's West 56th Street building. After a rehearsal, flutist Tom Nyfenger dropped him off at the corner of 99th and West End. "A lot of musicians live around here," Nyfenger said. Just as Bobby slammed the car door, a pretty blond bass player he knew turned the corner and pulled him into her building, the Allendale, to meet rental agent Rudy Rudolph. The Allendale was run-down, but a three-room flat in the huge building that the landlords owned next door was far more refined. It was a lot of money, Bobby thought, writing a check for $280 rent, a month's security deposit, and a $300 bribe, but with a doorman, thick walls, and windows facing residential West End Avenue, he was definitely moving up.

Sam was moving up too. He and Rhoda found a large prewar place just south of Bobby, on West End at 83rd and Rhoda gave birth to a little girl they named Sophie. Sam's schedule was exhausting: Town Hall one night with Rose, Rockefeller University with Bobby the next, a three-city tour of Florida and then off to Peoria, Utica, and Galveston with Itzhak Perlman.

Sam never got over his nerves, combating his fear with obsessive practice. He drilled pieces endlessly, in myriad variations of rhythm, tempo, and phrasing. Practice was a matter of survival, and he rehearsed every chance he got. Practice was his master, practice and Valium, which "brings me down from a wild panic to a mild hysteria," he said.

Sam started practicing in a friend's soundproof apartment after midnight, so he would have more hours at the keyboard without being interrupted, returning home each morning at sunrise to sleep. When he woke at lunchtime, he either took a cab to Juilliard or packed his tuxedo between sheets of tissue paper and headed to the airport for a short concert tour with Itzhak, with whom he was playing ever more frequently as time went on.

After one run-out performance in North Carolina with Itzhak in 1978, Sam was packing up the hairbrush, address book, and wristwatch he always set out in precise parallel formation backstage before the concert, as a good-luck ritual. After a long week of concerts, he was eager to get home to see his young daughter Sophie, especially since he hadn't been feeling well, and he was growing anxious hanging around while the ladies' club shook Itzhak's hand.

As Itzhak put on his coat, Sam glanced back one last time to make sure nothing was left behind. Just as it looked like the two men could finally leave, a local girl who'd studied piano with someone he knew approached. She wanted to talk to him, but like so many music students she had nothing to say.

4

New World Symphony

SAM SANDERS HAD succeeded despite huge physical odds. Born with a life expectancy of nine years, he twice benefited from medical advances that saved his life at the eleventh hour. The credit for his musical career, however, was his. Though he rose to prominence, Sam still had to piece together a living, artistic or not, by playing radio and television variety shows, performing an array of recitals, and recording whatever paid best.

When Sam started out in the 1950s, few financial resources were available to classical musicians. No federal or state arts council would exist until 1960. With so few meal tickets, Sam learned to rely both on the musical network that brought him work as an accompanist and the social circle whose money backed organizations and performance projects.

Musicians like Sam earned good fees playing community concert series, but the money was whittled away by expenses. He might earn $450 for a performance; after paying the presenter and manager fees, piano rental, hotel, travel, advertising, promotion, and buying formal wear, he'd have no more than $75 in his pocket. Health and retirement benefits were luxuries.

During the 1950s, music groups began extending their seasons, and philanthropic organizations formed to offer support. New competitions sprang up, offering cash awards, debut recitals, and concert management contracts. Until this time, only two major contests in America existed in the entire classical music community: the Naumburg Prize, founded in 1926, and the Leventritt Prize, founded in 1940. In addition, faster jet flights were now allowing a soloist to fit in more concerts—and paychecks—than ever before.

Musicians like me, born a generation after Sam, entered a very different music business, one filled with greater opportunity compared to earlier eras. During the 1960s, funding mushroomed for arts education, performing groups, and concert series. Jobs were still not plentiful compared to many nonmusical professions, but the improvement was so dramatic I assumed that a fairly active arts world had always existed, complete with big audiences who clapped in all the right places.

"The American attitude toward the arts has completed a 180-degree turn since the end of World War II," wrote Alvin Toffler in *The Culture Consumers*. "From one of apathy, indifference, and even hostility, it has become one of eager, if sometimes ignorant, enthusiasm."[1]

The apathy, Toffler argued, had begun in Puritan days, as settlers came to value work above idle pleasure. Statutes forbade plays, dancing, and "unprofitable" books, along with smoking, drinking, and gambling. Even so, theater, painting, and music had emerged by the late 1700s as villages grew to cities and hardscrabble lives became more comfortable. In 1789, George Washington urged Congress to "accelerate the progress of art and science; to patronize works of genius," but his plea inspired little action at the time.[2]

American arts paid their own way until the late nineteenth century. Market demand drove impresarios, who survived only by providing art that an audience could, and would, buy at competitive prices, like a retail product. Performers who were willing to trade low salaries for artistic gratification helped subsidize the production of entertainment in the nineteenth century, according to arts analyst John Kreidler.[3]

To please the audience, presenters bowed to popular taste, mixing Shakespeare and Mozart with drinking songs and circus acts. Applause, shouts, hisses, stamping, jeers, and whistles punctuated performances, inspiring the orchestra to substitute "Tally Ho the Grinders" or "Yankee Doodle" for the classical overture.[4]

European opera stars crisscrossed the country during the mid-1800s on lucrative tours, injecting popular tunes like "An Old Man Would Be a-Wooing" into a Rossini opera, which might then be followed by a comic play. Once English-language performances made their stories more accessible, the *New York Home Journal* could declare that "opera music has become a popular taste."[5]

Concert music, without the entertainment value of a story line, was still something of a Eurocentric rarity, and few instrumental concert performances were presented in the United States during the mid-nineteenth century. The wealthy traveled abroad for classical music. Members of the small middle class waited for European artists to tour America, while the workingman had neither time nor money for sophisticated entertainment. Bands and orchestras began forming, sometimes playing a few classical pieces, but the groups could not attract an audience without combining their Beethoven symphonies with polkas and popular music.

When the New York Philharmonic was founded in 1842, it gave four concerts a season. A workers' cooperative, its musicians maximized resources. They shared profits, chose their own conductor, and determined his salary. They substituted a violin for a missing oboe. They sold tickets even to rehearsals.[6] During their summer seasons in a Central Park beer garden, conductor Theodore Thomas had to juxtapose waltzes and Wagner, complaining that "circumstances force me to prostitute my art and my talents."

One Philadelphia paper in 1899 noted the general public wasn't interested enough in classical music to buy tickets for it, declaring "promoters must expect to pay the piper." Pay they did, as wealthy elites of the era began to fund arts groups in order to satisfy their own preferences. Maestro Thomas's yen for pure classics became a reality when orchestras began divorcing themselves from the marketplace through guaranteed funding. As the necessity of pleasing a paying audience diminished, "pure" elitist culture rose above the common entertainment, creating a wide gulf between the two.

Art became a lofty pursuit, and Americans began regarding concert halls as cultural shrines, music as uplifting mysticism. "The sermons in behalf of the arts then preached (and which continue to be preached) laid a heavy moral burden on an experience that elsewhere was considered simply sophisticated entertainment," wrote author Alice Goldfarb Marquis in *Art Lessons*.[7]

Elites then controlled cultural policy by forming nonprofit organizations, which served as central clearinghouses for financial arts support. Under the aegis of these board-run operations, orchestras formed in St. Louis, Cincinnati, Minneapolis, and San Francisco.

The nonprofit model pasted "an altruistic, morally chaste veneer over basically self-serving activities," wrote Marquis. Arts marketing was born. By selling culture as snake oil for the masses, elites could engineer a city's artistic life to separate themselves from commoners, creating a smokescreen of cultural ritual that also distanced performers from their audience.

The New York Philharmonic's musicians finally relinquished control to a board of directors in 1908, accepting a $90,000 note from Andrew Carnegie, J. P. Morgan, and Joseph Pulitzer, who also left them ten times that amount upon his death, but only if their programs included his favorite musical warhorses.[8]

A new system of American taxation in the early twentieth century further changed the business of philanthropy. When the country's first income tax bill was enacted in 1913, charitable giving dropped when wealthy scions had to find the money to pay large sums to the government. There was a positive side to the 1913 bill, however, which gave nonprofit organizations like orchestras the new benefit of tax exemption. A second tax bill, in 1917, created a deduction for contributions to those nonprofits, and the resulting tax incentive once again spurred philanthropy.

When the 1929 stock market crash devoured fortunes, donations to the arts by foundations declined from $1.4 million to $740,000 between 1930 and 1933. Only a few organizations funded culture during the Great Depression, among them the Carnegie Corporation, which provided 82 percent of all foundation donations to the arts until it virtually withdrew in 1943.[9] In the following years, audiences sought such lighter fare as movies, radio programs, and stage shows, which were popular as relief to the grim realities of the era's everyday life.

World War II immigration built a fervent audience of European Americans, many of them amateur or professional musicians. As the war ended, a renewed sense of democracy diffused the elite's monopoly on artistic taste, opening the concepts of high and low culture to debate and often mixing the two. Operatic legends Lauritz Melchior, Risë

Stevens, and Ezio Pinza appeared in Hollywood films, soprano Beverly Sills hawked Rinso soap powder on the radio, and dancers Agnes de Mille, Jerome Robbins, Gene Kelly, and Fred Astaire moved between the worlds of Broadway and ballet.[10]

The Eisenhower era produced four million children each year, born into a healthy economy where luxuries were commonplace and technology freed the growing population to enjoy leisure activities. Real income had grown 50 percent between 1941 and 1952. The 1944 GI Bill spent $14.5 billion to educate 7.8 million veterans, guaranteeing free tuition to a generation rapidly gaining the knowledge and income for art appreciation.[11]

Americans of all ages participated in the arts, with one in six involved in cultural pursuits. One symphony's 1955 demographic survey revealed 54 percent of its audience was under thirty-five.[12] Between 1940 and 1960, musical instrument sales quintupled, and more than half the world's orchestras were located in America.[13]

In this environment, the nonprofit Ford Foundation budgeted $57 million in 1951 for programs promoting peace, democracy, world economy, education, and interpersonal behavior. The foundation's first five-year arts and humanities program spent $2 million annually, starting a tab that would total $320 million by 1974. A private foundation, Ford was not accountable to taxpayers in its choice of artists, often giving large grants to develop a nascent organization over many years.

America declared superiority in technology, education, and industry, but the U.S. government saw the Soviets' cultural wealth as a threat. Echoing nineteenth-century "arts religion," government leaders promised spiritual and social benefit for any community that launched an active cultural life. Bach and Beethoven would provide sublime revelation, or, in the words of one *Life* magazine story, "impose form and meaning on the increasing complexities of the human experience." Europe and Russia had something America did not: a complex creative class that had evolved over centuries. Not to be outdone, Americans wanted one too—right away.

"The sooner we can implement a program of selling our culture to the uncommitted people of the world as a weapon, the better off we are," said New Jersey congressman Frank Thompson in 1954.[14] Four years later, that "weapon" arrived, in the form of a Texan pianist so un-popular that Columbia Artists Management was considering dropping him from their rural touring program.

When pianist Van Cliburn won Moscow's Tchaikovsky Competition in 1958, he beat the Russians at their own game. New Yorkers threw him a ticker-tape parade down Fifth Avenue, and politicians declared the arts essential to a free society. Dwight Eisenhower signed a bill to build a National Cultural Center (later renamed the John F. Kennedy Center for the Performing Arts), JFK appointed an honorary arts council, and Jacqueline Kennedy brought Pablo Casals, Leonard Bernstein, Paul Hindemith, and Igor Stravinsky to the White House.

In the early sixties, The Rockefeller Brothers Fund examined the future development of the performing arts. Their published study, *The Performing Arts: Problems and Prospects*, suggested that a more active cultural life would benefit all classes of Americans, that

> the arts are not for a privileged few but for the many, that their place is not on the periphery of society but at its center, that they are not just a form of recreation but are of central importance to our well-being and happiness. In the panel's view, this status will not be widely achieved unless artistic excellence is the constant goal of every artist and every arts organization, and mediocrity is recognized as the ever-present enemy of true progress.[15]

The Rockefeller report did not analyze how to pay for the vast arts programs it promoted. However, New York's most powerful men did find a way to capitalize on the idea, with plans for arts centers that would profit them as businessmen while painting them as beneficent cultural patrons. By 1962, construction of at least sixty performing arts complexes was under way nationwide, increasing real estate values and development and pro-tecting a city's value and appeal as postwar residents were fleeing to sub-urbia. Although the centers looked like a boon to arts groups, they were a mixed blessing. The performing organizations would soon find that their elegant new surroundings increased operating costs dramatically.

"The raison d'être for Lincoln Center was dubious from the begin-ning," observed *New Yorker* journalist Paul Goldberger. "It originated with

Robert Moses, not Leonard Bernstein, and Moses didn't care much for opera, or theatre, or symphony orchestras. He just figured that they could serve as a magnet for development."[16]

America still exhibited an inferiority complex about its cultural life, so even the very structure of New York's Lincoln Center echoed the Eurocentric activity inside its buildings. Tennessee pink marble had been good enough for Washington's National Gallery in 1941, but Cold War concert halls had to be built from European bricks and mortar. For Lincoln Center, travertine marble was brought from the quarries that built St. Peter's basilica in the Vatican, with the Metropolitan Opera's enormous murals by Russian-French painter Marc Chagall taking center stage on the plaza.[17]

A multimillion-dollar industry revolving around performing arts complexes like Lincoln Center blossomed, providing new business for contractors, service industries, transportation, investment companies, law offices, and accounting firms. Moving companies provided exhibition tour packages, with insurance firms securing the precious artworks. Consultants peddled management surveys to orchestras, troupes, and civic organizations planning the arts centers, while manufacturers sold the centers' ingredients: carpeting, seats, lighting, concrete, steel, easels, and industrial tiles.

Paying for it all became a staggering prospect. Orchestra trustees accustomed to plugging a five- or six-figure deficit each year shrank in terror when confronted with skyrocketing costs, as groups mounted longer seasons and more elaborate productions within their costly new buildings. A New York City Opera performance at Lincoln Center's New York State Theater ended up costing nearly five times what it had at its old home, the populist City Center on 55th Street. Even though the opera nearly sold out its new house at sharply higher ticket prices, the company's annual deficit leaped from $325,000 to $1.8 million soon after the move.[18]

Paid for largely by contributors, the complexes themselves cost a fortune. Some $144 million of Lincoln Center's $185 million construction cost came from private sources. The Metropolitan Opera's $32 million construction estimate rocketed to $50 million, and putting on its operas consumed 10 percent of all music production expenditures in the entire country.

When President Eisenhower broke ground for Lincoln Center in 1959, he proclaimed that "a mighty influence for peace and understanding throughout the world" would grow out of what was then a $75 million complex. The cost had grown to $100 million one year later and $170 million by 1963. Private contributors, most notably the Ford, Rockefeller, James, and Avalon foundations and the Carnegie Corporation, continued pouring new grants into Lincoln Center's snowballing budget, but in its seventh year, the project teetered on bankruptcy.[19] A summer music festival and film series were canceled, staff was cut, and plans for an administration building were scrapped. At last two donors, John D. Rockefeller III and Lawrence Wien, gave $1.25 million apiece, which, with more foundation, city, and individual funds, finally paid off Lincoln Center's building fund. Nearly ten thousand donors had contributed to the Lincoln Center project.[20]

As Lincoln Center's crisis was averted, its administrators now faced the problem of paying for sharply increased operating costs, which totaled $40 million annually for all the center's constituents. Amyas Ames, chairman of Lincoln Center's executive committee, predicted in 1970 that the complex's total deficit would increase from $11 million to $20 million in a mere three years, only a fraction of which could be recouped by higher ticket prices. If the arts were a public good, as their businessmen architects claimed, the government had to step in.[21]

Interest in federal arts support was nothing new—George Washington and Thomas Jefferson had proposed a government role—but the country saw little real application until the 1960s, except for a brief post-Depression period. From 1935 to 1943, Franklin D. Roosevelt established employment programs for artists under the Works Progress Administration (WPA). The WPA's Federal Music Program (FMP) concentrated on providing employment for musicians, spurring the formation of the Buffalo Philharmonic and the Pittsburgh, Springfield (Massachusetts), Oklahoma City, and Utah symphonies, and encouraging new works by Aaron Copland, Virgil Thompson, and others.[22] Musicians of the FMP worked steadily by 1938, earning $23.86 for a 45-hour week.[23]

Government money and creativity were bad bedfellows from the beginning, proving to be more controversial than expected. When the Federal Theatre Project produced prolabor anticapitalist plays critical of the government that funded the program, the House Un-American Activities Committee muzzled WPA arts programs, which Roosevelt later reviewed and canceled in the midst of economic recovery.

WPA arts projects had whetted an appetite for government-sponsored culture in America, and support for the arts began showing up throughout government agencies. Cultural programs were included in the Office of Education, the Social and Rehabilitation Service of the National Institute of Mental Health, the Labor and Interior departments, the Small Business Administration, the Atomic Energy Commission, and the Elementary and Secondary Education Act, which gave $41 million to cultural programs during the 1960s.[24]

Congress also provided ongoing funds for the operations and activities of the National Gallery of Art. The industrialist Andrew Mellon, seeking a tax break after the Depression, had founded the museum in 1941 by donating $14 million and his private collection, which centered around twenty-one masterpieces once owned by Catherine the Great of Russia.[25]

Jacob Javits and Hubert Humphrey unsuccessfully introduced bills for federal arts funding; Eisenhower and Harry Truman also failed with their recommendations supporting culture. Centralized support for public arts policy came with Lyndon Johnson's Great Society, a "place where men are more concerned with the quality of their goals than the quantity of their goods . . . beckoning us toward a destiny where the meaning of our lives matches the marvelous products of our labor," said Johnson in a 1964 speech. Johnson's Congress finally approved the National Council on the Arts in 1964, satisfying a growing constituency of arts board members who were also business, community, and corporate leaders. Though the 1950s McCarthyism (which blacklisted many actors) cast suspicion on the arts, the new organization was included under the umbrella of the National Foundation on the Arts and Humanities in 1965, spawning the National Endowment for the Arts (NEA).

The artists themselves remained cautious. Many disagreed with Johnson's Vietnam policies and considered government money tainted, anathema to the autonomous voice of protest in a time of drastic social change. The musicians' union, lobbying for jobs, supported the legislation, but 91 percent of American Symphony Orchestra League members had previously opposed federal funding in 1951, seeing the money as artistically oppressive. Theater critic Brooks Atkinson, *Harper's* editor Russell Lynes, playwright Thornton Wilder, painter Larry Rivers, and Beat poet Lawrence Ferlinghetti all argued that federal funding would tether creativity and lead to mediocre art.[26]

Ironically, Richard Nixon—active in Joseph McCarthy's Hollywood witch hunt—became the NEA's messiah. In 1971, he increased the agency's budget eightfold, to $40 million. "It struck me as politically wise to build up the Endowment," said Leonard Garment, the clarinet-playing lawyer who had become Nixon's special counsel. Garment advised the president that such a dramatic increase could win the political allegiance of arts groups' board members, who were usually influential corporate and community leaders as well.[27]

Nixon imbued the arts with the power "to help heal divisions among our people and to vault some of the barriers that divide the world." The agency's new chair, Nancy Hanks, added that "the lives of the people should be advanced in freedom and in comprehension of the tough and soaring qualities of the spirit," declaring the arts to be "not a luxury; they are a necessity." In rhetoric intended to lure arts board members, one Nixon-era official promised that symphonies, ballets, and stage plays would "rid our society of its most basic ills— voicelessness, isolation, depersonalization—the complete absence of any purpose or reason for living."[28]

With such a broad agenda, it was not surprising the NEA started out by assigning funds indiscriminately. In its infancy, the NEA gave $350,000 to the American Ballet Theater but also proposed $400,000 for a new chamber orchestra to compete with already struggling groups, as well as subsidizing a musicians' booking agency that would steal business from existing managers. Some $100,000 was allocated for artists' housing, $80,000 for helping art school graduates, $50,000 to preserve

Hawaii's natural beauty (through a conference on development), and $10,000 to help a poet move to a warmer city.[29]

Seed money from the Ford Foundation provided what appeared to be limitless growth for performing arts groups, spawning new foundations to fund an ever-increasing number of projects. Ford's unique invention, the challenge grant, saw great success in raising money by asking donors to match foundation giving. The rate of growth was breathtaking as performing arts centers were erected, radio broadcasts brought concerts into every home, and legions of students earned fine arts degrees. Cultural growth sped ahead with little examination of the arts' genuine or practical value to society. Why classical music? Why orchestras? Is the expense worthwhile? Few asked for fear of being labeled barbaric.

A 1975 Harris poll about public participation in the arts revealed Americans thought highly of the arts, much as they did of religion, with almost all respondents saying that cultural facilities were important to local quality of life and to the economy. Half expressed respect for professional musicians, but few actually attended concerts. The culture boom was fizzling, yet the business of the arts was gaining momentum.

5

Apollo's Flophouse

A NEATLY DRESSED BLACK man had just left the rental office. Inside, the agent looked up from his handwritten ledger, files spilling from bookshelves sagging overhead. "I always turn people *like that* away," he said, winking slyly. My father, a southern history professor, set his jaw and looked at the floor. Someone in the apartment next to the office pounded out piano arpeggios.

The Allendale was our best hope. Juilliard, the Mannes School of Music, and my own Manhattan School had no dormitories in 1978, and Upper West Side apartments meant astronomical rents and brokers' fees exceeding $1,000. "Three hundred dollars under the table," my NCSA teacher had said. Should I literally do that? I looked for a passage beneath his desk.

The Allendale—together with the separate fifteen-story annex its landlords owned next door—had become the Ellis Island of classical musicians. A few musicians came in the sixties lured by cheap rents. Friends dropped in to rehearse, catch rides to a gig, or sublet. Lucky ones signed their own leases, and the building became a community, with its own social strata, immigration laws, public assistance, civil wars, and even two dictators. Spontaneous musicales ignited nightly; someone always brought an extra music stand, the Reicha quintet's missing horn part, leftover sesame noodles, or a joint for inspiration. No one complained about loud practicing or the building's decrepitude.

There was an official Allendale just west of Times Square, which had opened just a few months before. Construction on Manhattan Plaza, a 1,700-unit forty-six-story apartment complex, had stalled during the energy crisis and the fiscal woes of New York City, which had financed construction with a $90 million mortgage.

In *The New York Times,* Molly Ivins wrote that a federal subsidy to fill the place with performers and stagehands was being considered. By opening day, demand was so great that only one in four applicants got in, paying between 10 and 30 percent of their income on a sliding scale. The makeup was 70 percent artists and 30 percent elderly. Single folks got a studio, married couples a one-bedroom, and unmarried duos shared a two-bedroom—all with parquet floors, modern appliances, and access to the facility's full-service health club.

The building's priorities in seedy Hell's Kitchen angered the neighborhood. Even the General Accounting Office noted that Manhattan Plaza's high-quality housing, built under a measure meant to mix economic classes, invited "resentment on the part of the taxpaying public who see their subsidized neighbors living in better accommodations than they themselves can afford."[1]

The Allendale, however, wasn't city-funded official housing. It boasted no swimming pool or fancy appliances. Its self-selecting population endured poor maintenance, and its noisy-musician renters were hesitant to complain about one another for fear of retribution in their closed society.

My parents and I followed Mr. Rudolph to the lobby, where he punched the elevator button. Inside, graffiti was scratched into the elevator's Formica paneling. As we passed the second floor, I heard a violinist practicing Paganini; on Four, Ravel's piano *Sonatine.* Dark viola tones drifted from the stairwell as we walked down a gray sixth-floor hallway, lit by a few fluorescent lights.

The hallway was dark, but when Rudolph unlocked apartment 601, brilliant sunshine washed the corner living room's expanse of oak parquet, highlighting its mahogany inlay. Down West 99th Street's canyon, tugboats passed in the Hudson River like toys, stark red against New Jersey's palisades. Except for an ugly pink bathroom, the two-bedroom apartment was airy and spacious, its central kitchen and foyer perfect for sharing. The building filled with classical music felt as familiar as my high school dorm. There was plenty of room for me and two roommates, one of them the gay male friend my parents trusted to keep their eighteen-year-old daughter safe. My mother looked somewhat relieved.

"It's official, then! Our little girl's going to take New York City by storm," said my father, as he watched me scribble a check on my new Citibank account for $450 as a security deposit equal to one month's rent.

When the Allendale opened in 1910, its Carnegie Hall-style tower, stucco detail, and fierce stone lions stood above a valley whose nadir marked West 96th Street. The area was quickly being transformed from a sparse group of small houses and open land to an upscale neighborhood offering new luxury apartment buildings of twelve stories or more. At the Allendale, wealthy families snapped up opulent ten-room apartments, paying $250 for a place with fourteen closets and three baths on a residential street promoted as "the West Side's Fifth Avenue."

Although the Allendale was extravagant, income tax laws had downsized lifestyles by the 1920s, when the building next door, which the Allendale landlords would one day purchase, went up. More police blotter than society page, the annex rented five-room flats to the workingman. During Prohibition, the Mob snuffed out one of its less law-abiding tenants at the 45th Street speakeasy he owned.

Between 1920 and 1960, New York lost a quarter of its population as new suburbs, and the bridges and tunnels that made them accessible, lured city dwellers away.[2] Retail sales and jobs followed them, eroding the neighborhood's elegance. By the mid-1970s, robberies and muggings infested Upper Broadway, an area rich in burly transvestites, drug dens, and welfare hotels housing psychiatric patients dumped during the state asylums' purge between 1965 and 1979.

A new landlord divided each of the Allendale floor's three stately apartments into twelve tenements leasing for $150 a month in 1961. This man, Mr. Geizhals, installed brown Cookmaster gas stoves and Hotpoint refrigerators with flimsy aluminum freezer compartments. Obsolete gas drying racks crowded the basement's laundry room, hosting rats and the stray cats hunting them. Tenants who threw out battered wood and vinyl furniture later found it in the lobby, where iridescent black wallpaper accented puce carpeting and a lone plastic plant gathered dust.

Geizhals died, but his style lived on. Surveying the kingdom from their balcony office, his daughters refined their father's negligence to high art. Boss lady Brunhilde, a brassy lawyer nicknamed for Wagner's screaming Valkyrie, bellowed at suspected subletters and Puerto Rican doormen. Recently, she'd diversified by hiring Jules, a scrawny East Indian doubling as the Geizhals spy.

"Get-ting chilly," Jules droned, as Brunhilde's sister, whom we nicknamed Yoda for reasons of appearance, not wisdom, heaved through the lobby, bangle bracelets clanking like the radiators upstairs. Jules's eyes shifted to the elevator, noting where two strangers got off. Yoda stopped a sweet girl from the eighth floor, bleating about prostitution.

"No, that's not me," the girl replied, indignant. "She's on Eleven."

Angelo, a superintendent with no discernable skills apart from reproduction, lived in a sprawling basement hellhole. I often found one of his thirteen children from three different mothers smoking dope in the cellar's maze. Angelo's teenage kids produced grandchildren with impressive frequency. When temperatures plunged in winter, Brunhilde sent him for sweaters and blankets at Goodwill. He layered them around the roof's labyrinth of pipes but could not stop our hot water from freezing fourteen days straight. Nearly half the tenants withheld rent and filed suit against the Geizhals.

His helper, Hippolito, haunted the stairwell after dark, peering through the keyholes of old service doors long sealed shut and jerking off into a filthy rag. He favored the third floor's revolving cast of beautiful South Korean girls, earning Juilliard degrees prized as dowry back home before passing their apartment leases on to cousins and friends. Harpist and writer Judith Kogan noted the phenomenon in her exposé of Juilliard culture:

Juilliard was a finishing school for some of [the Korean girls]. They all played piano—and some played incredibly well—but their primary goal was to catch a husband. Their parents thought the Juilliard name would attract a successful Korean man.[3]

Brunhilde liked the Koreans too, raising the rent with each new crop. Between peeps, Hippolito slipped rent receipts under our doors. When wind gusts from leaky windows blew them back into the hall for tenants' perusal, we could see that, though transients like the Koreans got charged $1,200, old-timers paid less than $200.

Since the lease was mine, I claimed the corner living room, with its river view. Two other oboe students moved into the bedrooms. I didn't see much of Lionel, who probed the glory days of Crisco Disco, Studio 54, and the Ramrod. Missy took the smaller room. We painted the faux wood kitchen cabinets white and scrubbed our grimy stovetop. Teetering on a folding chair, I reached for a clock over the fridge that had stopped long ago. Cockroaches jamming its warm motor swarmed up my arms. I shrieked. The clock started ticking.

Some of New York's hot tickets started in the Allendale. Julian Fifer ran Orpheus, the conductorless chamber orchestra, from his apartment on Twelve, and one of its violists, Sally, lived on Five. Getting the music before performing on *A Prairie Home Companion* meant an elevator ride to Eleven, where music director Rob Fisher churned out his arrangements. Visitors included James Galway and Mischa Maisky. Some tenants were en route to stardom. Violinist Ida Kavafian, violists Kim Kashkashian and Steve Tenenbaum, Metropolitan Opera French hornist Julie Landsman, and pianists Stephen Hough and Robert MacDonald all stayed in the Allendale before moving on.

Still, lifers also populated the Allendale. Jorge left the thick Cuban cigar smoke of his poker game only for an occasional gig on his contrabassoon, a woodwind known for its farting timbre in *The Sorcerer's Apprentice.* Dick, an occasional tubist, muttered to himself as he shuffled cassettes at Tower Records to support his "passion," and a violinist named Peter crammed wife and infant into an alley one-bedroom until the child, ripe with material, escaped to an MFA writing program.

The place also bred miserable spinsters who'd moved into the Allendale years before as ingenues like me. Joan waddled nightly on the sidewalk outside with two stinking matted dogs, a secretarial job having eclipsed her singing career. Her apartment was exactly the same as mine but on a different floor. It was crammed with bric-a-brac, piles of magazines, and ruffled floral curtains and pillows that smelled moldy.

Marni walked her psychotic dog when she plodded to Gristede's in polyester muumuus, the gray roots of her carrot-red hair always showing three inches. Once, I fed her mangy cat, which cringed between towers of unsold LPs from her independent record label (featuring women composers and an all-girl bassoon quartet). I peeked in a jumbo box of children's books languishing in the corner and read the copy:

> Come with us on our lighthearted romp through history, music and art with Roxanne, Ben, Bach, Beethoven, Vermeer, Brueghel, and of all things, that scamp—Benjamin Franklin! There is no age limit, for our guest of honor, Johann Sebastian Bach, is over 300 years old!!

I'd seen Marni carrying a violin but never playing it. The source of her income was unclear. A combination of the record label's tax-exempt status, subsidized by Allendale rent, and arts grants tweaked into salary may have explained it.

Betty, a frosted fireplug of a bass player, was most ominous of all. Once, she burst from the elevator after thirty minutes between floors, spitting like a demented white tiger. Approaching fifty, Betty's middling career covered her Allendale rent, a vacation, and not much more. She played bass in the New York City Ballet Orchestra, filling in income gaps by hiring musicians for Basically Baroque's concerts. Betty was cloyingly friendly or vitriolic, her scent sometimes broadcasting Hong Liquor Store's special of the week. No one visited her except an aging tenor who lived in the West Seventies with his wife.

A stunning flutist moved into her own apartment on the opposite side of the building from mine. A dead ringer for supermodel Cheryl Tiegs, Sydney's blond hair sparkled and her huge blue eyes were perfectly spaced in an oval face. Nearly six feet tall, her confidence inspired respect even from strangers, her polished style elevating her above her contemporaries.

Fresh from conservatory, Sydney had already made finals at major orchestra auditions. Even her instrument was special, a gold and silver Powell flute that her teacher had played on some of the most famous recordings of his day. She dated a bassoonist from a wealthy family that ran a scientific foundation, and he'd given her a diamond ring. Neither would worry about money if they married, though she'd be fine on her own. She played in the city's best chamber orchestra, won a woodwind quintet position, and substituted with the American Ballet Theater orchestra. With her reputation as a fine musician and colleague, she'd be a member of many more groups before long.

In the mid-1970s, the cultural prophecy came true as iconoclastic chamber music groups and orchestras formed. The twenty-six musicians of Orpheus played without a conductor, and the Orchestra of St. Luke's also rose quickly. Another chamber orchestra was organized at the 92nd Street Y, while the American Composers Orchestra dedicated itself to playing new works. Sydney hadn't arrived in time to land any of those permanent jobs, but more groups would surely form in the 1980s.

Sydney wasn't only looks and talent. Growing up in an affluent suburb, she had the social graces of a cultured young woman. She spoke fluent French. Her manners were impeccable, her graceful smile and gestures capable of putting the surliest colleague at ease. Sydney personified America's new Cold War fantasy: a home-grown American goddess of the European fine arts. She was everything a classical musician should be—refined, charming, accomplished. In the music business, and to the men around us, Sydney was unquestionably a muse.

With so many tenants who knew each other well, the Allendale offered many inside dating opportunities. A conductor invited me to erase string bowings in rental music in return for dinner. He forgot his wallet but remembered to grope me. A saxophonist who was marketing a CD he'd produced, *One Jew's Views*, for sale through his toll-free number, 1-800-586-SAXY, made it clear he wanted to cheat on his fiancée. Manhattan School of Music's piano tuner, sporting a comb-over, started dropping in too. Installing himself at our reed desk, he stared at me and at my roommate Missy, scooting his chair closer and closer until we lied and told him we were lesbians.

One boyfriend, a scrappy midwestern fiddler, played in second-violin sections all over town: Queens Symphony, Long Island Philharmonic, and Basically Baroque, which was an Allendale connection. The place he shared with a black mutt, left over from his divorce, celebrated 1970s bachelor decor. In the bedroom, a massive laminated dresser and mirror, part of a bedroom suite from his former marriage, dominated one wall. His living room featured a carved wooden sofa in tones of cherry Nyquil. Red panne velvet bordered Moorish arches along the back. An orange phone, meant to match, sat beside his Heathkit ham radio set and telegraph key.

I woke up here many mornings.

At thirty-seven, my boyfriend had never smoked pot. In fact, since he wouldn't smoke anything, I made pot brownies. I'd heard that sautéing weed in butter released its best properties, and I embarked on a culinary production using an entire ounce. Their smell billowed into the hallway, and when they were done, I cut the pan into nine big pieces. We each savored one and, four hours later, another. Finishing the pan, we settled into the sofa to watch Marilu Henner on *Taxi*.

It was dark when I woke up. The radiator hissed like a python. Python. Oh, I could eat a snake! My boyfriend ricocheted off the dresser, shot into the other room, and crashed to the floor.

Face down in the hall, he lay completely still. I turned him over, scooting velvet cushions under his head. He stirred, breathing audibly, and I relaxed.

He started convulsing. The dog yelped maniacally.

"I'm calling Nine-one-one," I said.

My boyfriend mumbled something about cops. Being stoned isn't illegal, I assured him. We were in this very fix because the evidence was gone.

At 4 A.M., two officers wedged themselves in the door, exploding backwards into the hall like Keystone Kops and crashing into the paramedics. I doubled over laughing. My boyfriend's hands opened and closed involuntarily. His tongue lolled. The dog barked.

The poor man recovered in a day, but Jules reported to Brunhilde.

Inside the Allendale, everything went public. Near the garbage a corpulent clarinetist's love letter to Sydney peeked out from coffee grounds. Wolfschmidt vodka bottles spilled from Betty's trash. On the roof—one went there for air, to smoke dope, watch fireworks, sunbathe, or escape roommates—I saw, in a painter's studio over in the annex, half-finished pictures of the Allendale's tenants and stone lions propped on his easel.

From the outside, we were invisible. Our windows were obscured by nearly a century of filth, a barrier not unlike NCSA's high fence. I could see into the expensive co-op apartments across West End, though. One couple drew their shades nearly to the sill, leaving a nine-inch gap where their hips beat away on the bed. In other apartments, I saw candlelit dinner parties, fancy sofas, and stay-at-home moms in lives that changed and grew. Waiting in my Honda during alternate-side-of-the-street parking, I saw them anxiously hailing cabs or pushing strollers to Riverside Park. They bought tickets to our concerts yet did not recognize us.

It was warm now, the May air pleasant. Waiting for the street sweeper, I flipped through *People* magazine, stopping at a picture of Itzhak Perlman. Big news—he'd broken a string. Behind him, Sam Sanders grinned from the piano. A halo of curls framed his face like a Lab puppy's big ears. Why had he snapped at me back in Greensboro?

Tossing away the magazine, I locked my car. I'd seen Sam hailing a cab in front of the Allendale, where he visited some singer. His concerts with cellist Leonard Rose got written up in the *Times,* and he was featured in recent stories about accompanists in *The Wall Street Journal* and *Piano Quarterly.*

Sam was handsome, powerful, and probably rich.

I leaned against my car. Sydney's liquid flute tone, as golden and silky as her hair, spilled from her windows. The building seemed alive, its walls singing as if it might break free from its foundations in an elegant dance. My eyes swept the building's stately exterior, the Gothic iron ALLENDALE APARTMENTS fixed into beige sandstone. Ivy clung to the curlicues of carved masonry and decorative balustrades.

Like most people, I did not look closely, or I would have noticed how the vines tangled, untended. Brown leaves dropped to barren planters flanking the entrance. Cardboard patches covered jagged basement windows. The stucco flaked and eroded; ivy tugged the rusty fire escape from its moorings. The bricks were falling out, one by one.

Elixir of Love

I HEARD MUSICIANS practicing piano arpeggios, clarinet long tones, and bassoon excerpts in apartments down the side streets as I walked the mile uptown to school. After passing the stone buildings of West End Avenue, I walked beyond the gates of Columbia University, Barnard College, and two theological seminaries, places where other eighteen-year-olds were starting lives very different from mine.

Manhattan School of Music, founded on the East Side in 1917 as the Neighborhood Music School, changed its name and first offered bachelor's degrees in the 1940s. After the Juilliard School of Music moved to Lincoln Center in 1969, Manhattan School took over its old building near Harlem, tucked beside Riverside Church and Grant's Tomb.

Before housing Juilliard, the structure was built for the Institute of Musical Art in 1910. Now, sixty-eight years later, the Claremont Avenue Edwardian was showing its history. When Manhattan School moved in, the first weathered-beige granite block was removed from the name JUILLIARD SCHOOL OF MUSIC and a new white stone inscribed with the word MANHATTAN was shoved in its place, its color standing out starkly from the rest of the façade.

Although many music students considered Manhattan inferior to Juilliard, the school trained big names, among them composers David Amram, Anton Coppola, and John Corigliano, conductor George Manahan, divas Dawn Upshaw and Lauren Flanigan, and violin virtuoso Elmar Oliveira. Unlike Juilliard, Manhattan School also boasted a jazz department; its alumni included Herbie Hancock, Yusef Lateef, Herbie Mann, Max Roach, and Ron Carter.

Settling into his new Philharmonic gig, my teacher from NCSA, Joe Robinson, had accepted an exclusive faculty contract at Manhattan School. His studio window overlooked Union Theological Seminary and was soundproofed by double walls and cork flooring. Arriving late by a half hour or more each week, Robinson started me on a fourth year of the same long-tone D, adding an occasional sixteen-bar melodic study from my dog-eared *Barret Oboe Method.* Robinson gave each of his students exactly the same routine, regardless of the oboist's individual strengths and weaknesses.

Though moving to New York signified a quantum leap in my lifestyle and opportunities, my lessons hadn't changed a bit. Each Thursday at two I still had to put my hand on Robinson's belly, just below the belt. He hadn't stopped commenting on my "small lungs" and had even added a new feature to my lessons by describing in exquisite detail the breasts of the Philharmonic's new flutist.

The boob talk at least cut down on critiques of my reeds. I'd spent the summer in Georgia taking reed-making lessons from the Atlanta Symphony's principal oboist. Living alone in the Georgian Terrace Hotel for $12 a night, I had just enough left over to pay for instruction and my Greyhound bus fare home. Making reeds all day every day, my skill should have improved, but it hadn't. My reeds still made sounds like dying fowl.

However, I loved being in the center of New York City's rich smorgasbord of classical music performances. Whereas visiting artists like Itzhak Perlman had come through North Carolina rarely, in New York I could hear internationally renowned soloists, opera productions, and orchestras at Carnegie Hall or Lincoln Center any week of the year, for the price of an inexpensive student ticket.

The rest of my classes at the Manhattan School of Music were a snap, as we repeated the same music theory, sight-singing, and ear training I'd already studied at NCSA. No math or science was offered, and the few humanities courses—mostly taught by adjuncts—left much to be desired. Foreign-language classes, filled with vocalists who sang entire operas in Italian, French, and German, didn't progress far beyond present tense. The art history teacher misspelled *Renaissance.* Yet Manhattan School's tuition ($24,500 in 2004) was nearly as high as an Ivy League university like Harvard ($27,448 in 2004).

Even if my reed-making needed work, I was advanced for a freshman oboe student, with excellent technique, rhythm, and an ear for playing well in tune. Robinson didn't assign me the music that would develop these skills while learning the basic oboe repertoire. Because his students played little more than the same old D in lessons, only a few had the wherewithal to perform even a short solo work. Fortunately George Manahan, a talented young conductor on the school's staff, immediately placed me as principal oboe in one of Manhattan School's orchestras.

We began our first orchestra rehearsal in the school's art deco Borden Auditorium. A time capsule, the hall had been designed by the Empire State Building's architects in 1931 and not altered since. Manahan drilled the orchestra's first violins on Bizet's Symphony in C. The fiddlers scratched away, falling apart as winds and brass watched silently. Although Manahan was a dynamic conductor, most of his violinists lacked passion, talent, or ambition and weren't about to win one of the few orchestra jobs available once they graduated.

The Manhattan School orchestra was far less polished than the one I'd played in at NCSA. I needed to find a way to gain experience, and fortunately, good oboists were in demand elsewhere. Just down Broadway, Columbia University's shortage proved a boon and I joined one of their student orchestras. Before long I was not only playing regularly in their symphony but performing as a soloist in J. S. Bach's *Concerto for Oboe and Violin* with violinist Ralph Morrison, who was a literature undergraduate already holding down a Broadway pit job and heading off to a job in the Los Angeles Chamber Orchestra.

The plucky group of Columbia University musicians partied hard, its lively dinners in West Side apartments bursting with talk of history, politics, culture, and literature. Manhattan School's students paled in comparison, with nothing but musical mechanics on their minds. I was happy to meet some smart new men, too. Though my roommate and I had rebuffed Manhattan School's piano tuner by lying about being lesbians, our ruse backfired when he spread the gossip around school. Since everyone assumed we were gay, no male student had yet showed any interest in either of us.

I was already spending little time at Manhattan School when I won one of three oboe spots in the National Orchestral Association (NOA) in a highly competitive audition. NOA was a training orchestra for the crème de la crème of New York's best young players, and I was honored to suddenly find myself among them. Founded in 1930 by philanthropist Mary Flagler Cary and maintained by the Cary Trust, the group even paid me and its other musicians a small amount, funding performances of several concerts at Carnegie Hall with soloists like Richard Goode and Ruggiero Ricci.

Leaving NOA rehearsals, which met three afternoons a week at Juilliard, I discovered the real action took place at Lincoln Center. In the evenings, I'd seen Leonard Bernstein walking to work. It felt like I was watching a movie, especially when I saw the violin star Pinchas Zukerman racing across the plaza and Luciano Pavarotti gliding by in a stretch limo; none of that excitement infected Manhattan School. Here, clarinetists, violinists, and trumpeters rushed to their stage doors at 7:30 P.M. I couldn't wait to join them.

All those worlds collided at the Allendale, where students from Juilliard, Mannes, and the Manhattan School could fraternize with music professionals. On any night, impromptu chamber music parties erupted, given a little Mozart sheet music, some kung pao chicken from Hunan Balcony, and a joint. One night, I played through the Mozart *Oboe Quartet* with my neighbors, beers at our feet, and so it was not surprising when we all ended up in bed together. Much of New York's classical music community did this with equal abandon, as the lines between music and passion blurred.

Instrument players had a sexual style unique to their instrument. Neurotic violinists, anonymous in their orchestra section, came fast. Trumpet players pumped away like jocks, while pianists' sensitive fingers worked magic. French horn players, their instruments the testiest of all, could rarely get it up, but percussionists could make beautiful music out of anything at all. One of them even specialized in making instruments from refrigerators, auto taillights, and other castoffs he'd found at junkyards.

Oboists crossed an incestuous line, speaking a language of reeds, articulation, and the challenges of playing Ravel's *Le Tombeau de Couperin*. Because of our obscure shared experience, the relationship between oboists could be comfy as old flannel, giving the deceptive illusion of safety between competitors.

I had first met Jayson at a reception for musicians of the newly-formed American Philharmonic. Twisting his wedding ring, he whispered to me that I should pretend to be an old friend, so no one would know that he'd hired me purely on the recommendation of my teacher, Joe Robinson. I felt privileged to have landed the gig and to be in on the intrigue of Jayson's con game. Jayson would have done anything to make Robinson happy. As principal oboist of the New York Philharmonic, one of America's five biggest symphony orchestras, Robinson was in a position to hire freelancers like Jayson to substitute in his orchestra on a week-to-week basis. Since New York Philharmonic players were also offered lucrative studio work before freelancers were called, Robinson might recommend Jayson for jingles and film soundtracks as well.

The American Philharmonic gave its first performance in the autumn of 1979 at the Brooklyn Academy of Music, under Rohan Joseph, a Sri Lankan conductor of questionable ability who had launched the orchestra. Fortunately, Rohan's musicianship was counterbalanced by enormous talents of persuasion, as he schmoozed wealthy board members into bankrolling his project and talked musicians into volunteering their services.

I was too naïve to understand how freelance musicians landed gigs through networking. What I did know was that the concerts I played at Carnegie Hall and Washington's Kennedy Center over the following months trumped anything I'd play at school as a nineteen-year-old undergraduate. What's more, I shared every aspiring performer's dream: to join a professional orchestra that promises to grow. I overlooked the fact that by rehearsing for free (we were paid only for concerts), we perpetuated the classic scenario of artists subsidizing a performing arts group, the only way such a group can come close to paying its own way without substantial funding.

Jayson, who like Robinson and me was also a Southerner, was extraordinarily friendly. At thirty-four he was considerably older, but had taken the job as a way of improving his résumé with a principal oboe position. In addition, other freelancers who might hire him for work would hear and see him play the prominent oboe solos in orchestral music.

Although Robinson wasn't particularly supportive of me or any of his other students, he liked knowing one of us was already playing at Carnegie. At the same time, Jayson flattered Robinson by taking a few oboe lessons. The two men became closer by playing golf afterward. Jayson was likable, and Robinson soon added him to the New York Philharmonic's sub list.

Jayson was moving in on me too. After rehearsing Anton Bruckner's Third Symphony at a public school on West 77th Street one afternoon, he invited me to his place to make reeds. First, we shared drinks at the fireplace bar at One If by Land, a romantic restaurant housed in Aaron Burr's historic coach house on Barrow Street. By the third Chivas, I had melted against him on the sofa, gazing at the candlelight reflected in his eyes. Winding down Grove Street, we climbed five flights to his walkup across from Chumley's. His dancer wife was out west, on a six-month tour with American Ballet Theater.

I unzipped my bag of reed tools. Jayson reached around, taking the kit with one hand while unbuttoning my blouse with the other. Ambidextrous but gym-phobic, he was all love handles and bad posture, but none of that mattered as we climbed past the makeshift closet, where his wife piled leotards and dance skirts, and up to their loft bed. We flailed away, laughing as we kept hitting the ceiling. I looked up to Jayson as an older mentor in love and work.

The tryst was the first of a three-year affair. I devoured books about loving a married man: the tragedy and, for the lucky, the triumph. Every time we spent the night together, I got another gig shadowing him in the second oboe chair. With his wife gone half the year, it was only a matter of time until he left her.

Jayson had something very different in mind. His marriage included an influential father-in-law, an iconoclastic architect who ran a utopian colony in Arizona, a man with social connections that would serve any performing artist well. I was simply part of his grand networking plan, though I offered fringe benefits that Robinson and his father-in-law did not.

Our liaison was already unimaginably glamorous and romantic to me. At a fundraiser in the swooping modern building at 9 West 57th Street,

Jayson and I swam nude in the skyscraper's pool, taking in the glittering skyline. Tipsy and dripping, I joined him in a formal woodwind octet performance for couture mogul Xavier Guerrand-Hermès and his friends. When Betty hired us both for a Basically Baroque church gig, we spent our break making out on the chaplain's darkened office floor.

"The section that lays together plays together," Jayson panted, his hairless chest heaving. We slipped quietly by Betty's music stand as she screwed tuning pegs back and forth on her double bass, sawing away purposefully with a gargantuan bow.

"Bach," she declared, eyebrows knitted sternly. "A lot of fun, this cantata. A *lot* of fun."

I sat quietly next to Jayson in a 57th Street studio as we recorded music for the first feature film produced by Mary Tyler Moore Productions, called *A Little Sex*. The plot paralleled New York's early eighties lifestyle, which was iconic for its sexual promiscuity. In the film, a young married man struggled to stay faithful while being challenged by temptations of the flesh.

Behind the glass window, director Bruce Paltrow bent over a huge mixing board, gesturing toward a video monitor. The film was Paltrow's first. An engineer cocked his head, changing the balance by sliding bars along the console. The recording studio was cutting-edge, its owners recently having invested in the latest analog equipment. It was 1982, and digital technology was not yet advanced enough to be used much in recording studios. Even though IBM's first home computer hit the market earlier that year for $1,595, it was really for business accounting and college term papers.

Between film and jingles, recording had become a significant source of income for musicians in the 1980s. Studio work had been around since the 1930s, but an expanding global economy had caused explosive growth in the field. The money was so good, several members of the New York Philharmonic quit their contracted positions to play only recording gigs.

A copyist was distributing our parts in handwritten manuscript form. A few composers tried printing out their music using programs from new personal computers, but the dot-matrix printouts were virtually illegible. The computers reduced a copyist's graceful arcs of slurs and clef signs to a pileup of angular lines.

Although the film's cast had finished shooting, some of them had come to watch the session, including John Glover and Wendie Malick. Before we started recording, the actors and musicians viewed one scene on a video monitor set up in the studio. For me, art eerily imitated life as I watched Malick playing a frosty, calculating oboist named Philomena who beds the married man, played by Tim Matheson.

Philomena's movie apartment was everyone's idea of a classical musician's pad: slick, expensive, painted in ocher with a few plants scattered about. Its enormous rooms must have been shot in one of those expensive prewar buildings that had thick soundproof walls. I watched Matheson's character luxuriate onscreen in bed after their tryst as Philomena crossed the movie bedroom in pink panties and an open shirt to "play" soulfully on her oboe. Jayson would record the actual oboe solo she was acting out.

Jayson tried to catch Malick's eye. Earlier, he'd bragged to the other recording musicians about teaching her to fake playing the oboe in that scene. He left out enough details that I, and the other musicians, wondered if he'd had any sexual success. In the early 1980s, classical musicians were venerated as the ultimate in sophistication. Jayson was working his musician image for all it was worth, but Malick remained polite but distant.

Surrounded by movie people and expensive microphones, I pinched myself to make sure I wasn't dreaming. Millions of people would hear my oboe playing on this film soundtrack. I didn't want anyone to know it was my first recording gig, so I imitated Jayson, donning the studio headphones asymmetrically. My left ear started clicking. "Four, three, two," the producer counted off through the phones. We played the music in front of us, an arrangement of Handel's *Water Music* measured with a click track, metronomic audio beats used to time our performance so it would fit the video segment.

Jayson looked wistful as Malick put on her coat and slipped out of the studio as the session ended. My adoration of him was starting to turn sour. He and I took the elevator down to 57th Street and split a cab uptown. As we approached the Allendale, I wished my place resembled Malick's film apartment in even some little way. My plants were dead. My parquet floor needed refinishing, and a tannish stain was turning brown on the bathroom ceiling. I remembered tracking a fluffy mound of cane shavings across the floor that morning, and I knew the bedroom smelled of rancid oil from honing my reed knife.

As Jayson and I walked into the Allendale, I saw the pianist Samuel Sanders hail the taxi we'd just vacated. He didn't recognize me from our unpleasant backstage encounter four years ago, but I ran into him periodically. I'd been seeing him a lot recently in my neighborhood, always nervously flagging down cabs at the corner of 99th and West End. I figured he was working with some musician who lived nearby.

Jayson and I took the elevator upstairs. I unlocked my apartment door, and flute music soared out. In the living room, I caught a glance of my current roommate, John-Sebastian, playing flute duets with Sydney. Jayson blanched. Would Sydney tell Jayson's wife? We sealed ourselves in my bedroom, but Jayson fidgeted nervously, nothing like Philomena's movie lover. As he undressed, the unflattering physical comparison was unavoidable from his concave chest and love handles on down. I looked away, focusing on the window across West End where the torsos once thrust away in the sliver between shade and sill. The sex had stopped last year. Now the woman nursed a baby.

Jayson slid on top of me, and we began to kiss. As we embraced, he stole a glance at my alarm clock once, twice, and then froze when the flute duets stopped. His wife would return home from her own ballet performance in an hour, I guessed. As he grabbed his shirt and rushed for the door, I thought about rising to serenade him like Philomena. It wasn't worth wasting a good reed.

As morning light filtered through the stained glass, Dennis Keene, music director of Fifth Avenue's Church of the Ascension, sat in the front pew waiting until it was time to start rehearsal. He often hired the Orchestra of St. Luke's to accompany his chorus. After only a few years, its young musicians had turned their passion into exciting, edgy performances of Baroque and classical music.

Playing in St. Luke's for the first time today, I thought about how much better my career was going than my disappointing affair with Jayson. Just then, Jimmy slid into the principal oboe chair, rolling up the cuffs of his tux shirt. Twenty-seven years old, he was magnetic and sexy, and I was drawn to him immediately. There was something darkly intriguing about him, a fragility hidden behind his confident façade. As we started playing Bach's *St. John Passion,* Jimmy's sinuous bobbing and weaving put me at ease. I'd saved my one decent reed, and it sounded dark and rich in the church acoustics.

Like many other freelance classical music gigs in New York, this job paid a set union wage called "single engagement concert scale." In 1982 the rehearsals, which were usually two and a half hours long, paid around $18 an hour, and concerts were just under $100. In addition, scale included contributions to the union's pension fund and its health benefits plan, although it was difficult to do enough work to qualify.

Sydney was playing today too. I observed her carefully, because I wanted to emulate her professionalism and style. Sydney was a trusted musician whose preparation never failed her. Marking her part meticulously, she checked intonation, watching and blending with the principal flutist's tone. I thought she'd probably move up to principal when he left for his new gig with the San Francisco Ballet.

We took a break after an hour and a half of rehearsing. By the time I snapped my oboe case shut, the other musicians had already cleared out. Jeweled light dappled the silent nave. I peeked through a door into the church office and then out onto the street. Out of twenty-five musicians, not one was on the corner. Nor were they buying coffee in the deli or using the pay phone. I went back inside and studied my reeds in the quiet.

At exactly eleven-thirty, voices burst the silence as bodies raced through the sanctuary and back to their seats. French horns and trumpets warmed up kinetically. The morose, sedentary principal flutist babbled. Behind me, a bassoonist sniffled, and Kleenex made the rounds, from cellos to harpsichord. "Hey, where were you?" Jimmy asked, as he slid into his chair.

Soporific arias sped at uncharacteristically fast tempos, and even the viola da gamba, a soft string instrument, played with abandon. The group energy transformed what had been a slow-paced rehearsal. Self-expression won out over precision as players added unique touches. One hunched over her modern viola, holding the bow with a peculiar center grip usually reserved for Baroque instruments. She hee-hawed her laugh at a bassist who could double for Jack Nicholson at his most diabolical.

"Dennie," said Jimmy, "can you play a little softer?"

"Jimmy? What do you think?" he replied, smirking.

"Honey," whined the violist, addressing her husband, who played harpsichord, "you're too fast!" Although the harpsichordist's name was Bob, the entire group had been calling him Honey for some time.

Billy chimed in with comments about the tempo, along with Stevie, Jennie, Markie, and Davey. The group's familiarity was charming; they behaved like a family. Packing up after rehearsal, people seemed sleepy and grouchy. I caught up with Sydney halfway down Tenth Street.

"Where did everybody go?"

"Out. You know, out," she said, touching one side of her elegant nose and exaggerating a sniffing sound.

She pulled a luxurious rope of golden hair from under her flute bag strap and it cascaded over her shoulders. We walked toward the subway. I felt silly in my dress-for-success uniform of tweed jacket and 1980s bow-tied blouse, especially next to Sydney. She was artful and luminous in a burnished suede jacket, fashionably cut trousers, and a silk scarf. Two men in reefer coats stopped talking, their mouths agape. One bumped her arm, pausing to look her straight in the eye. She smiled, and we continued on our way to the subway.

Sydney was far more open now that I'd showed up on this job, which many considered the inner sanctum of classical freelancing. She mentioned her favorite shopping haunts and the European tour she was hired to do. She even told me about breaking up with her boyfriend. He was moving west, but Sydney decided to stay in New York, because it offered more musical opportunities. I was surprised she didn't want to compromise, because I thought they'd been such a tight couple.

I wanted all of Sydney's beauty and success. My imagination went wild. If I hung with Sydney, I'd learn to dress right and imitate her confidence, poise, and grooming. Maybe soon I'd be playing concerts every night, enjoying my pick of admiring men. My checks would pile up, just like hers. Then I'd leave the Allendale to find a better apartment. That must be how this worked. There was so much work to be had, Sydney didn't even have enough time for practicing anymore.

Halfway up 99th, I could hear loud plodding scales coming from the Allendale. Some new pianist with annoying practice mannerisms had moved in.

Rounding the corner into our lobby, we heard Betty screaming. She had cornered Carlos, a violinist from Colombia, by the mailboxes. Poor Carlos had done his laundry on Betty's dime—quarters, really. From what I could deduce, Carlos had found the coins orphaned on the folding table and fed them into the dryer to start his own load. When he returned, Betty started to berate him. Her roar peaked as she followed Carlos to the mailboxes: She would never hire him for Basically Baroque again. Brunhilde appeared on the lobby balcony to see what the fuss was about.

Sydney rolled her eyes. It was one of Betty's bad days, probably fueled by a hangover. Yesterday, she had been overly sweet. With such personality swings, staying in Betty's good graces was one of the Allendale's challenges, if you wanted her to hire you.

As Sydney and I waited for the elevator, I listened to the mishmash of piano, flute, and trumpet practice. Faintly, I could hear Jimmy Madison practicing drums in the insulated booth he'd built inside his apartment. I felt warm and secure, living at the Allendale for four years now in a community of offbeat people just like me. We epitomized New York's artistic community. Everyone had passion but little money, and most behaved like eccentrics. In a few months, I would graduate from college and be a full-time member of the club.

The Rite of Spring 7

"BLAIR, WAKE UP." My new roommate, a pianist named Elizabeth, poked me. I changed roommates at least once a year, and it took a minute to remember her name. The clock read 7:05 A.M. "The Philharmonic's on the phone."

Like most musicians, I had recurring performance nightmares. I was onstage as a soloist but held a violin, or I performed a recital of unfamiliar music. This particular dream was an old one. I was drunk at a bar halfway across town five minutes before the concert.

As I struggled to wake up, I realized it was no dream. It had been a late night. Why not? I'd thought, when my third martini arrived at 1:30 A.M. I'd just skip class tomorrow.

Now, a very mature voice on the telephone was telling me I wouldn't just be cutting solfège but playing second oboe in the New York Philharmonic this morning. Their regular second oboist was sick and my teacher had told them to call me, even though I was only twenty-two. I didn't feel so great, and my reeds sucked.

I rooted through piles of the jeans I usually wore to school. Finally, I found the black jacket, which looked somewhat respectable and pinned my long hair into a barrette. My head throbbed as I took the elevator to the lobby. I could hear Sydney practicing a Vivaldi piccolo concerto.

The stench of urine on 99th was worse than usual. My shoe slipped on a condom. On Broadway I passed Sloan's grocery and a few boxes of rotting produce in front of ¡Caramba! Mexican restaurant before disappearing into the 96th Street subway. Crammed on the local train with New Yorkers going to their mysterious jobs, I felt nauseated until the train finally stopped at Lincoln Center. I escaped out the 66th Street exit beside Juilliard and reached Avery Fisher Hall's stage door at nine-forty-five, where the guard absently waved me in without asking for ID.

I slipped into the second oboe chair, where the cacophony of eighty musicians warming up made me even dizzier. I was relieved to see Jayson sitting in the first oboe chair instead of my teacher, who must have called in sick as well. Robinson would have been on my case from the beginning, making me even more nervous. Tchaikovsky's Fifth Symphony blurred on the stand. It had only been eight hours since that third martini, and I wondered if I smelled of gin. This morning's rehearsal should have been an exciting triumph for me, but instead I slouched in shame.

Klaus Tennstedt strode smartly across the stage and opened his score. I tried to become more alert. Defecting from East Germany ten years earlier, Tennstedt had quickly earned respect in Göteborg, Hamburg, and London, working his way west to the United States. On his debut with the New York Philharmonic, he received rare attention and cooperation from the musicians. Filled with some of the world's finest ensemble players, the orchestra showed most visiting conductors no mercy.

I'd never played Tchaikovsky's Fifth. In the andante movement, Philip Myers's ecstatic horn solo floated above the strings, and Stanley Drucker's clarinet tone wove soulfully around it. I'd never felt this sensation: being physically part of such a glorious sound. It was fabulous. I desperately wanted to feel every second of it, in case this was my only chance to sit in the middle of the New York Philharmonic.

Yet I was terrified. These confident musicians knew one another well and played together like a precision machine, each one adjusting to the others. I was a good student, but not nearly as seasoned as these musicians. I tried to fit my tone underneath their timbre and finally started to relax in my anonymity.

Then I saw it: the low C-sharp, naturally a loud nasty sound the oboist must wrestle into the submission. It was marked pianissimo—supersoft—at the end of a long exposed phrase. Guessing that everyone would be able to hear me clearly when the moment came, I stuffed a piece of cloth up the bell on the end of my oboe in an attempt to muffle the tone.

The work's texture began getting thinner. The brass dropped out and then the violins, until the music became very soft with just a few musicians playing the delicately orchestrated passage. My hands shook, and my forehead was clammy with sweat. I couldn't breathe, and my stage fright worsened. My low note, not even part of the melody, must come out cleanly, softly, in tune, and with a dark tone. I sucked the extra saliva out of my reed.

Journalist George Plimpton once described this sensation as the most frightening thing imaginable. Already known to have tried everything from pro football to bullfighting, Plimpton had convinced Leonard Bernstein to let him play triangle and gong during Mahler's Fourth, documenting his insider's view for the *Bell Telephone Hour*. "The music is rushing along, you have to come in at a certain moment, and if you lose your place it becomes even more acute than physical pain," he told *The New York Times* in 1968.

Plimpton let his audience in on a few secrets. Behind the scenes, he said, oboists make reeds for thirty hours a week yet hate the results. Also, orchestral playing looks easier than it is. Plimpton quaked, playing in a rest, lagging behind the beat and producing a harsh tone. "One of my major problems was that I found myself staring at the music instead of Lenny," confided Plimpton, who hung on to the score like a life preserver. If it's right, no one cares. Play something wrong, and everyone knows—as Plimpton discovered when even Bernstein literally applauded his resounding *bong*, played too loudly and in the wrong spot, from the podium.

I didn't know about Plimpton at the time, but his words describe my experience as the music's mood turned devotional. Slowly, the chorale faded. The winds were ethereal, perfectly balanced. I hung on to the long-tone A, which was not such a low or recalcitrant note—good, good, almost done. This reed sounds pretty nice, I told myself.

"When I hit this clout," as Plimpton had described his bombastic gong, "it made all the musicians in front of me jump up like beans on a griddle."

My mouth muscles were tiring. I was losing control. And I was scared out of my mind. I braced for the low C-sharp, knowing I needed to blow slightly harder and open my teeth a little farther apart. That way, the reed would vibrate just enough to attack the note delicately.

"Spleeeee-YAHHHHHHH!"

Tennstedt stopped, glaring. Starting with the second violins, heads rippled in my direction. In cutting my musical fart, I'd also quacked a spectacular wrong note. Tennstedt raised his baton again. When repeating the passage, the winds sounded beautiful but this time I was too frightened to play anything at all.

I rushed home, humiliated by what seemed to me my miserable failure. Yet neither Jayson nor Tennstedt were in a position to hire me. The personnel manager had promoted me to the top of the list based on Robinson's recommendation, and a few hours later, the Philharmonic called to hire me to play third oboe in Stravinsky's *Rite of Spring* with Leonard Bernstein.

I felt as if I was dreaming. Bernstein had been a hero of mine ever since his televised children's concerts, which introduced the boob-tube generation to Mozart. Bernstein had also had a late night before his Philharmonic debut in 1943. Assistant conductor of the orchestra at the time, he partied after his new song cycle, *I Hate Music*, premiered at Town Hall. Soon after dawn, he got the call to step in at Carnegie Hall for an ailing Bruno Walter. Without any rehearsal at all, Bernstein conducted a live concert that was broadcast nationwide, featuring Schubert's *Manfred Overture*, Wagner's Prelude to *Die Meistersinger*, and Strauss's tone poem *Don Quixote*. Expecting the twenty-five-year-old conductor to follow the orchestra instead of leading it, Philharmonic musicians were astonished to find themselves swept away by Bernstein's musical spirit. The audience, warm enough at first, rioted with cheers by concert's end.

Bernstein defied the highbrow crowd, turning newcomers on to Mahler. As a composer, his music crossed ethnic and class lines, from the Chicano gangs of *West Side Story* to his soundtrack for Elia Kazan's *On the Waterfront*. An American Jew, Bernstein's affiliation with the Vienna Philharmonic spoke deeply about how musicianship can transcend ethnic conflict. Tom Wolfe chronicled his relationship to the Black Panthers in *Radical Chic*, adding to a thick FBI file detailing political views written into his *Mass*. He crossed other boundaries too. Writing a bisexual role into his 1983 opera *A Quiet Place*, Bernstein himself became openly gay once his wife died in 1978.

As I waited with the orchestra at the *Rite*'s first rehearsal, I studied my unusual sheet music part, one of a set the Philharmonic kept just for Bernstein, its complex meters repackaged into neat bars of 3/4 and 4/4. Bernstein strolled onstage thirty minutes late. On the podium, a cough rattled him for minutes, wracking his distended belly. He was in his sixties, and his body showed the effects of an exuberant lifestyle. Still, Bernstein lived for music.

Although the *Rite*'s shocking images of human sacrifice, jarring dissonances, and irregular throbbing rhythms had outraged audiences at its 1913 premiere, the piece has become part of a standard repertoire. Not Bernstein's version, however. Lenny's *Rite* was primitive, sexual, exhausting, and thrilling, an orgiastic feast. Even the most apathetic musicians rode his raw energy as he clutched emotion from thin air, dancing like a drunken sailor, moaning and snorting. The performance was more than just the music. It was an orgy that threw the heart, the soul, and all the senses into a superhuman sphere. When it ended, a boy stood backstage and toweled the maestro off between bows, keeping a lit cigarette for him to puff in the wings. The players blushed at their white-hot abandon, and Bernstein burst into the woodwind section, embracing the players. Reaching the oboe section, he kissed my ear. The *Times* raved:

> Finally, *The Rite of Spring* [was performed], which Mr. Bernstein likes to play for all the cataclysmic shock it can possibly deliver. This was an explosive performance of the sort that is alleged to have brought the following sardonic review from Stravinsky the first time he heard it: "Wow!"
>
> [Bernstein] evidently wanted, and certainly got, great crunching, snarling chords from the brass and thundering thumps from the timpani. One could argue that the work can make its Corybantic effect with something less than a frenzied approach of this sort, but Mr. Bernstein has always sinned, when he did sin, in the right direction. The essence of *The Rite of Spring* is its solar heat, which this performance brought out, even at the expense of orchestral finesse.

After a week like that, I was hooked. Sometimes the phone rang just before 8 P.M., like the night second oboist Jerry Roth, dad of CNN's Richard Roth, suffered an accident involving a roller-skating waiter, scalding hot soup, and his lap. I sight-read the concert; he recovered.

Over the next year, I played with European and American stars who guest-conducted the Philharmonic, including Andrew Davis, Erich Leinsdorf, and Pierre Boulez. The Czech conductor Raphael Kubelik brought Leŏs Janáček's grim opera *From the House of the Dead* to America for the first time, and Giuseppe Sinopoli made his New York debut conducting Mahler's tragic Sixth Symphony, looking exactly like the composer himself.

I could barely believe my good fortune. Just four years earlier, I had predicted a grim future for myself, and here I was substituting with one of the world's great orchestras. My success was not only a résumé entry but, more significantly, a source of great spiritual growth and delight, a unique high that eluded words.

Roth nursed his ailing wife for much of my final year in college, often calling the Philharmonic at dawn to cancel an evening's concert or an entire week. Playing classical masterpieces with the world's best musicians was terrifying and enthralling at the same time. Learning on the job, I began feeling more at ease onstage with the Philharmonic; rushing to Lincoln Center after school soon became second nature.

After playing with the Philharmonic for a number of weeks, I needed to transfer my union membership. In North Carolina only a couple of hundred musicians belonged to the union local, which operated from someone's kitchen table in Raleigh. The New York City chapter of the union was housed in a four-story building. It published an inch-thick directory of members that represented 10 percent of the hundred thousand union musicians nationwide.

"Two hundred eight dollars," said the old man behind the glass divider as he scratched his mottled, flaking face. I wrote the check, while the man trumpeted his bulbous nose into a handkerchief and inspected the result. I took my new union card and pushed my check toward him, making sure our hands didn't touch.

LOCAL 802, AMERICAN FEDERATION OF MUSICIANS read the little card. I peered over my shoulder, where old men sat at every desk behind the payment window. I felt conspicuously young and female.

I headed back to the union's front door, where jazz music was starting to spill out from the 52nd Street clubs during happy hour. The exit route was circuitous and skirted a gallery that overlooked the Roseland Ballroom, which was once used as the union's exchange floor. Back then, dues were $24.

Roseland's dance floor was still as a tomb, with the sheet covering some amplification equipment lending a ghostly touch. In the 1950s, this room would have been bursting with action three days a week. Hundreds of men jostled for engagements in the afternoon and contractors hiring for various fields each gathered in a different part of the cavernous room: cruise ships, high-end club dates, scrappier nightclub gigs, recordings for commercials and Muzak, and single-engagement classical concerts. Yorkville restaurants hired three to eleven sidemen, paying $90 a week. A bank of pay phones lined one wall, and a switchboard operator in the center paged musicians next to a booth selling black or white bow ties.

Since then, the focus of employment for musicians had shifted. Local 802's exchange floor had shut down in the 1970s after LPs, radio, television, and rock 'n' roll acts gradually replaced big bands, many club dates, and other once-popular genres of live music. The union was representing musicians' interests better than ever now by negotiating contracts, organizing for benefits, and lobbying for musician-favorable public policy. However, it was more practical for its members to find work through auditions and personal networking efforts than the old-school exchange floor.

A typical 1950s *International Musician*, the union's national paper, ran 5,000-word features detailing music in every part of the country. The stories focused on groups filled with community residents who were also part-time musicians. "Music in Idaho" revealed a state bustling with Basque folk musicians, cabaret acts, and the Boise Philharmonic, photographed showing teachers, bankers, farmers, and other workers holding violins and wearing their Sunday best. In these communities, classical music wasn't a rarity, but few people expected to make a full-time living playing it.

Around the United States, postwar European immigrants were eager to hear concerts in America and perform as amateur musicians themselves. The most influential landed at American universities. Paul Hindemith taught composition at Yale, Igor Stravinsky in Los Angeles, Kurt Weill at Juilliard, and Nadia Boulanger at Harvard. Most were less famous but kept music alive wherever they lived, by playing for free or supporting their musical life with a day job.

Savannah lured musicians to its twenty-week season with a "wonderful winter climate," and sought those "able to accept other employment." At the same time, the Norfolk Symphony—established for forty-four years—was hiring strings, oboes, harps, bassoons, and French horns who could fill local vacancies, including teachers for civil engineering and history, a secretary, and a mechanic.

In 1950, the Chattanooga Philharmonic paid $600–$1,000 to play its October–April season. Its musicians rehearsed in the evenings for its twenty concerts, with many players combining the salary with a local university scholarship to finance nonmusical degrees. In the same month, the Boston Pops advertised for "a doctor who is an instrumentalist, probably a string player, to join this group to be of good enough standard to take his place on one back-stand position in the string section; attractive offer."

The New York Philharmonic became the first American orchestra to go full-time, starting in 1964, when it paid musicians $10,000 a year. Many other symphonies were able to expand their seasons in 1966, when the Ford Foundation approved $80 million in matching grants to establish endowments for sixty-one orchestras. Seemingly overnight, classical musicians could view an orchestra job as full-time employment, complete with health and pension benefits and paid time off for illness and vacation.

American orchestras started hiring more women too, after largely barring them from their ranks for much of the twentieth century. Some conductors had complained that females made the stage look like a kitchen, and they would faint from the foul rehearsal language anyway. Critic Donal Henahan described the scene in 1983, a year after I began subbing in the Philharmonic:

Younger readers may not believe it, but symphony orchestras were not always bastions of tolerance and enlightenment. Traditionally, in fact, both here and abroad they were the musical equivalents of those all-male clubs where old gentlemen still gather to nurse their gout and to lie to one another about their war records and their sexual adventures.[1]

There had been exceptions. In 1935, the Philadelphia Orchestra hired a lone female cellist, Elsa Hilger, who occasionally substituted in the principal chair during her thirty-five-year tenure. A few more women filled vacancies during World War II, taking over spots for male musicians who were serving in the military. In 1952, a woman won a principal position in an American orchestra for the first time when flutist Doriot Anthony Dwyer, a descendent of suffragist Susan B. Anthony, joined the Boston Symphony.[2]

Some European orchestras still prohibited women from auditioning at all in the 1980s. In 1983, musicians of the then all-male Berlin Philharmonic had vetoed hiring its second female member, Sabine Meyer, a twenty-three-year-old clarinetist. (The orchestra's first female musician, a Swiss violinist, had been hired months before.) Countering their action, music director Herbert von Karajan canceled all but six contracted appearances with the orchestra and cut out additional orchestra services that would have been lucrative for its players.

The New York Philharmonic hired its first female member, a bassist named Orin O'Brien, in 1966. By 1982, the number of women had grown to eighteen. There were even more at other symphonies; of fifteen hundred American orchestras, large and small, women made up 40 percent.

Times had changed since the exchange-floor days, when few women would have arrived looking for work as musicians. I tucked the union card into my wallet. All the older New York musicians I'd met talked about the "good old days," an era of varying dates which was thought to have been preferable to modern times. For really old guys, it was the silent film epoch, when theaters hired live orchestras to accompany movies. Middle-aged men spoke wistfully of radio stations that kept an orchestra on the payroll and of the time when every orchestra was recording standard repertoire for the first time on the new long-playing records that came out in 1948.

Unlike older players, classical musicians of my generation didn't speak of the past. Never had musicians enjoyed more diverse, well-funded, and plentiful opportunities. The 1980s were unquestionably a golden age for the music profession, and I was right at its center.

I sipped the herbal tea Sydney made me and studied a poster-sized photograph of her meant to advertise a concert series. In the image, she beckoned like the Pied Piper, feet bare, playing her flute in a white dress, her luxuriant mane blowing in the wind.

Sydney's two telephone lines had been a boon for her as she wearily fielded calls, putting one contractor on hold for another. Three months of checks were piled two inches deep on her desk.

"If only they'd give me a minute to myself!" she moaned.

Six years younger than Sydney and living in New York for four years, I was still a full-time student. However, once I started playing in the Philharmonic, the calls came quickly and I was also swamped with work. I was hired for oratorios with the Orchestra of St. Luke's, run-outs with Philharmonia Virtuosi to Florida, and Brandenburg concertos with the Y Chamber Orchestra. Orpheus, the conductorless chamber orchestra, had just hired me for their tour of Florida.

The poster of Sydney reminded me of Arleen Auger, in her Queen of the Night costume back when I was seven. Sydney and I really were living out the fantasy of my magic dress. We rushed between Carnegie Hall and Lincoln Center in beautiful evening gowns that were as much our work uniform as other young women's blazers and skirts. Everybody wanted us; the phone never stopped ringing. The demand for my skills made me feel as if I floated above people I saw on the street; I figured they were office drudges.

A typical day started at a morning rehearsal with the New York Virtuosi, moving on to a matinee substituting in a Broadway pit, followed by a one-hour jingle date at studios in the art deco Edison Hotel. At night, a concert at Carnegie Hall with a freelance group like the St. Cecelia

Chorus and Orchestra. Together, the gigs could add up to $400 or more in a single day. One French horn player boasted one-day earnings of nearly $1,000. At 8 P.M., he played the overture at the Philharmonic; at 9, the second piece at New York City Ballet; around 11, he slipped into costume for stage band at the Metropolitan Opera.

The work came in like magic. Unlike soloists, freelance musicians don't use agents but rely on word of mouth, especially through others who play the same instrument. Although full-time groups like the Philharmonic were required to hire through audition, tryouts for freelance orchestras violated Local 802's bylaws.

Typically, another flutist would ask Sydney to substitute for her or play second flute. As a freelancer, Sydney's personality was strong enough to hold her own yet savvy enough not to threaten the principal player who hired her. They always liked what they heard and saw and always invited her back. The flutist would approach the group's personnel manager and ask that he call Sydney directly in the future.

New classical music groups like Orpheus and the Orchestra of St. Luke's that had been founded in the mid-1970s filled up with musicians just a few years older than I, the music students who were graduating while arts funding was on the upswing. With matching grants spawning the creation of more arts organizations and more donations, the money seemed limitless.

When my first recording jingle check arrived, along with hundreds more from the Christmastime gigs, classical music suddenly looked lucrative. Now I needed to shop for some professional items.

Since work—no one called it *playing*—came through telephone calls at home, I used some of my $860 weekly Philharmonic check for one of those new cassette answering machines. I spent $150 on a crinoline-lined embroidered floor-length black skirt trimmed with velvet. Another $200 went for four black concert blouses, and I put the rest away to save for a new reed-gouging machine, which cost $900. Maybe it would solve my reed problem.

I fussed with the roses I'd brought Sydney, a thank-you for a big favor she'd done for me that morning by fetching my music. Arriving at Philharmonic rehearsal at 9:45 A.M., I realized I'd left the only copy of handwritten sheet music to a contemporary music piece at home. Even though

I woke her, Sydney promised to let herself into my apartment and taxi it down to Lincoln Center. For the first fifteen minutes of rehearsal, I glanced at the first oboe part for inspiration and hoped the composer—who was conducting this rehearsal of his own music—wouldn't notice. At last, the door behind the double basses cracked open, and the music was passed to me by the cellists and violists.

Music director Zubin Mehta was celebrating Witold Lutoslawski's seventieth birthday by conducting the Polish composer's *Concerto for Orchestra*, which had become something of a classic along the lines of Béla Bartók's work by the same name. The composer himself rounded out the program by conducting some of his more recent music.

While Lutoslawski's *Concerto* invoked romanticism with its lush harmonies, his *Novelette* was jarringly atonal, the sort of work that was sometimes thrown into a subscription package to hold the audience captive for music they surely wouldn't like. The musicians didn't particularly enjoy it either.

"Shit, I thought that would never end," said the orchestra's blondest first violinist after the first concert, as she slipped off her expensive velvet jacket and hung it in her locker beside ruffled blouses and long skirts.

The violinist's locker was a reminder of the Philharmonic's dress code, which required floor-length skirts with long-sleeved, high-necked blouses and simple jewelry. Anyone wearing pants was sent back to the locker room to change. Men didn't have it much better, buttoning themselves into mandatory white tie and tails.

Climbing onto the M-104 bus across from Juilliard after the concert, I stumbled on the front hem of my puffy taffeta skirt. A Chanel-suited woman clutching her Philharmonic *Stagebill* stepped on the fabric trailing behind me and glared, unaware we'd spent the last two hours together.

Stuffing yards of my voluminous skirt beneath my thighs to fit in one bus seat, I watched a young woman across the aisle with pity. Wearing eighties *Flashdance* regalia—torn T-shirt and leg warmers—she held a new Sony Walkman, bobbing happily to music I couldn't hear. Now there's someone who'd never buy a Philharmonic ticket, I thought, proud that I couldn't identify a pop song from the Beatles to Blondie.

I rustled off noisily in front of the Metro Theater, which had been converted to a porn palace. *Blow Some My Way* and *Here Comes the Bride* were playing. Scurrying past the homeless man who'd staked out the northwest corner of Broadway and 99th with a broken beer bottle, I hurried up the block. Reaching the Allendale, I stopped to listen. I heard Sydney's distinctive Powell flute, playing long tones, her sound marred by the banging keyboard player. God, when would that awful pianist move out? As I stared up at the Allendale's rutted bricks, Jean, a neighbor who was a massage therapist, caught up with me.

"Wow, look at you!" she said, her eyes following my puffy skirt to its floor-length hem.

I wiggled with pride in my fairy princess outfit, feeling as if I were playing a movie role, in costume and living among the romance of all these bohemian musicians.

"I can't play my high school flute with all you pros around," Jean said, as she got off the elevator. "I'm getting rid of it." I started to say something, but the elevator door slammed between us.

8

A Midsummer Night's Dream

"I'LL TAKE IT," I said. I folded the sofa bed back and plumped its cushions. The man who'd advertised the secondhand couch flirted with me while I rooted for money. He asked where I'd seen the ad and what I did for a living.

"Classical music," I said, adding that I'd seen his notice on a bus stop. "I play the oboe in freelance groups."

"You don't play in St. Luke's, do you?" I pulled myself erect, proudly mentioning the *St. John Passion* in the Village. Expecting the usual awestruck reaction, I was surprised when he became agitated instead.

"But you're not really *one* of them, are you?"

I bristled. Didn't he know that St. Luke's considers itself the best group in town?

"I heard that concert," he continued, voice rising as he mentioned the cost of buying two tickets. "The musicians really turned me off. The weird violist, all her private jokes with that creepy guy playing bass." His words spilled out angrily. "It was as if they were excluding the audience, the paying audience!"

I shrank into the corner as the movers I had brought rolled the sofa into the hall. The cute man, now scarlet with rage, stood by the door, his body language suggesting that I leave immediately. He took a deep breath, as if to calm himself before continuing.

"I will never, ever, go hear you people again," he said. I stumbled out the door, which closed quickly. Three locks clicked behind me.

*　　*　　*

Bums were sleeping on grates on West 41st Street behind the Port Authority Building. Buses rumbled overhead. Passing the post office employees' entrance and their favorite bar near Ninth Avenue, I opened the door to Carroll Studios. Inside, the schedule listed rehearsals for American Composers' Orchestra, the Bach Aria Group, and a new Broadway musical, *Sunday in the Park with George*. Orpheus was in the first-floor studio.

A few musicians were arranging chairs inside the room. Four timpani crowded in the corner, behind a rack of black metal music stands, a wooden harp crate, and piles of quilted mover's blankets. Bending over a box of music, Julian Fifer, who lived on the Allendale's twelfth floor, waved at me. A few years back, he'd organized Orpheus as a democratic alternative to mainstream symphony orchestras. Sydney's bassoonist ex-boyfriend was a member too; he had returned from his new job in California to play this tour.

Following a centuries-old tradition, Orpheus played like an enormous chamber music group, with the concertmaster, or first violinist, acting as the conductor. Everyone took responsibility for leading and programming the performances, and seating revolved according to the players' own wishes. Like St. Luke's, Orpheus took the stuffiness out of classical music and replaced it with the same electricity Leonard Bernstein generated. Its twenty-six spirits accelerated toward their blissful collective outcome during concerts, a phenomenon rapturously described as a "headless wonder."

I sat in the second oboe position. Jimmy, whom I had only seen once before at the St. Luke's gig, arrived and told me I'd be playing first oboe on a few pieces. As I moved into the principal chair, I thought about the *St. John Passion* we had played and about the man who had sold me the sofa. Despite the man's anger, I felt fortunate to be living in a city where so many people cared passionately about classical music.

A few days later, we flew to Florida for concerts, starting in Melbourne and crossing the state to Tampa and Fort Myers before reaching West Palm Beach. Florida was a hot touring market. In an area filled with music-loving retirees (in the 1980s, many of them European Jews) our Florida audiences would be as knowledgeable and loyal as one in New York.

The orchestra filed off our bus and into the West Palm Beach Performing Arts Center. The place doubled as a sports arena, but the acoustics were better than in most gyms. For the concert, a red velvet curtain had been hung across the length of its oval space, creating a cavernous and private backstage. Jimmy and I watched the last musicians troop onstage to play a Mozart violin concerto that didn't include oboes. I heard muffled applause in front of the curtain, then the sounds of tuning up. Jimmy twirled the turkey feather he used to clean spit out of his oboe. He probably suspected I found his mannerism annoying. I fell into the camp of oboists who pulled a cloth swab through my instrument instead.

"Wanna get stoned, Blairie?" asked Jimmy, reaching into the breast pocket of his tailcoat for a joint.

It wasn't that anyone would catch us. All alone, there was no chance we'd be interrupted by anyone, since the only access was from the stage. We still needed enough brain cells to play after intermission, however.

"You're not serious." I laughed, massaging my bare toes on his calf. The concrete floor was cold against my feet. Jimmy unhooked his white bow tie and opened his tux shirt.

He lit the joint, inhaling with the deep lung capacity of a woodwind player, then clamping his mouth shut while passing it. "I've never played stoned," I said, but I sucked in a long toke anyway. If the other oboist was high, I'd be all right. Maybe my concert jitters would go away. If only there really were a drug for stage fright.

"It'll add a whole new dimension." Jimmy grunted and held the inhaled smoke in his lungs. He leaned forward an inch from my face. Was he mocking me? Or flirting? He fiddled with what was left of the joint, making a roach clip by jamming the stub into a tube we used for the bottom half of oboe reeds. He sucked in a long inhale, then put out the joint as the Mozart finished and the orchestra clomped offstage loudly down a plywood ramp.

After intermission, I felt like a zeppelin straining to break away and float over my chair as I waited for the orchestra to finish tuning. When we started playing the first movement of Schubert's Fifth, the music quivered with sensation, not only washing over me but through my bones, weaving itself into thoughts and passion. Wow! As I noticed how the piece seemed to be taking forever, my usual stage fright ballooned to paranoia.

Only twenty minutes more. Breathe!

The concertmaster raised her bow to start the work's "Menuetto" movement. The jolly D-major arpeggio in 3/4 time had begun perfectly at each rehearsal, but tonight the violins raced off, then trailed into silence. Ashen, the concertmaster signaled to cut off. I was relieved that the accident happened before either oboe was supposed to be playing, as they stopped and started twice more. Jimmy and I dissolved into giggles through the end of the Rondo.

The audience leaped to their feet in a wild ovation, accepting rough edges for a chance to hear the risky thrills of Orpheus. Gathering my things backstage, I followed the other musicians out a side door and onto our bus, where Jimmy locked his hand around my upper arm and led me to seats in the rear.

"I'll come by your room at the hotel, okay?" As Jimmy barricaded me in the back corner of the bus, Liang-Ping, a violinist, shouted from the front seats to ask how Jimmy's wife was feeling after giving birth to their first child last month. Jimmy looked sheepish but did not move away.

Nearly an hour after returning to the Holiday Inn, I'd changed into jeans, but Jimmy was still in his tails when he pushed open the door of my room. He sat in the desk chair, pushed aside the first oboe part to Rossini's *Italian Girl in Algiers,* and tapped a pile of cocaine on the glass. Rolling up a $5 bill, he looked at me and raised an eyebrow.

I didn't want any. In fact, I was genuinely terrified of the stuff, the result of an antidrug lecture given to my seventh grade by a North Carolina state patrolman that was for some reason delivered during art class. Marijuana leads to worse sins, the officer said, looking over my shoulder at my painting of Palomino ponies at sunset. "And horses aren't pink, little lady," he said menacingly.

I didn't do any coke that night, but Jimmy snorted both lines noisily. He split a Heineken between two plastic motel cups. "Rossini sounds good, Blairie, sounds like you got me beat," he said. I naïvely thought he was serious. In the next room, I'd listened to him practicing the same music to audition for the Cincinnati Symphony next week. Orpheus booked hotel rooms in score order. Flutes were assigned to adjoining rooms, all the way down through cellos and bass. I would always be in a room next to the other oboist.

It was nearly 2 A.M., and I rode the wave of Jimmy's sudden energy, my schoolgirl crush growing by the minute despite knowledge of his family situation. He sure wasn't behaving like anyone's husband and father. We left the hotel and dodged across the highway to a bar. One Dewar's, then another, then a third. The yellowed arm of Jimmy's tux shirt crept around me as the bar owner drove us back to the Holiday Inn at closing time. The sun was rising as we fell into bed together, ripping off our clothes.

It was nearly 7 A.M. and the bus was leaving. We'd have to wait until Cincinnati.

Back at the Allendale, Jayson insisted on coming by to gouge cane. I was exhausted and napped through the evening as Jayson sat at my reed desk. Cane shavings flew from the new machine I'd bought, which my teacher had adjusted especially for me. By using cane prepared with this special gouge of Robinson's, Jayson was looking to find some secret key to my teacher's success. My eyes fluttered open, and I could see him quietly sifting through drawers in the desk, occasionally shooting a look in my direction to make sure I hadn't seen.

"Why are you so tired? It's not like there's jet lag from Florida," he said, when I awoke.

After months of sleeping with Jayson, I had grown weary of being used for access to Joe Robinson. Jayson used jokes and charm to cover up his shtick, throwing me vague promises whenever he sensed my frustration. I'd realized sometime back that he would never divorce his wife. He was a busy boy too, spending plenty of time with another attractive oboist my age. Since it was the early eighties and everybody in every profession was swinging, he couldn't possibly have a problem with my other boyfriends, I figured.

I wasn't much more ethical than Jayson, since I kept our relationship going despite my dissatisfaction. I still had trouble meeting single men my own age. At Manhattan School, the rumor that I was gay persisted and no one approached me. In the freelance world most everyone was considerably older. At some level, I knew that keeping Jayson in my life would keep the gigs coming in. Without considering my plan in depth, I also sensed the amount of work I was offered would double if I added Jimmy to my dance card. I imagined touring the world with Orpheus, then earning big money sitting beside Jayson on all his New York studio dates. Both men were married, so it wasn't as if I was expected to be faithful.

I dozed, waiting for Jayson to finish gouging and join me in bed. He was zipping up his oboe case and packing away tools. In my torpor, I vaguely heard the floorboards creak and sensed the lights going dark. When I woke in the middle of the night, he was gone without a goodbye.

The Cincinnati Symphony vacancy was for associate principal oboe, and it was my very first orchestra audition. I'd heard the event would be held behind a screen. The process of winning an audition for one of the country's larger orchestras was completely different from the routine of networking (and trading sex or drugs) for gigs in the New York freelance circle, where union regulations prohibited auditions for most orchestras.

Fifty-one orchestras fell into the "larger" category and were organized within the American Federation of Musicians as the International Conference of Symphony and Opera Musicians. By organizing, these groups could trade information and function somewhat collectively when negotiating their individual contracts. ICSOM members include a range of orchestras. The New York Philharmonic is a member (in 2004) with its $51 million budget and fifty-two-week season, but ICSOM also represents smaller orchestras like the thirty-nine-week Syracuse Symphony, which runs on a budget of only $5.3 million. The fifth oldest orchestra in America, Cincinnati's symphony falls in the middle range. Its $31 million budget includes nine weeks of paid vacation during a fifty-two-week season and pays a minimum of $85,000 to one hundred musicians.

The audition's anonymity was supposed to bypass the kind of nepotism I was enjoying in the New York freelance scene. Screens were also intended to prevent discrimination against women and minorities, although, in 1983, American orchestras included fewer than 2 percent blacks and Latinos, partly due to a dearth of music students from those ethnic groups. A unique job interview, the screened audition also overlooked appearance, age, and even résumé and experience. Success in blind auditions for the ICSOM orchestras depended solely on performance.

The screened audition had changed the way orchestras hired their musicians, and not everyone agreed with it. "Several of the majors have had a tradition of filling vacancies with students of their own players, students who have gotten to know the orchestra over a long period," wrote orchestra consultant Philip Hart, a comment that described my situation as substitute for the New York Philharmonic.[1] On the other hand, a screen could help me. The number of women employed by orchestras had grown dramatically since blind auditions became commonplace, although the increase could also be attributed to a 1970s explosion of working women across all industries.

As I pushed open the Cincinnati Music Hall's stage door, the butterflies in my stomach grew. I tried ignoring my jitters, taking a deep breath and summoning up the obnoxious, if false, confidence I'd adopted recently. Jimmy was leaving. He'd already been eliminated, so we agreed to meet up after my preliminary round. Inside, the warm-up room buzzed with sixty more oboists playing the hit tunes of the oboe world: the Brahms Violin Concerto, Strauss's *Don Juan*, Ravel's *Le Tombeau de Couperin*, Rossini's *La Scala di Seta*.

After I warmed up, the personnel manager led me to a small lounge where a folding screen blocked most of the room. The setup felt strange, as if I would be performing for an empty space. As I riffled through the music, a male yawn on the other side of the screen broke the silence.

Picking out the reed saved just for this moment (in reality, the only one that worked), I tried a scale to test the room's acoustics. It was dead, with all that carpeting. Everyone was in the same boat. But everyone had not just played with the New York Philharmonic, I boasted silently to myself, but my hands had started shaking with stage fright.

First came two minutes of Mozart's *Oboe Concerto*. "That's enough," droned a disembodied voice. "Now the excerpts." I opened the orchestral parts. They were all difficult, technical "finger gymnastics," the quantitative stuff of classical music. I loved the showiest excerpts and had practiced with a metronome until they were faster than anyone else's.

My heart was pounding as I tore through "Ballet of the Unhatched Chicks" and then "Tuileries," from Mussorgsky's *Pictures at an Exhibition*. Despite a brain foggy from nerves, I thought my tempo, technique, and tone were perfect.

"Let's hear that one again," the voice said. I repeated the solo, two lines of carefully measured sixteenth notes. My hands were shaking a little less now; I had nailed it.

"Look carefully at the music," the voice said. I sped through the excerpt again, cocky now. They want to hear me do it three times in a row!

"Thank you," the voice said, seven minutes after my audition had started. They hadn't even needed to hear me for my full ten minutes! I strutted confidently down the hall back to the warm-up room.

Settling in to wait for the audition results, I listened to the other oboists warming up. Bored, I flipped through the *Chicago Tribune* as a man slowly practiced "Tuileries."

"Hey, you're playing a wrong note," I said, tossing the paper aside. He peered at his music.

"No, it's definitely an A-sharp," he said, turning back to his practice. *So that's why they wanted to hear it three times!*

I sulked in the lounge where the seven other oboists in my round were waiting. They talked about reeds, guzzled coffee, and looked suspiciously at one another. The music hall was supposed to be haunted and built on a potter's field, said one, who was sure she'd felt a ghost in the audition room. I wondered if she was trying to freak out any opponents in the next round. The lounge door swung open.

"Numbers thirty and thirty-four, stay for the semifinals," announced the personnel manager. "The rest of you, thank you."

I bolted quickly from the room to avoid seeing anyone, tears stinging my eyes. After walking back to the Marriott, I was pouring my second Dewar's from the minibar when Jimmy arrived.

"You were in the next motel room all last week," I scolded Jimmy. "Why didn't you tell me I was playing a wrong note in "Tuileries?" Jimmy turned up one corner of his mouth and looked at the floor.

"I didn't hear it, Blairie." He looked up, his gaze stopping at my breasts. "Honest."

Jimmy dug into his satchel. Oboists carry reed tool kits: knives, mandrels, pliers, sharpening stones, plus cigarette paper for leaky keys. He shook a plastic film canister filled with water for soaking reeds. He put it aside and grabbed a second canister, tapping out some pot to roll a joint. We smoked dope, got naked, and embraced.

"Blairie, do you want to do the New England tour in March?"

In that moment, I believed I was a sensational talent. I did not yet admit to myself the link between the sex and the job offers or the triangle of competitors I'd created—the very people I relied on for work. I didn't care. I was living inside a romance novel.

Jimmy did a line and turned on the TV. We'd gone back to his room, in case his wife, home with their infant son, called from New Jersey . I dozed, but he never slept.

At the Cincinnati Airport, security waved me on but opened Jimmy's oboe case. He watched helplessly as his $3,500 Loree tumbled to the floor. Scrounging through his reed-making kit, which was identical to mine, the guard inspected sharp knives, razor blades, and awls, pulling out a film canister.

I walked away, as if I were traveling alone. Out of the corner of my eye, I could see Jimmy was nervous. I held my breath as the guard shook the container, smelled it, and popped the lid open.

Water poured out.

At the gate, Jimmy was pale. "Thanks for the support, Blairie, really," he said, squeezing my upper arm and pulling me just a little too hard down the corridor to the airplane.

In residence at a 1984 New Hampshire chamber music festival, I listened to the other oboist, Randy, practice in the room next door. In the past six months, I'd flown to auditions in San Francisco, Detroit, and Atlanta, never making it past the preliminary round. Preparation had become a full-time job and an expensive hobby, each trip costing hundreds of dollars.

One of many festivals dotting the summer countryside, Monadnock Music featured different combinations of strings, winds, and piano in rural churches. Flipping through the festival schedule gave the audience a wealth of choices: string trio and piano, or string quintet and oboe, or Benjamin Britten's Serenade (for nine musicians and tenor).

A local ex-hippie named Ruth opened her house to us, having added a wing with four extra bedrooms. She baked bread and roasted granola, spooned up with local Stonyfield Farm yogurt. I sat on her sunny deck, looking west toward Mount Monadnock. Randy had driven up in his rented car, a Sunfish lashed to its roof. He brought two violinists, Evan and Rolf, and a cellist named Dan who liked to sleep out back in his tent. Ruth's house was Allendale North, only with clean sheets, great food, and a far more inspiring view.

Randy had graduated from Philadelphia's elite Curtis Institute of Music, which is housed in four Beaux Arts mansions on Rittenhouse Square that were once owned by the Drexel and Sibley families. I'd seen the ornate molding and intricate ironwork inside their wood-paneled rooms during an unsuccessful audition for Curtis in 1978. The school attracts the best young musicians worldwide, with a $60 million endowment allowing every student free tuition for personalized study with high-profile artists. As an alum, Randy had not been a disappointment, landing a job as principal oboe with the New York City Ballet and later becoming a member of Orpheus.

Though Randy was a professional success, he'd told me he had recently emerged from a serious drinking problem. Like many people who spend their lives steeped in art and emotion, Randy had been drinking excessively, behaving erratically, and risking his gigs before finally stopping cold in detox. For the last few months, Randy had to learn to cope with everyday life without chemicals, his raw emotions contrasting with the order of most adult lives around him. He was thirty-seven, unmarried, and childless. A recent tempestuous relationship with a ballerina had plummeted him into depression, and for hours every day he consumed music like he once drank liquor, taming his moody temper by practicing for hours in screaming renditions of Bach and Handel.

In the room next door, I scraped reeds, read, listened to Wagner's *Ring* cycle on my Walkman, and waited for Randy to finish practicing. Finished, he emerged calm, ready to go exploring on country roads. We turned down narrowing dirt lanes, passing colonial churches, farms, and roaring creeks. He liked getting lost on purpose. With Jayson and Jimmy left behind in New York, I decided to get lost with him.

At the end of one lane near Hancock, the waters of Lake Nubanusit spread out in front of us. We swam in the sunshine that afternoon and decided to return at night.

After playing a concert, we drove back to the lake. Wordlessly, we peeled off our clothing and slipped into the water's strange warmth, floating beneath stars piercing the sky. I'd never seen so many shades of blue and gray. Our relationship changed when Randy finally reached out for me, yet our embrace felt childlike and pure.

Randy and I returned several times, in secret trips powered by our post-performance energy. Our platonic status was growing into something larger, and we concocted a plan worthy of our wild emotions. We would return tomorrow night for a midnight sail. It was crazy. No one sails at night, but surely no one had felt these intense stirrings either, Randy said.

We played our concert, a performance of Igor Stravinsky's opera *The Rake's Progress* at Peterborough Town Hall. The libretto was by W. H. Auden, based on eighteenth-century illustrations by William Hogarth. A lurid fable, the opera describes the moral descent of Tom Rakewell, a young man whose life blows apart after receiving an unexpected windfall. Rakewell falls into the clutches of the devil. He abandons his values and true love in exchange for a life of gambling, sexual deviance, and marriage to a bearded lady, at last landing in the lunatic asylum at Bedlam. I hoped the plot had nothing in common with our real life.

We rushed from the concert to his car, retracing our route to the tiny beach. The lake suddenly seemed truly vast, its shores shooting up sharply from its edge in peaks that looked larger than I remembered. I felt danger. I wanted to back out, at the same time that I wanted to sail into the darkness. In the car's headlights I made out a rusted sign:

KEENE STATE UNIVERSITY WILDLIFE PRESERVE

NO TRESPASSING. NO FIRES. NO OVERNIGHT CAMPING.

Randy nosed his car into the bushes to park. Without the moonlight I could barely see his silhouette dropping his tux pants, pleated shirt, bow tie, and cummerbund in the back seat. I peeled off my chiffon gown and pulled on jeans as Randy untied the Sunfish from his roof. Together, we heaved the 130-pound sailboat to the beach and slid its hull into the inky water. We loaded his tent into the cockpit and pushed off into darkness, rocking perilously as we rigged the sail. Something dropped overboard. It was so dark, I couldn't see my own hand or Randy's, only a black velvet background and the sound of water.

We floated without wind or direction for an hour. At last I heard the rustle of trees, perhaps a deer in the bushes, as the centerboard scraped a sandy bottom. Without flashlights, we blundered through the brush to what felt like a clearing and struck camp, pitching the tent blindly. Inside, our breath beaded on the nylon walls. I felt for Randy's face in the blackness. We had already crossed a boundary musically, a natural dance that sparked when we played together. Gracefully, it now evolved to lovemaking, slow and sensuous.

Streaks of pink light were streaming through the birch trunks circling our tent when I woke. Randy was sleeping peacefully, his long dark hair tangled over his face. I felt a warm glow that was turning to love as I watched him. Randy was a real lover, unlike Jayson and Jimmy. Though twelve years older—I was twenty-five—he was unmarried. I adored his discipline and serious nature. My fantasies unfolded as the tent's olive skin turned spring green in the rising sun, and I fast-forwarded through an imagined life together. We could have a beautiful child.

Picking hatfuls of wild blueberries, we crashed through brambles, sated, then thirsty. I couldn't wait to go public with our relationship, but Randy said no. "It's our little secret," he murmured, stroking my hair. I was sick of "secrets" after my illicit affairs with Jayson and Jimmy, but Randy said that, if anyone knew, our relationship would look like nepotism. Didn't I want to work with him on more gigs?

The next weekend, we stayed the night at The Ram in the Thicket, a romantic local inn with organza bed canopies and claw-footed tubs in its rooms. In the restaurant, Randy ordered coffee for himself and brought me a Courvoisier, which he asked me to describe in detail. Outside the veranda a doe grazed. Other couples whispered in the candlelight, exchanging intimate glances. Other couples! Was I finally part of a real couple?

Under the covers, Randy whispered plans for tours together. Did I want to record a Mozart Divertimento with Orpheus? Could I start subbing in his ballet orchestra?

We returned to Ruth's house the next night and to our "just colleagues" routine. Ruth loaded her table with organic salads, tabbouleh, broiled trout, and chicken stir-fried with snow peas and sprouts. Everyone dug in, without questioning where Randy and I had been all those nights.

Evan, the violinist, took a third helping of fish, praising Ruth's cooking. He'd had intestinal problems all summer, growing skinnier even since we started rehearsing this week's Boccherini Quintet. He said Ruth's healthy menus made a tall guy like him lose weight. I knew something else was terribly wrong. When visiting Jayson on Bedford Street, I'd seen gay men around Greenwich Village who were skinny like Evan, with skin blotched by grotesque skin lesions. Middle America might be clueless, but everyone in the arts knew the look of AIDS by now.

Soon after returning to New York, I sat in Carnegie Hall's top balcony, a steeply raked expanse of inexpensive seats. Jimmy sat next to me, on one of the last nights he'd be in New York before taking the job he'd won with the Houston Symphony. Perhaps "won" was too strong a word; a few members of the audition committee had come to New York without advertising the position, inviting only a handful of oboists to play for them. It was a loophole in the audition system that allowed symphonies to hold "invited" auditions if they selected no one during the cattle calls.

Jimmy and I had bought these tickets in the spring, before I went to the summer festival with Randy. Sitting beside Jimmy, I began feeling uneasy. I was in a pickle, involved with three of the city's most powerful oboists, each of whom could make or break my career. My scenario with these men had felt like wildly romantic fantasy, as if I were starring in a film about the music business. Now it was turning into a bad dream that affected my livelihood.

As the music started onstage, I thought about the New York City Ballet Orchestra subbing Randy had given me. Warming up next to him before our first performance at Lincoln Center's New York State Theater, I had wondered why an usherette stared at me so intently, without smiling, from the pit railing. Randy and I had made love the previous night on a sheepskin he'd spread over the bed in his 70th Street apartment: the start of something wonderful and new.

Sitting beside Jimmy made me nervous because I did not know how to end our liaison gracefully. Maybe it would just fizzle out when he left town. As the oboe soloist Heinz Holliger finished the middle movement of Mozart's Oboe Concerto, my eyes drifted from Jimmy's hand, nearly hidden beneath my skirt, across Carnegie Hall's top balcony. There I saw Jayson, alone. I smiled at him, wondering why he wasn't with the other oboist he liked or with his ballerina wife.

As the Rondo drew to a close, I saw a rush of understanding in Jayson's eyes. He turned away. He had finally realized why I toured with Orpheus and he did not, why St. Luke's hired me without calling him. As the audience burst into applause for the oboist who had performed, I scurried across the balcony in pursuit of Jayson. He stumbled over the ladies in his row, tripped on his way up the deeply angled steps, and disappeared.

CHAPTER

9

The Damnation of Faust

THE NARROW STEPS led me down to Possible Twenty, the bar beside a popular sushi restaurant on West 55th between Broadway and Eighth. I'd come to pick up some sheet music from another musician who was stuck in Midtown between recording sessions. It took a minute for my eyes to adjust from the sunlight to the bar's dim lighting, but I could make out a cello case and a trombone gig bag in the corner. A French hornist I knew sat at the end of the bar with a martini, marking something in his date book.

I sat a few stools away and waited for the cello's owner to appear. He and the trombonist must be in the bathroom doing blow. The horn player sniffled and scribbled. I'd tried working my way into the coke scene since drug use had become a way of networking with the top freelancers. Jimmy had once given me a little to rub on my gums in my bedroom at the Allendale. Not feeling any effect, I snorted half a line. Immediately I felt out of control. I hated cocaine, and as a nonuser I felt uncomfortable in a place like Possible Twenty, one of several 1980s Midtown pit stops for drugs.

Musicians hit several haunts like this to kill time between gigs and score coke, tempering its effect with a drink or two. After tonight's Broadway shows finished, Possible Twenty would open up its jazz club upstairs. China Song on 50th was another popular spot. So was Café Un Deux Trois, with its proximity to RCA Studios across 44th, west of Sixth.

Cocaine use raged across New York City's industries and class lines in the early 1980s. Most classical musicians had not been able to afford the drug until the commercial music market exploded, providing even the busiest classical musicians with additional income as studio players. Although the phrase "an hour with a possible twenty," indicated an extra twenty minutes of overtime on a session, it also epitomized an era of power and excess. Classical, jazz, and pop musicians all shared the title of studio musician, recording music together for films and ad jingles. As studio musicians, racing between Midtown dates at the Hit Factory, Clinton Studios, and the RCA complex, they all felt empowered by the money pouring in from sessions and residual payments; drugs made them feel downright superhuman, as it did for drug-using stockbrokers, night-club owners, and bankers.

Certainly drug use among musicians was nothing new. From the 1930s, jazzers had provided a soundtrack for experimentation, with Cab Calloway's "Funny Little Reefer Man" and Benny Goodman's "Sweet Marijuana Brown." There was no question that rock 'n' roll carried its own torch with alcohol and drugs. Yet few outsiders suspected the musicians in the rarefied world of classical music, although we were playing the same twelve notes as everyone else.

Substance abuse was almost a badge of honor. Players formed a drug-using community that was impossible for newcomers or outsiders to penetrate, a phenomenon that sometimes evolved into an orchestra-sized dysfunctional family. An Orpheus tour booklet meant for musicians' eyes only included a cartoon reprint of catatonic male musicians wearing sloppy tuxes amid beer cans in a radio studio as the emcee announced, "You have just heard the Second Brandenburg Concerto performed by the Pro Harmonia Antiqua Society under conditions similar to those prevailing at music festivals in the time of Bach."

That cartoon's message sprang to life one night at Bargemusic, a floating chamber music venue moored beneath the Brooklyn Bridge. I'd stood next to Jayson at the railing to see the lights of lower Manhattan just across the water. Tonight, he would play second oboe on Bach's Brandenburg Concerto no. 1 and I would play third oboe.

The audience was just filing in when Honey, the St. Luke's harpsichordist married to the violist with the hee-hawing laugh, burst from the barge's restroom and noisily sniffled his way outside. His energy level took up far more space than his slight body warranted. Hyperkinetic,

Honey popped open a Heineken and almost simultaneously lit a joint. He chugged with one hand and toked with the other to counteract the cocaine he'd just snorted. "Gotta find the balance, man," he said, twitching. The Fifth Concerto's harpsichord cadenza, a classical version of a solo jazz riff, would zip by at breakneck speed tonight.

Honey had almost certainly shopped at Donald's Claremont cocaine den, the hub of 1980s classical drug activity. Or he might have visited Metropolitan Opera violinist Seymour Wakschal, another classical dealer arrested in 1982 for selling a half ounce of coke to a narc in his apartment right across from Lincoln Center. Cops found four more ounces of blow, three pounds of pot, and 540 Quaaludes in Seymour's pad. Despite the charges, Wakschal slipped free within the year.[1]

Studio players may have been casual about their drug use, but substance abuse among classical musicians sometimes had tragic consequences. Clarinetist Lou Gompertz was found shot dead in his Manhattan apartment after a drug deal gone wrong. In Cleveland, baritone Edward Russell White hanged himself from a psychiatric hospital's sewer pipe after overdosing on panic meds because of a bad rehearsal.[2] California violinist Cynthia Taylor was murdered in San Francisco's seedy Tenderloin district after a lifelong struggle with booze and cocaine, while an Oregon Symphony violist overdosed on a speedball, a mixture of heroin and cocaine.

Classical music celebrities weren't immune, either. The conductor Michael Tilson Thomas was arrested in 1978 at Kennedy Airport carrying coke, pot, and amphetamines. Violin soloist Eugene Fodor was found with heroin, a dagger, a hypodermic needle, and pills in an empty hotel room on Martha's Vineyard, a unit he'd entered through an unlocked window. A student of Jascha Heifetz, a full-scholarship recipient at Juilliard, and winner of top honors in the 1974 Tchaikovsky Competition, Fodor had turned to cocaine after trying to meet the superhuman expectations of his audience. Until the charges were dropped, managers avoided hiring him because Massachusetts' mandatory drug-sentencing laws would have put him behind bars for several seasons.[3]

There were plenty of reasons for musicians to get high—to soothe the frustration of spotty employment or to dull the repetitious nature of practicing and performing the same works again and again. For others, it was the pursuit of perfection in an art whose quality cannot be measured.

As tall and beautiful as Sydney, Bonnie studied at Juilliard with master cellist Leonard Rose, playing Carnegie with the American Symphony and her chamber group, The Music Project. Practicing for hours daily, her meticulous discipline bled into the rest of her life. Bonnie wore designer blouses while catering elegant chamber music fêtes in her huge apartment overlooking the Museum of Natural History, parties where cocaine flowed as freely as the Premier Cru Chablis she served.

She started dating my friend Rob, an oboist who sometimes played in American Philharmonic when Jayson quit after two years. Rob was devoted to her, and soon the couple was engaged. On one bus trip to Kennedy Center, he was distraught; she had seemed ill, and he couldn't locate her before leaving for Washington. Her absence that day was a small and early sign of troubles to come.

Rob and Bonnie married, producing an adorable blond baby. Over the next two years Bonnie's financial struggles surfaced. Her debts were curious for someone earning nearly six figures freelancing and playing at *Phantom of the Opera*. Soon, money began to disappear from purses in the *Phantom* pit or downstairs at Town Hall during concerts with Philharmonia Virtuosi. Bonnie grew gaunt and started missing concerts. *Phantom* fired her, and Philharmonia soon followed. Rob filed for divorce and took custody of their son.

She started freebasing, moved into a crack house, and sold her body to pay for the drugs. Arrested for prostitution and theft, Bonnie was ravaged by bronchitis. She descended into street life, sometimes visiting crack dens in Jersey City. At about this time, novelist Richard Price described a drug-abusing violinist from Broadway's *Phantom of the Opera* in his crime novel *Clockers:*

Her face seemed to belong to two separate women, as if a see-through hag mask had been superimposed on the features of a Nordic milkmaid.

Bonnie's retired father took her to Florida but could not stop her cycle of dependency. She moved in with a one-armed addict who foraged through their carpeting for crack. She stole meat from a supermarket while wearing a silk Oscar de la Renta party dress, then sold her designer clothes to prostitutes for more crack. An alcoholic chain-smoker, she lived in her car and then in the woods, taking breaks to hitchhike and turn tricks.

Suffering from a paralyzing depression, Bonnie checked into a county detox, where doctors diagnosed her as HIV-positive. Through it all, she kept her eighteenth-century Testore cello worth around $350,000; in recent years, the von Trapp family (real-life subjects of *The Sound of Music*) has helped raise money to support Bonnie's drug treatment. Bonnie reached her fiftieth birthday and now lives in Idaho with a new husband and seventeen pets. She has started playing and teaching again.[4]

Drugs were not the only plague sweeping the mid-1980s classical music scene. I hadn't seen Evan since the summer festival, and by the time I ran into him on Broadway in November, he'd shrunk to the size of a scarecrow. "It's just an intestinal bug," Evan said weakly.

We both knew better. Paul Jacobs, the Philharmonic's pianist, had looked just like Evan before dying the previous year. A 1950s prodigy like Sam, Paul was finally seeing success as a soloist, with his Debussy solo recordings earning rave reviews. Paul started showing up at Avery Fisher Hall looking rail-thin and died a few months later. Before long his disease had a name: AIDS, which was killing gay men in the arts.

When Paul died in 1983, some 2,100 AIDS deaths had been reported in the United States. At the time, the disease seemed distant to most Americans, but inside the arts community, as more young men succumbed to what was then an automatic death sentence, panic, anguish, and rage took hold.

My ex-roommate Lionel died of AIDS in Venezuela, where he had taken an orchestra job. Vinson Hammond, a spectacular pianist I'd played with at Manhattan School, died at his parents' house in Alabama. Freelance violist Karl Bargen went home to the Southwest and never returned. Bruce Ferden, one of my conductors from Manhattan School, passed away, as did New York City Opera music director Christopher

Keene, one of seventy-five New York City Opera employees lost to AIDS. Pianists Jorge Bolet, Joseph Villa, and Thomas Lorango, a bisexual who'd married a girlfriend of mine, all died. Michael Dash, a countertenor known from his appearance as the boy soprano in the televised premiere of Bernstein's *Mass*, performed for the 1971 opening of Washington's Kennedy Center, died. So did Ross Allen, a Broadway keyboard player; Kent Jones, an oboist I'd known at NCSA; baritone William Parker; and organists by the dozen including Calvin Hampton, Eugene Hancock, and the Philharmonic's own Leonard Raver.

I had been keeping a list of people—all gay or bisexual men—I knew personally who had died of AIDS. When it reached one hundred names, I threw the list away.

During my first years in New York, gay men visited clubs for anonymous sex, fucking faceless partners through "glory holes" punched between stalls in "cruisy" bathrooms, while straight couples experimented with bisexuality and mate-swapping in local bathhouses. Birth control pills had eliminated the risk of pregnancy, and most sexually transmitted diseases could be cured with antibiotics. Whether gay or straight, hardly anyone used condoms anymore.

My ex-roommate Lionel and many other gay male musicians had picked up men at Village bathhouses and, late at night, in Riverside Park. Heterosexual musicians kept most of their casual sex within the classical music community, although a few tried out Plato's Retreat. Gays and straights both felt comfortable when they hit the road together, however. On one 1980s Solisti New York tour, that chamber orchestra enjoyed a hotel-room orgy featuring almost every sexual position and combination, a night that would be gossiped about even as its participants went gray two decades later.

AIDS was something entirely new. New York City closed virtually all the city's bathhouses, most of them specializing in homosexual sex. Gays cried discrimination but women suffered too, many not realizing they were also susceptible. The health department didn't add vaginal intercourse to its list of risky practices until 1987. No AIDS drug therapy had yet been approved by the FDA, and taking an AIDS test could red-flag insurance companies, which then denied coverage or raised rates.

Many of my women friends were beginning to realize that they were at high risk because of bisexual former partners. I knew that Sydney's ex-boyfriend, the bassoonist who'd moved to San Francisco, had surprised everyone when he came out of the closet there. I didn't know Sydney well enough yet to ask her if he might have been bisexually active when they were dating, or if she was worried about having contracted AIDS. I wasn't sure about several of my former partners either, so I signed up for one of the anonymous AIDS tests offered at city health centers.

As a freelancer I bought my own hospitalization insurance, but never the expensive plan that paid for outpatient doctor visits. The only medical professional I knew was the physician's assistant at a city health clinic, a woman who gave me free birth control pills and antibiotic prescriptions for me to self-treat recurrent respiratory and urinary infections.

Live chickens squawked from a corner shop as I crossed 126th Street, feeling conspicuously white and female in Harlem. I found the facility on a tiny lane in a late-1950s cinder-block public works building much like the Lenox Avenue clinic where I'd taken a free pregnancy test years ago. It was the only Manhattan site then offering completely anonymous AIDS tests. Inside, a nurse seemed startled by my presence as she handed me a plastic jar and anonymous identification number. In the epidemic's early days, I guess she saw few women.

Over the next two weeks I felt the same butterflies as stage fright, which then intensified into stomach pain. Finally the day arrived when I could claim my results. My chest tightened as the city bus passed the Columbia campus, which was where I last saw Evan. I pictured him warming up on Ruth's balcony in New Hampshire. He was tossing off a Paganini "Caprice," the sunset behind Mount Monadnock beaming a halo around his body like a Renaissance painting.

Evan had died last month. Would I be next?

As the adviser opened my file, I read posters on the wall, their messages aimed at gay men. I thought about the irony of sitting onstage at Carnegie Hall in a ball gown and, in the same month, in a plastic chair at a free Harlem public health clinic. What if I were sick? I didn't have money for medications or doctor visits. What was taking so long? It must be bad news. I imagined myself an ashen skeleton. With credit-card debt from traveling to orchestra auditions, I had no savings. Would anyone help me? At what point do dying people commit suicide?

"Let's double-check your ID number," the adviser said grimly. I handed him my slip. My heart pounded in the silence as he read a file for what seemed like an eternity.

"Negative," he said finally. He handed me a pamphlet and a fistful of colored, ribbed, and extra-large condoms. I promised myself I'd change my wild ways. Suddenly my romances with Jayson and Jimmy looked not free-spirited but shameful and dangerous.

Randy, the third part of my oboe triptych, soon rejected me entirely, demeaning our summer relationship as an affair even though he was not married. Obsessed, I paced West End Avenue at 2 A.M. I went as far as his door, where I heard a woman making coffee for him, probably the usherette I'd seen hanging over the pit railing.

What does she have that I don't?

Randy and I subsequently went to Puerto Rico on an Orpheus tour, which was arranged while we were in New Hampshire together months ago. He would not speak to me, turning his chair away during rehearsals of the Rossini overture we played. The curse of score order once again booked us in adjacent rooms; his voice on the phone to someone new was torture.

Months passed before I saw Randy again. It was the final gig he'd hired me for, a European tour with Orpheus. Deutsche Grammophon followed us from the Mozarteum to Montreaux, photographing the orchestra for its new sixteen-disc recording contract. On the album cover for a Mozart *Divertimento* we'd recorded so fervently together last year, today's photo in Salzburg would show Randy leaning away from me. As we boarded the bus in all-white outfits for the photo shoot, the orchestra joked that we looked much like the sperm in Woody Allen's *Everything You Always Wanted to Know About Sex*. I knew a quarter of the sperm intimately, if the blond horn player from last night's Lucerne hotel room counted. I'd had a crush on the hornist for some time and hoped he would provide a diversion from obsessing about Randy. Unfortunately, I had yet to learn that one-night stands aren't the best path to a relationship.

Photograph taken in Salzburg, 1987. I am in the front row, third right of center. (Schaffler, Salzburg)

I wasn't the only scorned lover on the bus, however. My hornist had, a few years ago, nailed a cellist, who promptly turned lesbian. Later, the horn player would divorce and land the bassist's ex. The bassist, in turn, cuddled with a younger violinist on the bus in front of his ex-wife. A female violist who lived in the Allendale was in the process of leaving her pianist husband for an Orpheus cellist, and a revolving list of subs like me added even more variety. All this intra-orchestra familiarity may have provided a musical benefit on this tour, because Spanish newspaper *ABC* reported that "the ensemble from New York transcends any name that carries any sense, or meaning, of plurality. It is—again without hyperbole— one instrumentalist. With only one body and only one spirit."

During a free week, I cashed my per diem check and headed to Menton, on the French Riviera, with two girlfriends. Randy took the same train, en route to Nice with Guillermo, a Puerto Rican violinist who'd shared our house back in New Hampshire. Traveling together in an Italian rail car, the five of us lay down for the night, Guillermo, on one side of me, became friendlier with my harpsichordist friend; Randy, on the other, put his sock feet in my face.

I had made the fatal mistake of becoming involved not just with one but with three of my most influential colleagues. Jayson would never again hire me for his studio dates. Other oboists would penalize me for the work Jimmy had provided me and denied them, and I wouldn't play with Orpheus or in Randy's pit again for some time.

When we returned to the United States, Randy quickly married an oboist from California, someone cuter, younger—and a crackerjack instrument repair technician to boot—who was now carrying his baby. However, his insistence that our relationship remain secret made it appear to others that he'd rejected me for my musicianship. I'd destroyed my connection with almost every freelance group in the city. I was only twenty-six years old.

Second Movement
Rhapsody in Blue

The cinder blocks and missing roof of the Allendale's water tower.

West Side Story

10

Two NEW KOREAN cellists got off the Allendale's asending elevator on Three, and a man stepped forward to punch the CLOSE button. He mussed his hair in a self-conscious way that gave him the appearance of a teenager.

"I haven't lived here long," he said, extending a bony hand as the lift creaked along. He was so skinny, like Evan and Paul before they died, that I hadn't recognized him until he told me his name.

"My name's Sam Sanders. What do you play?"

Sam's thick hair curled over his gray turtleneck, and his brown eyes sparkled with enthusiasm. I could tell he didn't remember meeting me nine years ago in Greensboro, and there wasn't a hint of the short temper I'd seen then. Perhaps moving into the Allendale after living in a grander place had humbled him.

I found him irresistible, even though his mannerisms reminded me of Woody Allen. His weight loss emphasized the resemblance even more—his bony nose had become even more prominent—but his energy level was magnetic. Juilliard students I knew gossiped about Sam's friendship with Bobby White, but he was certainly flirting like a straight man today. As the elevator stopped on Six, Sam held the door open and invited me to lunch the next day at the neighborhood café where he always ate.

Arriving at Marvin Gardens, I found Sam sipping a Diet Coke in one of the rear booths. He looked handsome in his turtleneck, though it was an odd wardrobe choice for 70-degree weather. I slid onto the seat opposite him and ordered a salad.

"Bassoon's my favorite instrument, oboe next," he was saying, when our food arrived. He pulled at the American cheese melted between slices of white toast and ate his sandwich piecemeal. He asked about my career and training. Did I know Margo Garrett from NCSA? She'd come to Juilliard in 1969, having grown up in North Carolina like me. She was such a star, so sweet. How did I like Orpheus? The Philharmonic?

He was animated, bouncing between topics: composers, restaurants, the Juilliard accompanying department he'd started, and his efforts to get equal billing and better pay for collaborative pianists. "Some soloists won't even hire women pianists," he said, explaining that old-school artists think women will upstage them. He fell silent for a moment to sip his soda.

"Sam, how did you end up in the Allendale?" I said. Surely a Juilliard professor who toured the world with Itzhak Perlman could afford something nicer. Sam set down his Coke, swallowed, took a deep breath, and chuckled nervously.

"My wife—well, she was my wife—and daughter live a block away on West End," Sam said. "Split up for now. I needed someplace to stay."

From Sam's behavior in Greensboro, I guessed that his wife may have found him difficult to live with. I'd seen his temper firsthand. I'd also heard Sam was a ladies' man; most recently there were rumors about Sam and a dark-haired flutist. The two had recorded George Crumb's *Voice of the Whale*. The flutist was married as well, with a daughter who was turning into a star pianist. It was all messy and incestuous in the minuscule world of classical music.

"I got the Allendale place through Bobby White," said Sam, clearly eager to change the subject. From what he said, it sounded like Sam had moved into conductor Neal Stulberg's old place on Nine. "You know Bobby? Second floor, tenor."

I'd heard him singing Irish songs. Bobby charmed landlord Brunhilde to rent flats to all his friends. In fact, he'd found apartments for half the Allendale's tenants, surrounding himself with the supportive community he'd started building years back.

Sam asked if I knew guitarist Fred Hand, who lived across the hall from him. Or the Korean cellists who studied with him at Juilliard and turned pages sometimes? Could I turn pages this Friday for a benefit with Itzhak on the Upper East Side?

"Sure, I'm free Friday," I said. I wanted to hear Perlman up close and check out a Fifth Avenue apartment. Sam was a class act and wouldn't live in a dump like the Allendale for long. I thought he made a fortune playing with such stars.

"What a beautiful tomato!" Sam exclaimed, as he poked at the cottony-pink slices beside his unfinished sandwich. I checked to see if he was joking, but Sam was enthusiastic about everything he encountered, regardless of quality. Observant, he missed nothing. There's a lesson there for me, I thought.

When I hauled out my wallet, Sam snatched the restaurant bill. On the street, he pressed money in my hand for a taxi. What a contrast to our first meeting nearly a decade ago, when he had snarled at me. I must have been wrong about him. He was generous, disciplined, passionate, and kind.

I hung the Yves St. Laurent cocktail suit far away from my reed desk to avoid staining it. There'd been an entire wall of them for fifty bucks apiece in the basement at Fowad, a 96th Street firetrap stuffed with designer evening wear whose origins were always a mystery. Spreading a ragged hand towel on my lap to protect my skirt from oil smears, reed shavings, and steel filings from sharpening my knife, I turned on my high-intensity lamp. Pulling my thread tight against the desk leg, I had begun tying on another reed when the phone rang.

Damn! I dropped the thread spool, shooting cane across the room while trying to reach the phone.

"Hello?"

"Hold on, I'm getting another call," Sydney's voice cried over the phone. The line fell silent. I scanned the floor for my cane, eyeing the time. After a couple of minutes I hung up, and the phone rang again immediately.

"Yeah," I snarled, expecting Sydney again.

"Claire Kendall?"

"Blair Tindall," I corrected her.

"Whatever," said the high-pitched voice. "This is Fern? At the Orpheus office? I'm hiring for the next tour?"

As we spoke, I pictured the latest intern in the orchestra's airy loft at 80th and Broadway. Not bothering to learn an instrument herself, she was a new recruit in the arts management army, gazing out the window overlooking Zabar's at violinists scurrying to the subway with cases slung over their shoulders.

If she climbed the ranks, Fern would earn up to seven times more than any of them as CEO of a major orchestra, a theoretically nonprofit organization whose administrators' annual salaries would rise to $700,000 by the millennium. If she were *really* smart, she'd study conducting and make up to $2 million for just fourteen weeks of work, leaving plenty of time for one or two other $2 million gigs in other cities.

I spied the cane just under my bed.

"Well, Claire? We've tried *everyone* else in town? We'll be *stuck* if you can't do it?"

"Okay. And it's Blair. *Blair*." I sighed and hung up. At least there was no confusion about my place on the Orpheus list these days. No new work came in either. Groups that had sprouted like toadstools in the 1970s seemed an anomaly in the late 1980s, their musicians permanently epoxied to their chairs. Only a narrow age category had been in the right place at the right time.

I gathered the grimy towel on my lap into a wad that rattled with the tools I'd been using. They included four reed knives, since I could never seem to get any one of them sharp enough to shave off the last hundredth millimeter of cane required without tearing off the reed's tip. I dropped it on the desk, turned off the light, and set to the task of transforming myself with the discount Yves St. Laurent suit.

It was time to go. I met Sam in the lobby and hopped into a waiting limo. Its crystal decanter rattled as we pulled onto 90th and Riverside to pick up Itzhak. I sat quietly as the famous violinist, crippled by polio during his childhood in Israel, pulled himself inside, laying his aluminum crutches against the leather seat.

Cruising through Central Park, the two men rattled off baseball scores and news of their children, only then moving on to music. "A lady in the audience last night told me my Strad sounded beautiful," joked Itzhak. He'd held the violin to his ear, shaking it. "Really? I don't hear a thing!"

I had a feeling we were about to meet a few more ladies like that. The car turned down Fifth Avenue, stopping just past the Met. As we made our way upstairs to the host's apartment, Sam carried Itzhak's precious fiddle across the lobby, since the violinist needed both hands for his crutches. Itzhak followed, his leg braces creaking gently.

An elevator opened directly into the apartment instead of the usual hallway or vestibule. The place looked like a museum, full of furniture pieces that looked as if they should have braided cords surrounding them for protection. I peered through an archway that framed a series of doorways beyond it. I'd hate to lose my keys in this apartment, I thought, as we passed through rooms whose tabletops and étageres were arranged with objets d'art. Oil paintings hung on nearly every wall.

In a spare bedroom, I gazed through sheer curtains at the street, trying to give Sam and Itzhak privacy for their preparations. Something in the room ticked irregularly, like one of those old pyramid-shaped pendulum metronomes. I looked around for a clock but didn't see one.

Sam stood at a mirror, fussing over his bow tie with trembling fingers. He rustled tissue paper in his bag, extracted a hairbrush, and used it to fluff up his curly hair. He then carefully lined up his brush, glasses case, and date book on a mahogany side table, just as he had backstage in Greensboro. It was a study in right angles. Turning away, he rooted through a Dopp kit, tapped out eight pills, and threw them back dry.

More drugs, I thought.

Itzhak seemed as confident as Sam was neurotic. He wrapped his enormous hand around the violin's neck, plucking each string, then clamped the Strad between chin and shoulder, tuned with broad bow strokes, and sent rivulets of scales down the fingerboard.

I turned back to the window, focusing on the luxury building across 82nd Street. As I pulled the sheer drapes aside for a close look, Sam was right behind me. He snatched off his glasses to peer at five naked couples kissing, guzzling champagne, and massaging one another in a Jacuzzi. Itzhak glanced but went back to his fiddle.

Sam reddened, whipping his tux jacket shut.

Most definitely not gay, I thought.

"It's time, Mr. Perlman," called a chipper blonde. Her huge diamond-stud earrings glinted, and her hair was perfectly combed behind a tortoiseshell headband. Itzhak handed Sam his Stradivarius and hoisted himself onto his crutches. I grabbed the pile of sheet music and followed him; Sam lingered by the window until the last second.

Applause rippled through the audience, seated on the faux-gold bamboo chairs that fancy caterers bring with them. These were the richest and most generous New Yorkers, who supported the Carnegie Hall Foundation, the Metropolitan Museum of Art, and other cultural treasures.

Itzhak sat down and arranged his legs, laying his crutches on the floor and taking his instrument. Sam's rigid posture softened at the piano. His hands, that were shaking backstage, were still. I placed Pablo Sarasate's "Zapateado," op. 23, on the piano and sat to his left. Sam poised his weird, clubby fingers over the keyboard.

That ticking again! And in a faster tempo than this piece.

Sam launched into the Spanish dance, drawing out strong octaves in his left hand, a saucy folk tune in his right to set up Itzhak's dramatic high Es perfectly. Sam, who had appeared almost frail backstage, became a powerhouse as he accompanied one of the world's great virtuosos. It was as if he banked every shred of energy for his music.

He didn't just play the piano, he wove playfully around Itzhak's dark-sounding tone as if his life depended on it. His passion took flight. He wasn't merely an accompanist; he was a collaborator in a breathtaking performance.

I stood up and reached to turn the page where Sam had marked. I was one eighth-note late, but that was surely close enough. Sam grunted, slapping my hand and flipping the music himself. I took more care with the next page.

Next came Fritz Kreisler's showy "Caprice Viennois." The piece was included on an album Itzhak and Sam had recorded that was nominated for this year's Grammys. The audience responded to this performance with polite applause. An evening like this was more about networking than music. In 1986, philanthropy was hotter than the stock market. Wealthy New Yorkers needed the tax breaks that came by donating to nonprofit charities like music groups.

Itzhak Perlman and Samuel Sanders. (Julian H. Kreeger. Courtesy of the Juilliard School archives.)

Afterward, Itzhak's stretch limo glided back to the Allendale. As we pulled up beside the hydrant, our doorman Jules was mute, gawking at the limo. I stepped out in my designer suit, feeling the car might turn into a pumpkin at any moment. We turned to go inside.

"Wait," said Sam, gesturing with his head as we stood in the foyer. Just ahead of us, Betty waited for the elevator. Sam wanted to avoid her as much as I did. She was usually alone or wheeling her double bass. Tonight an older man clutched her elbow.

"Isn't that—?"

"Yeah. They've been having an affair for years," said Sam, studying the contents of his battered mailbox. I recognized the man from old photographs of him as a New York City Opera star of the 1950s, although his health had declined since his glory days.

As I got off on Six, Sam held the elevator door, which bucked against his hand with a greasy smudge. "Want to come up for a drink?" he asked. Hearing him play had turned me on, and I accepted.

Sam's apartment looked like a smaller version of mine, with an equally pink bathroom, bare-bones kitchenette, and cheap marble-patterned green linoleum. His possessions, however, were far more elegant. A nineteenth-century display case was filled with antique glassware, and another cabinet held toy soldiers, Yankee memorabilia, and a baseball autographed by lefty Whitey Ford.

Sam had made the large corner bedroom into his piano room, carpeting the floor and adding plaid curtains to soak up the sound for his neighbors' sake. In the other bedroom, an enameled Japanese screen hid his bed, leaving only a kitchen table for socializing. Above the table hung a photo of Sam at the White House, shaking Jimmy Carter's hand as cellist Mstislav Rostropovich looked on.

"People give me booze, but I don't drink much," he said, picking a fat bottle of German Goldwasser from a high shelf crowded with liquor gift boxes. He tapped one of the crystal glasses, which made a ringing sound. "C-sharp," he observed, pouring a half inch in the goblet. Golden specks fluttered to the bottom.

There was that ticking again!

"Sam," I asked finally, "did a metronome get turned on in your bag?" He held up his palm, signaling me to be still. The irregular beat continued.

Click-clack. Click-clack.

"That?" he asked. I nodded.

"It's just my heart," he said. "There are ball bearings in there. And pig valves." He seemed to relish my look of shock as he started telling me the story of his childhood as a blue baby and the pioneering surgery in Baltimore in 1947, when he was nine. He also recalled his 1965 operation; it hadn't turned out to be the "final correction" his doctor had expected, because his heart problems reappeared in the late 1970s.

Even that operation wasn't his last. Onstage at his new chamber music festival on Cape Cod in 1980, Sam had realized something was terribly wrong. The veins in his hands were pounding, and his pulse raced to two hundred beats per minute. He was rushed to specialists in Alabama, who diagnosed full heart failure. Rare in a former blue baby, coronary artery disease had ravaged him. No one was hopeful. Rushed into surgery, he got new heart valves from pig donors, fitted with the latest technology in stainless steel ball bearings.

"That's what you're hearing now," Sam said.

In intensive care for two months, Sam had hallucinated and gone in and out of a coma. He didn't remember, but he was told that he swore and screamed. He remembered the unbearable pain, though. After he swung at an aide, nurses tied his arms to the bed. Blood transfusions topped eighty pints at a time. His brother, Martin, rushed to his side, only to receive a phone call from New York informing him a Chinese food deliveryman had bicycled into their mother, killing her.

After two months, Sam came out of it, returning home to his wife and daughter at their new 83rd Street apartment. It took months to get used to clicking in the wrong tempo, and his internal beat, audible to others, drove Sam's collaborators nuts. It was like trying to perform with a metronome set at the wrong speed.

The pills he'd taken before the concert were diuretics, blood pressure medicine, and other prescriptions. Well, the blue one *was* Valium, he admitted. The kids at Juilliard thought he was skinny from AIDS, Sam said, flashing that grin I'd begun to adore. He must keep his weight under a hundred twenty-six pounds, though. He would simply die otherwise.

"Enough of this old story," Sam said. "When I saw you in the elevator, I told myself you were one of the unattainable ones." Sam squeezed my hand gently with his strange, clubbed fingers. He apologized for slapping my hand at the concert and tipped my chin toward him. I tasted blood as we kissed.

"My gums bleed from the blood thinners," Sam said, wiping his mouth and leading me behind the lacquered screen where geishas peeked shyly from their fans. He lit a candle on the windowsill over the empty spot where he'd removed his broken radiator. Light flickered against his spare cast-iron double bed, antique table, and chair.

"Promise me you won't run away," he said, removing the two top studs from his tux shirt. A row of rectangles protruded a half inch from his sternum, like a zipper you'd expect to see on Frankenstein's monster. Now I understood why he wore turtlenecks so often. Removing his tux shirt, Sam explained the chronology of his scars. There was the diagonal one from the 1947 operation, a north-south number from 1965, and so on. His entire torso was laced with incisions.

"Everything works, though," he said sheepishly, his voice crackling as he looked down his body. I already knew that from his response to spying on the Jacuzzi scene at Itzhak's soiree.

Sam handled me gently, kissing my neck, stroking my long hair, and caressing my shoulders as he slid my blouse onto the chair. We climbed into bed and made love. Afterward, we lay on our backs, our arms tangled around each other.

"My damn circulation," he said, looking away. He'd rejected the doctors' various suggestions for a permanent implant or for a shot in the dick each time he wanted to make love. He kissed my forehead.

"I understand if you want to go home."

I didn't care about the sex. All I saw was Sam's courage, his dedication and discipline, his taste. I stayed. His heart clicked away beside me in bed until I dozed off. At midnight I faintly heard him close the apartment door, leaving to practice as he said he would.

In his nightly routine, Sam hailed a cab downtown to a huge apartment in the San Remo. There, he practiced on a rich man's Steinway every night until the sun rose behind him over Central Park, its orange rays glinting off Essex House and the other buildings diagonally across the park. In return, the man had access to Sam's nubile Juilliard students. A female Chinese pianist without a work visa had just moved in with the man, trading sex for financial support.

After several hours, the night sky began turning pink. Glancing at the picture window over his shoulder, Sam placed his hands on the keys to repeat his banging practice. Just once more and he'd be perfect.

* * *

After nearly a decade in the Allendale, I had an assortment of neighbors' keys—including Rob Fisher, Sam, Sydney, Marni, Jorge, and Joan—and at least five sets to flats now full of Korean cellists. Everyone distributed their keys to neighbors, since as musicians who worked together we might as well have been family. This way a quick phone call could arrange for a friend to water the plants, feed the cat, or collect the mail. Picking out Sam's key, I turned off the bathroom light, eyeing the brown stain that was spreading across the ceiling.

Heading down the hall, I pushed open the stairwell's swinging door. It was early for Hippolito, but there he was, rag at the ready. The stairwell's elaborate faux-Greek mosaics barely showed through thick dirt, and years-old sludge coated the windowsills and window glass. Hearing me, Hippolito jerked away from the keyhole and furiously polished a doorknob down to solid brass shine.

On the ninth floor, I let myself into Sam's apartment. I'd overheard his intense practice sessions without knowing it was Sam. Once I knew, I adapted parts of his routine to the oboe. Knowing Sam these past two months had dramatically changed my habits. Watching him try to maintain his health was an eye-opener and made me grateful for my own good health. Unlike Sam, *I* could exercise. I vowed to put a lifetime of crash diets behind me and started running several miles a day.

"Almost ready, honey, " he said, and rushed around the piano room. Despite the building's decrepit condition and sloppy conversions, many of the rooms retained their original spaciousness. Sam leaned over the suitcase he'd take on tour tomorrow, carefully smoothing the lapel of his tux jacket, folding tissue paper saved from the dry cleaner over it. More tissue lay stacked in the closet next to a box of odd shoes, orphaned as a result of the difference in his feet, an effect of his childhood surgery.

"Almost ready, honey," he repeated nervously. Switching off the space heater beneath his splintering window, he penciled one last fingering onto music that seemed to have numbers over every note, reviewing his work before closing the score. He lined up a pile of arias on the lid of his glossy black Steinway, nudged the papers in perfect alignment, then rubbed away a dusting of ceiling plaster. Looking over the room one last time, he turned out the light.

"Um, ready, I think," he said.

In the taxi's backseat, Sam, at forty-nine, looked boyish in his turtleneck and blazer. No one would have ever guessed his age, all the more remarkable, given his physical ailments. We pulled up in front of a building on Central Park West and went upstairs to an Argentine investment banker's birthday fête—just the kind of party, filled with intellectual, fashionable people drinking sophisticated cocktails, that I'd dreamed of attending back in North Carolina.

The hostess knew Sam through Bobby White's circle of journalists, executives, old-money scions, and artists. Ana loved classical music and had served as chairman of the board during the first season of a chamber festival Sam had launched in 1980. Now in its sixth season, the Cape and Islands Festival was firmly established, and Ana's fund-raising efforts were a big part of its success.

I recognized newscaster Garrick Utley, who was far taller than I'd imagined. Bobby White stood in the kitchen, chatting with someone in a black sheath dress. Sam introduced me to General Foods CEO Jim Ferguson and his wife, Esther, a tiny blonde with an energizing South Carolina lilt.

This fête was nothing like the parties thrown by most freelance musicians. Our events took place in small dingy flats. The guests were orchestral musicians like me who schlepped in wearing dowdy black dresses and tuxes that smelled funky from many nights of performing. Refreshments came in the form of Chinese takeout containers and liters of jug wine. Conversation revolved around gossip or who was contracting gigs and how to get on their hiring lists.

Ana's party took place in a huge co-op apartment overlooking Central Park. Her caterer had adjusted the lighting, arranged flowers, and created a spread of tiny hors d'oeuvres, each of which included at least four ingredients and looked like a miniature work of art. The guests wore elegant clothing.

As Sam and I crossed the room for a glass of wine, I heard bits of conversation about bank mergers, a Connecticut regatta, and the dealings of a museum board of directors. I imagined people were making appointments to play golf together or to bankroll some new company. The room was alive with power and progress. Unlike my freelance-musician parties, where much of the activity consisted of complaining and getting drunk, big things were *happening* at this event.

While the hired bartender opened a new bottle of chardonnay, I observed the action. This party looked a bit like the ones a cellist ex-boyfriend of mine named Fred sometimes attended, where the rich and powerful interacted with artists, journalists found a good story, and performers made connections for funding and publicity.

Fred had existed on a higher echelon of the music business than that of freelance orchestral musicians. He was more of a soloist and chamber musician, and he hung out with other musicians who had won solo competitions and had big management. Even if I had been the most talented player, I could never have fit in with his circle of famous string players and pianists, since there simply wasn't the same demand for oboe soloists. I would always have to settle for lower-paying orchestral work, where I had to depend on contractors to hire me instead of creating my own path.

Still, I had found Fred's network intriguing. One of its members, Marya, a flutist, ran the Bridgehampton Chamber Music Festival. The *New York Times* had lavished 3,500 words on the three-week series, explaining how it got started after the flutist had married an investment banker. The banker had urged his wife to start a festival in the Hamptons so she could spend the summer with him instead of jetting off to other festivals.

Ana's bartender handed me the wine, and Sam and I plunged into the crowd. I stayed quiet after he introduced me to a management consultant, listening hard to learn what such a person did. In fact, his work sounded far more interesting than I'd expected. I was curious to find out more about what investment bankers and lawyers did too, since I rarely ran into people with these jobs. I felt out of my element, but I desperately wanted to belong.

Sam talked knowledgeably with a man who sold Oriental antiques and had just returned from Hong Kong. A documentary filmmaker started talking with the antiques dealer about Mongolian nomads whom China had forced to stop wandering and settle in communes. She was looking for a way to finance a film about it. I sipped my wine, which was tasty compared to the swill I usually bought for myself.

The filmmaker talked about Tibet, the Dalai Lama, Chinese Muslims, and other subjects I'd never considered. Wearing a red mandarin-style sheath dress and dangling silver earrings, she was a magnetic presence in the room. As several guests wearing business suits gathered around her, she skillfully turned the description of China into a balance sheet of what her film would cost. Pretty slick, I thought with admiration. A Merrill Lynch banker and his wife joined us. They'd known Sam for many years and donated money to his summer festival.

"Old boy, how do you get to Carnegie Hall?" The husband guffawed.

"I don't know. How?" Sam smiled blankly, as if he'd never heard the old chestnut before.

"Practice, old boy, practice!" bellowed the banker and slapped Sam on the back, nearly knocking him over. The banker's wife turned to me and exclaimed that she loved the sound of an oboe. Her husband interrupted, now addressing me.

"Danny Kaye—you're too young to know him." He continued, in a gravelly smoker's voice, "Now let me get this right: He said the oboe's an ill wind that no one blows good!"

I laughed, although the joke wasn't funny anymore. I had actually played with Danny Kaye once at the Philharmonic. The comedian had stolen Zubin's baton to conduct the *Fledermaus* overture. We had great fun playing with Kaye's exuberant beat, and he didn't once insult the oboists.

Smiling sweetly, I squeezed Sam's hand. He squeezed back, as if in code. No doubt Sam was silently rehearsing a comic impression of the banker, which he would deliver in a sidesplitting performance at home later.

Sam dazzled the crowd as he talked passionately about film, books, and his teenage daughter's paintings. When no one was looking, Sam turned away for a handful of pills, returning in a graceful arabesque to ask about the other guests' lives, spreading the word about Bobby's latest album and introducing me as part of his "musical insider's" circle.

Although I liked most of the people I was meeting, neither Sam nor I had much in common with them. Except for Bobby and possibly the filmmaker, none would return to a dump like the Allendale tonight. Perhaps that accounted for the electricity between us all. Everyone offered something strange and useful to the others, whether money, influence, or creativity. As we gathered our coats to leave, I felt as if I'd just glimpsed a magic kingdom in which I could never afford to live.

"Love you!" The banker and his wife bade Sam goodbye at the door. He shook my hand; his wife air-kissed Sam.

"Love you," Sam replied, with alarming sincerity.

As my carpool turned toward Marlboro, October foliage lined the country road with splashes of orange and red. The sky looked even bluer against the white clapboard of Marlboro's meetinghouse and the brilliant bronze hue of hickory beside it. The Vermont town was sacred ground for classical musicians, who came here each summer for one of the world's top music programs.

I'd probably never participate in the famous Marlboro Music Festival, but I might come close during this autumn week by playing in the New England Bach Festival under the direction of Blanche Honneger Moyse. She had come to Marlboro in 1949 with a group of fellow Europeans to found the summer festival and make a home in Vermont. Although the festival's summer concerts were immensely satisfying for her, Blanche quickly grew restless during the long Vermont winters. To combat the boredom and contribute to her adopted community, in 1952 she launched the Brattleboro Music Center, a year-round educational mecca, in a house on Walnut Street that soon was filled with local people learning to make music. It had thrived ever since.

After an ailment ended her violin career in 1966, Blanche began conducting, making her Carnegie Hall debut at age seventy-eight. She devoted herself to local amateurs billed as the Blanche Moyse Chorale. These thirty-eight singers practiced all year long, coached by Blanche in the evenings after working their day jobs. Over time, their performances evolved into the New England Bach Festival, the set of autumn concerts in Marlboro I'd been hired to play.

I knew just how those singers felt. When I did concerts with Orpheus, the Philharmonic, or St. Luke's, I sometimes felt a kind of joy that only occurred when I was playing music. When I was feeling particularly emotional it came out in my phrasing. The fervency of playing could be explained as the difference between a dull reading of a passage from Shakespeare and one delivered by an actor who was not only skilled but who deeply felt the words he was reciting. At twenty-seven, I'd come to crave the musical rush, but transcendent moments were rare (particularly since I was handicapped by my bad reeds). This weekend's performances would almost certainly deliver that kind of revelatory music-making.

In Marlboro's Persons Auditorium, I found my chair. Out of four oboes, I was sitting second. In J. S. Bach's *St. Matthew Passion*, it was a big part, involving duet arias on oboe, English horn, and an alto instrument pitched in between, an oboe d'amore, which literally meant *oboe of love*. Some oboists jokingly called the horn a "love stick."

I was looking forward to playing with Steve, New York's first-call freelancer who would be playing principal oboe. He also lived in the Allendale and used to drop by my apartment to borrow some vodka in a jelly jar. Now thirty-eight, Steve was one of the musicians who had been in the right place at the right time, filling a sudden volume of New York music gigs in the 1970s. His virtual monopoly included principal oboe in Orpheus, Chamber Music Society of Lincoln Center, and St. Luke's.

As Steve warmed up with silly cartoon-music themes just minutes before the rehearsal would begin, Sydney burst through the back door and found her place in the third flute chair. Sydney usually sat at least second flute with these musicians, who were mostly St. Luke's members. She looked annoyed but quickly hid her disappointment. It would get her nowhere to act sour. She carefully adjusted her mohair sweater and smoothed out her wool pants. I didn't blame her for being upset. A flutist of her caliber and experience should be moving up, not down.

Her hair snowy white, Blanche hopped on the podium with the energy of someone half her age. An elegant blond woman followed. I hadn't bothered to find out who the soloists were, but there was something undeniably special about this one.

"Good afternoon," Blanche warbled, in her thick French accent. The blonde had turned to the orchestra, surveying every face to establish rapport with our ranks. "I would like to introduce our wonderful soprano—"

Just as Blanche announced her name, I recognized Arleen Auger's smile from Thanksgiving dinner in Vienna two decades ago. She'd had a wonderful life since then, spending years at the Vienna State Opera, singing at the televised wedding of Price Andrew and Sarah Ferguson, and touring Japan with the Bach conductor Helmut Rilling.

I was already older than Arleen had been when she rose overnight to international fame. I still struggled with my own career, which shone in some places but sputtered and failed in others. I got to borrow Arleen's figurative magic dress on occasion, but I was starting to think I would never have one of my own. The reality of my little-girl fantasy was often far less glamorous, but I had invested too much to turn back now.

As a soprano soloist, Arleen would always stand in front of the orchestra in a starring role. She spent much of her preparation time studying scores and shaping their musical interpretation with her creative mind. In contrast, oboists like me had few opportunities to perform as star players. Much of my career would be spent accompanying soloists as part of an orchestra, where decisions about tempo, phrasing, and balance between instruments would belong to the conductor.

Starting our aria, Steve and I fit our English horn lines under a flute solo. Arleen's thoughtful interpretation soared above, angelic. Where did she find such inspiration? Perhaps she already knew she was sick, with the brain tumor that would kill her at fifty-three.

Blanche was still sharp, though she was quite old. She was undeniably a deeply spiritual and committed musician. However, I questioned why the St. Luke's musicians described her as a world-class interpreter of Bach. I could barely make out her tiny gestures and concentrated on blending with Steve, trying to provide a solid bass line for his wailing incantations, since I had the lower-pitched part.

He couldn't complain, I thought, but he could keep me in my place by saying I wasn't playing musically. The "musicianship" criticism was subjective and hard to describe. Steve enjoyed a reverence from other freelance musicians that bordered on idol worship, and a comment from him about my musicality could tarnish my professional reputation and keep me out of his way as competition. How little had changed from the old NCSA "artistic policy," where musical critique sometimes masked the faculty's ulterior motives.

After rehearsal, I saw Sydney conferring with Steve, who hadn't yet discovered that she and I were friendly. "He says you're in tune but not musical," whispered Sydney, one of the few people here I trusted. She went on to complain about the seating. "It's the boys' club." Sydney nodded in the direction of her chair at the far end of the flute section. "The boys' club won't ever let me play. I quit!" As she rushed off to check her answering machine on the pay phone, I wondered what she was talking about. Boys' club? All the flutists here were women. Stepping into the crisp October air, I looked for Steve's car but found Eliot, the principal flutist's husband, instead. A recent MBA graduate, he now played cello part-time.

"You are so *lucky* to play with Steve," he said. I was feeling a little nauseated. Eliot was just one of the many New York musicians who showered Steve with adulation and assumed younger musicians like me could never compare. Like much of this orchestra, his attitude toward a select group of players approached religious fervor. "And Blanche. Blanche, Blanche, Blanche!" He sighed, casting his gaze up to the sky. Still awaiting a sign from above, he didn't notice when I moved away.

Steve picked me up in the Bach Festival's old Toyota, turned right at the Whetstone Inn, heading down Ames Hill Road, and parked in a wooden garage that must have been a stable at one time. All the St. Luke's wind players had been assigned to housing here; they formed an impenetrable tribe during the early eighties drug days. We convened around a rickety dinner table. Dennis, who was a gourmet cook and oenophile, opened a very good bottle of Bordeaux.

"My wife's coming up Saturday, Stevie," Dennis said.

"Great, Dennie, mine's coming too," Mark said.

"My squeeze is up Friday, Markie," Dave cried.

"Steve," I said, trying to sound casual, "Sam Sanders is coming too." I had a saggy double bed up in my room, which doubled as storage for broken furniture and the owner's boxed possessions.

Dennis drummed his fingers slowly, exchanging a long look with Steve.

"Sam Sanders? He can't stay here," Steve said grimly.

"But you . . . all of you. . . ." I trailed off. Sam, a more important musician, would outclass them and shrink the status of their carefully constructed clique. At the same time, they considered me an outsider who had to play by their rules.

"He can't come."

Foliage season? Where would I find a room? Ka-ching! I'd offer to pay, since I invited Sam. A fourth of my week's $600 salary. And how will we even get to an inn?

"I'll rent a room then," I said, controlling my anger. "Steve, may I use the festival's Toyota you've been driving to get there?"

"Absolutely not," Steve said firmly. "I'm driving it to save mileage on my car."

"Okay then," I said, my anger nearly boiling over. "Could you drive me into Brattleboro to rent a car?" Since Brattleboro was twenty miles of winding road, Steve relented and tossed me the keys. I grabbed them and turned away to search for local inns in the Yellow Pages. I got lucky on the first try, landing a room at the only place in Marlboro just as they'd received a cancellation.

On Saturday, Sam and I explored the Whetstone Inn. "I'd always wondered about this place when I was playing Marlboro," said Sam, looking over book titles on the dark wood shelves before choosing one. His bony fingers turned the pages, stopping when he found his own name printed in a Marlboro program from 1968.

There were other familiar names in the programs, including Betty, the Allendale spinster. Like Sam, she would have been around thirty then. I imagined her with long blond hair and slim hips, walking barefoot in the Vermont sunshine. What happened? Sam's career had taken off meteorically, while Betty played the tedious bass *oompah* offbeats of ballet music, drinking alone in her little Allendale apartment and devoting herself to someone else's husband.

Sam looked younger than ever, due to a combination of his slim figure and passionate outlook. The Whetstone's fire was reflected in his lively eyes. Together again with Sam, I relaxed for the first time all week. Sam believed in me and encouraged my musicianship. In addition, he was attracted to subjects like politics, art, religion, and literature. What a contrast to the musicians back at the house, who only veered from talking about themselves to discuss expensive gourmet cuisine, an interest that gave the illusion of elitism they wanted to cultivate.

I was relieved to be away from those depressing musicians as Sam and I cuddled on the inn's comfortable sofa, opening a bottle of Merlot and talking about Sam's favorite movies: *Prizzi's Honor, Belle de Jour, The French Connection*. He imitated Katharine Hepburn in the film *Stage Door*, trilling giddily, "The Caaaaaalla lilies are in bloom—"

"Let's come back here next year," Sam said, interrupting himself before lowering his voice. "If—if I'm still around, that is."

Yanking down our Murphy bed, we tumbled around on the mattress in our incomplete version of sex, and finally Sam fell into a rare deep sleep, relieved of any possibility of midnight practicing. Each deep breath gurgled. His body sloshed and clacked. I rose and walked to the window facing Ames Hill Road.

A half-moon had risen. Its soft light filtered through the red pines surrounding the inn, illuminating autumn leaves along the road. Four vials of Sam's pills cast a shadow across the windowsill. When Betty came here, she had been about my age. But my future looked brighter than hers ended up. The Philharmonic would have an opening soon, and I'd have a good chance after playing as a substitute for years.

Sam, sleeping, gurgled like a baby. We had been having an exclusive relationship for five months now, and I'd never felt more loved and respected. Unlike Randy, Sam had expressed a real desire to make a commitment. If we married, would I have to pay his doctor bills? How would we have children?

I was frightened. Other twenty-seven-year-old women out there were dating healthy men their own age. Probably the kids from my grade-school classes had careers that offered health benefits and retirement funds. They probably strove to excel in nine-to-five jobs where they were rewarded with promotions. My life felt very wrong. I didn't know how I was going to survive.

11
Mozart in the Jungle

THE ELEVATOR OPENED directly onto Alice Tully's apartment, which looked north over Central Park. I was here to turn pages for Sam's run-through with the teenage violinist Joshua Bell, whose half sister had been my roommate at NCSA. Josh grew up in Indiana, with as normal a childhood as any prodigy ever had.

His hostess had lived an extraordinary musical life spanning the century. Sam picked up a photo of Miss Tully curtsying before Queen Mary at Buckingham Palace in 1925. In another picture, she posed with Spanish princess Maria de Bourbon at her family's Minnesota estate. A Courbet landscape was hung on walls tinted green to match her Magritte painting of an apple. In the hallway, Steuben glass paperweights were enshrined in black velvet alcoves, symbolizing the origin of her family's wealth.

Her $3.3 million round Monet and $4.8 million Toulouse-Lautrec were rarities. One of her desks had even been created by Marie Antoinette's cabinetmaker. Heiress to the Corning glass fortune, Tully had plenty to lavish on art and music.

Holding her Maltese dog Tatie, Tully entered the room regally. She was famous enough to be a museum piece herself. So many people knew the Lincoln Center auditorium named after her that she was often introduced as Alice Tully Hall. Although she may have been the wealthiest person I'd ever met, Tully had a casual and friendly manner. She wasn't a dilettante but a trained musician. Born to a state senator and his wife in 1902, she used family money to study voice with Jean Périer and Thérèse Leschetizky in Paris, giving a debut recital at the city's Salle Gaveau in 1927.

It wasn't surprising that Tully had been attracted to Europe, which offered a centuries-old tradition of literature and the arts that the United States could not. European nations had a long history of patronage, in which churches and royalty commissioned music, statuary, paintings, and palaces. In pre-Depression America, the arts enjoyed none of that support.

European arts finally began to flourish in America only in the thirties, when the government established arts funding under the WPA. Tully returned to the United States. At her debut in 1936 at Town Hall, critics noted technical defects while applauding her intellect. By her third New York concert, it became clear that Tully would never be a top diva, so she stopped performing in public.

During World War II, Tully became a Civil Air Patrol pilot. She remained single, keeping company with a tenor for thirty years. After inheriting her estate in 1958, she decided to help other artists and became a modern-day Medici, giving away vast sums of money to help musicians.

Tully indulged many interests. She contributed to wildlife preservation funds, once visiting Ethiopia just to pet the emperor's lion. She donated anonymously through her Maya Corporation, a foundation set up in 1953 to underwrite struggling arts, education, and health organizations. Scrupulous about the use of her name, she insisted on testing the acoustics of Alice Tully Hall herself, choosing the decor and the organ builder and then creating enough room between the rows of seats to make even her six-foot-six tenor companion comfortable.

Moving into a small apartment in Central Park South's Hampshire House in 1959, Tully began buying the twenty-seventh floor's four other flats. Her fourteen-room home was completed in 1968 when she purchased Greta Garbo's apartment, last rented to a quarrelsome Ava Gardner and Frank Sinatra, who had bought it while Sinatra was filming *On the Town*. Since Hampshire House was a residence hotel, the 6,500-square-foot apartment came with maids and room service, which compensated for a minuscule Pullman kitchen. The five apartments comprising her home came with individual monthly fees totaling $22,800 in monthly maintenance. (When Tully died eight years later, the apartment listed for $7 million.)

Tully's apartment provided an extravagant backdrop for Josh, who looked more like an ordinary teenager than a violin virtuoso. His mother and father had come along too. While the Bell parents sat down, I sat next to Sam and helped arrange his music on the piano's music rack. Josh took out his Guarnerius violin, lent by New Jersey collector Herbert Axelrod, and began tuning. He and Sam were to play this program throughout New England and then record an album of showpieces. This run-through would give Tully a chance to meet the rising star. She'd long helped out individual artists like Bobby White, and gave soprano Jessye Norman the cash she needed to travel to Europe and "be discovered." Young stars counted on philanthropists like Tully to help them buy instruments; Josh was planning to purchase a $4 million 1727 Stradivarius violin.

Although I had confidence in my musical abilities, I knew I'd never travel in this sphere, a stardom reserved for singers, cellists, pianists, and violinists. They played the greatest repertoire everyone knew: Brahms, Beethoven, Sibelius, and Mendelssohn concertos. Even though I'd just won fourth prize in the Lucarelli International Competition for Solo Oboists, I knew there were few opportunities to strut my stuff. Oboists, with the exception of the Mozart Concerto, were limited to orchestra jobs or an occasional solo or chamber concert.

I still enjoyed meeting famous musicians and glimpsing their glamorous lives. Last month, in a fund-raiser for Sam's Cape Cod chamber festival in a Park Avenue apartment similar to Tully's, I'd played in Jacques Ibert's woodwind *Quintet*. When we finished, an elegant woman angled her French twist over my music stand. I smiled politely and looked up, expecting the Danny Kaye joke I heard so often. This woman's eyes were startling. Whomever she was, she connected deeply with the music.

"You are a very fine musician. That was the most beautiful sound and phrasing," she said quietly, decisively. "I'm Anna Moffo."

I snapped to attention. It really was the legendary soprano, here with her husband, RCA chair Robert Sarnoff. I started telling her how I loved her *Bachianas Brasileiras* no. 5 recording with Stokowski, and that I'd worn out her Rachmaninoff *Vocalise* record. Before I could go on, she was gone, lost in a blur of designer dresses. Like Tully, Anna Moffo was a link to the distant past.

Miss Tully was clearly engaged by Josh's virtuoso performance, which demonstrated musical sophistication far more mature than his seventeen-year-old age. I felt privileged to be in the room. As he and Sam finished their recital, Tully began talking in detail about the pieces they'd just played. I had a feeling that when she was present at New York Philharmonic board meetings, she was not only a source of funds but also a strong artistic influence.

We all walked to Tully's dining room, where the downstairs restaurant had delivered a simple dinner. We ate at a polished fifteen-foot table that was surrounded by Picasso sketches. Josh's father, a research psychologist at the Kinsey Institute, talked about his 1981 study linking biology and homosexuality. It was fascinating conversation, but even this could not keep Miss Tully, who was eighty-five, fully engaged. Seated at the head of the table, she nodded off for much of the dinner hour.

Tully wouldn't be able to bail out musicians for much longer. Her philanthropic style waned as modern American entrepreneurs earned millions but kept the cash. Those who did contribute gave to health, education, and technology, overlooking the arts they'd learned nothing about in school. The old school was dying off. "This extraordinary generation of New Yorkers, this generation of suffering, of memory, of the Holocaust and World War II, this heavily Jewish generation of goers and givers who have supported the arts so intensely, so generously, is not likely to be replaced," explained New York Public Library head Vartan Gregorian in a *New York Times* article.[1]

While philanthropists like Tully were fading away, arts groups still behaved as if they had an eternal supply of blank checks. Donations had steadily increased since the late fifties, with arts spending strengthened by the strong stock market of the eighties. Nowhere was this spending more evident than on an international tour with one of America's biggest orchestras that included me—sponsored, at least for the time being, by a corporate version of Alice Tully.

Rough waves crashed against Rio de Janeiro's Copacabana beach. The New York Philharmonic's tour bus drove us past women in tiny Brazilian "dental floss" bikinis, while men dozed in the traces of late-afternoon light. Up on Corcovado, the Christ statue blazed in the sunset against a graying sky. Rio was just one stop on the 1987 New York Philharmonic tour being sponsored by Citicorp. Three weeks in six South American cities would feature the full orchestra, with an additional week in three cities with the chamber group of fifteen.

I was still a substitute in the Philharmonic, but the orchestra's second oboist would be retiring soon. The orchestra had been hiring me for four years, so they clearly liked my playing. When the orchestra's job advertisement appeared in *International Musician,* the union paper, I would send in my résumé and reserve an audition time. Typically, hundreds of instrumentalists would apply for such a job; the orchestra personnel manager had to decide who would be invited to audition, who had to send a tape before being given an audition appointment, and who would be rejected outright. This tour would give me a chance to make an impression on conductor Zubin Mehta, who had the last word on who got in.

Sam had been unwavering in his support of my career, and he'd encouraged me to take more auditions. It wasn't as if I made a conscious decision, but our relationship had begun drifting closer to friendship than love in the weeks following his trip to Marlboro. His physical condition was problematic, and he spent all night practicing downtown anyway. I hoped the tour would put some distance between us before we had the inevitable talk about breaking up as a couple.

Last night in Rio I'd mailed Sam a postcard and then put my travelers' checks in a lockbox at the Othon Palace Hotel. Inside, I'd glimpsed the hotel's former safe, exploded steel fringing the six-inch hole blown in its side. Just a month before, twenty-six bandits brandishing submachine guns had commandeered the security room, tied up guards, and looted $56,000 from the safe as hostages cowered in $165 rooms upstairs. They must not have known that one month later, the same rooms would be home to millions in precious musical instruments.

The driver turned left, away from shore and toward Rio's vast green Flamengo Reclaim and the glass skyscrapers beyond it. A violinist sitting beside me on the bus massaged his hand, which had been the casualty of an Ipanema pickpocket the previous night. Two more violinists chatted about the best places to buy leather jackets in Rio. At last we crossed Avenida Rio Branco, pulling up to the Teatro Municipal's stage door.

Symphonies don't pack light. The New York Philharmonic's 113 aluminum traveling cases were strewn around backstage. In addition to these huge wardrobe valises were shipping trunks for the large instruments—basses, cellos, timpani, and extensive percussion—as well as four 200-pound trunks filled with music. The Philharmonic even brought cases for small instruments like mine, moving 23,000 pounds of cargo six times in three weeks. That didn't include the luggage of 110 musicians, thirty-seven relatives, three board members, a doctor, two travel agents, four stagehands, two librarians, and eight Philharmonic staffers. At least the contrabassoonist doubled as group photographer.

Built in 1909 as a replica of the Paris Opéra, Rio's Teatro Municipal was decorated in onyx, French stained glass, and fifteen hundred pounds of green Carrara marble. Painted pastel nymphs frolicked on the ceiling around a chandelier made with one thousand pounds of crystal.

Tonight we'd play the Eighth Symphony of Anton Bruckner, one of Hitler's favorite Austrian composers. The orchestra may have chosen the Austrian composer's work because so many European immigrants live in South America. Most of them were postwar immigrants, although a few exiled Nazis still lived in Brazil, Argentina, and Paraguay, protected by those countries' fascist dictators.

This was my second visit to Brazil. My first was with Orpheus in 1985. During that Orpheus tour, we'd played Montevideo's rickety Teatro Solís, where the theater's ancient harpsichord tilted precariously on the steeply raked stage. After performing, we left the stage door expecting a quiet walk back to the hotel. Instead, our audience flooded out onto the theater's marble plaza, surrounding us with bows, cheers, and wild applause worthy of a rock 'n' roll band.

While the twenty-six Orpheus musicians had juggled instruments, luggage, and snafus on a shoestring budget, the Philharmonic went first-class, its international touring costs topping $1 million per week. Stage-hands worked around the clock, shipping instruments to the next venue, as hotel staff whisked away suitcases that magically reappeared at our next destination.

In Rio my stomach turned bad, as it did on every international trip. I wasn't nearly cautious enough about my diet, insisting on trying native dishes wherever we went. When we had played in Argentina the previous week, waiters brought trays of raw meat for our inspection. I had chosen the mixed grill, which included testicles and a slice of cow udder. Then, in São Paolo, I had tried *feijoada,* a fatty Brazilian bean and pork dish that the hotel there served in a traditional Sunday buffet, offering vats of pig snouts, ears, and curly tails, all washed down with caipirinha, a drink made from cachaça—a liquor distilled from sugar cane—lime, and sugar.

Back at the Othon, my stomach in turmoil, I had headed for my room. Just as the elevator doors closed, conductor Zubin Mehta had slipped inside with me. I'd wished I felt good enough to think of something intelligent to say. I'd waited for this chance to connect with him personally before my upcoming second oboe audition. Our elevator ascended slowly, and we stood in silence. Ten, eleven, twelve. . . .

"How was the volleyball game?" Zubin asked. Looking out from his room, he must have seen us playing on the beach that morning. I concentrated hard on not throwing up, determined not to spray him in a scene worthy of *The Exorcist.* Before I could speak, the doors opened onto my floor. Covering my mouth, I ran, puking in the hall ashtray just around the corner. As I recovered, I heard a violent punching of elevator buttons and then the door slamming shut.

Flush with 1980s cash, Citibank was sponsoring the tour, in a routine started by AT&T in 1979 with its Orchestras on Tour program. The idea caught on; Isuzu sponsored the Los Angeles Philharmonic, Beatrice Foods underwrote Chicago Lyric Opera, and Merrill Lynch bankrolled recital series nationwide. To support the phenomenon of corporate arts sponsorship, another arts service organization was born, the Business Council for the Arts, Inc.[2]

By linking the Citibank name with a traveling arts group of the Philharmonic's stature, the corporation scored in two ways: the company associated itself with a luxury product like a major symphony, theoretically enjoyed by its wealthiest clients, and the advertising that accompanied our concerts provided Citibank with extensive public relations coverage across a wide geographic area. Parties, receptions, and exclusive events revolved around the concerts, with top clients awarded choice seats.

After Rio, we flew across Brazil's interior pink mesa to the Jetson-like capital city of Brasilia, which looked like an architectural mirage plopped in the center of a red soil desert. As we finished the airline lunch, a woodwind musician took an opportunity to poke fun at my oboe teacher Joe Robinson's stomach problems, which had on occasion caused him to leave the stage during concerts while the orchestra waited silently for his return. The woodwind musician threaded dried prunes and apricots on his swizzle stick and passed it down the aisle to Joe.

"Pass this to Ollie," the musician said (he had nicknamed Joe *Oliver North* for his clean-cut appearance). "I want to earn overtime tomorrow night." (Depending on the orchestra, overtime pay for concerts begins after two and a half or three hours.)

After we arrived in Brasilia, Citibank took the orchestra on a bus tour of the buildings Oscar Niemeyer had designed in the fifties, when the city was built. Next we were driven to the Academia de Tenis, where wine flowed freely and fresh seafood platters (in the country's landlocked center) appeared every few minutes. The opulent food and drink fueled exuberance in the musicians, many of whom were starting to tire after two weeks of touring. A percussionist started to dance. Before long, brass players joined in, then the violinists, and finally, the entire New York Philharmonic wiggled around the pool in a samba line.

On the bus back to the hotel, I noticed satellite cities—*favelas*, or shantytowns—off the highway. An underclass had started to surround this new utopian city, and no one had planned for them. By the time we finished Tchaikovsky's Fifth the following night, I realized that poor working people and relatively wealthy diplomats lived entirely separate lives here. No one who looked like our dark-skinned waiters and samba musicians from the dinner party were in our audience. I started piecing together how vast the expense of bringing us to Brasilia must have been, just to entertain government officials in this remote city.

The Philharmonic tour continued, with musicians snapping up shopping bargains in every city. They'd just finalized a new contract for 1987, earning a $980 weekly base salary. In Buenos Aires, they had bought nutria-lined gloves and antelope jackets, in São Paolo, aquamarines; and in Belo Horizonte, loose stones from the nearby mines. Even though I was only earning a Philharmonic-sized salary for a few weeks, I too bought my share of souvenirs, including an aquamarine ring and a custom-made leather jacket.

As the tour ended, most of the orchestra flew home to New York from São Paolo. I was one of fifteen musicians—staying behind for a chamber music tour of Panama, Ecuador, and remote venues in Brazil and Argentina—who hopped a puddle jumper with Zubin and five staffers. Zubin sat directly in front of me on the plane, and I listened as he planned programs three years ahead with his adviser, Frank Milburn. I'd imagined these decisions were a more bureaucratic affair, done with board meetings, arguments, and heated debates, but it turned out to be a simple conversation. The two men worked out which pieces worked well together, what tenor still got along with Kathleen Battle, what child prodigies might be ready by 1990. As the plane took off, one musician beside me listened to his Walkman, while another scribbled in his journal. No one noticed the bass and cello trunks disappearing to the size of silver specks behind us on the tarmac.

While we were in the air, Citicorp chair John S. Reed and six hundred guests—clients and executives—began arriving on the remote Iguassú Falls airstrip where Argentina, Paraguay, and Brazil meet. Tonight's concert, featuring Schubert, Villa-Lobos, and Mozart, would be an extravagant climax to the tour they'd sponsored.

We landed on a narrow runway in the middle of the jungle. Descending the plane stairs to the tarmac, I could see that the airport was surrounded by vegetation in all directions. A thick plume of vapor spiraled from the rain-forest canopy, probably in the spot I'd read about where the Iguassú's 270 waterfalls, over 200 feet high and two miles wide, plunge to the Devil's Throat, dwarfing both Niagara and Victoria Falls. I'd wanted to see this place during the Orpheus tour in 1985, but it was too remote to fit into the schedule. Since then, the spot became well-known from the 1986 film *The Mission*, which opened with Jeremy Irons's 1770s missionary character playing oboe in the nearby jungle.

The musicians identified their luggage, which porters hauled away. We waited. There was no sign of the trunks. Without cello and bass, the Schubert Octet couldn't go on. Concert clothes and another work's bassoon part were inside the trunks too. Looking worried, general manager Nick Webster shooed us into a large van for a tour of the area, staying behind to sort it out.

Our guide, Walter, ordered gourds of yerba maté tea for us at a Brazilian café perched over the Iguassú River. A dark-skinned Argentine expatriate living in Australia, Walter had returned to look for his father, one of the thousands who'd disappeared into General Alfredo Stroessner's Paraguay. Walter had a masculine take-charge energy that contrasted with the quiet demeanor of the musicians he was hosting.

After tea, Walter drove us to the waterfalls. On a wooden walkway, he led us over a broad mesa churning with the Iguassú River, where a half-million gallons of red water thundered to boulders below every second. The missing trunks were soon forgotten as Walter piled the five bravest musicians aboard his helicopter. We swooped through the mist, dipping below cliffs draped by dense lianas. Gargantuan coconut palms were dwarfed by two miles of roaring cataracts.

I was still officially dating Sam, but I was wildly attracted to Walter. He was probably around thirty and stirred an animal heat in me I'd never felt before. I sensed his breath on my neck as we walked down Puerto Iguassú's dirt road, his black eyes flirting with me. I could have offered to meet Walter after the concert tonight, or even just gone to lunch, but my obsession with impressing Zubin on this tour was even greater than my sexual urge. After all, the oboe section had a vacancy soon, and by having me substitute in the Philharmonic, my teacher had given me every advantage to win the job. I asked Walter to take me back to the hotel to work on reeds.

By this time, the hotel lobby was in chaos. Citibank had rented three jets back in São Paolo, and dismantled one to try and wedge the immense instrument trunks inside. No luck. The head of one of the world's largest global banks, South American aristocracy, and the continent's biggest presenter all could not bring the bass from São Paolo.

Wearing a motley combination of sequins and jeans, we could still play the Villa-Lobos *Duo* and Mozart's *Serenade* for eight winds, although the second bassoon part was in the missing cello trunk. Schubert's lush *Octet* score called for both cello and bass. Instead, clarinetist Stanley Drucker volunteered solo clarinet pieces by Stravinsky, a smaller but rare treat.

I spent the afternoon scraping reeds in my hotel room and watching a toucan perched on a tree outside. The other musicians were still sightseeing, but I needed to make sure I sounded great. We had recently played in Bogotá, Colombia, where my reeds didn't work at all. I had never realized how much high altitudes affect these quirky bits of cane. My old reeds hadn't been the same since we came back down to sea level, either. By 6 P.M. I had finally fashioned one reed that at least got the low notes out, although the tone quality was a little bright.

In the hotel's ballroom, the guests took their seats after enjoying a lavish buffet. Something about the ordeal of our day provided just enough adrenaline that all eight musicians playing the Mozart were at the top of their game, trading phrases playfully and putting extra emotion into the lyrical passages. We finished and the audience leaped to a standing ovation, lubricated by caipirinhas and Veuve Cliquot. Behind an enormous ice sculpture, Walter leaned against the wall. I would leave in the morning and never see him again.

As I packed up my oboe, I began feeling regretful to have missed out on a real adventure with Walter. I hadn't realized how starved I had been for a genuine sexual attraction to someone my own age. The concert, however, had been chillingly beautiful. If only every concert were like this, I would trade almost anything to play the oboe. I couldn't end up in the freelance ranks, where my career would mean schlepping between unsatisfying musical events, with no job security and little recognition. I had to win that Philharmonic job.

12
Twilight of the Gods

THE ARTS INDUSTRY in America had blossomed since the 1960s, as classical music, theater, fine art, and dance enjoyed more sources of support than ever before. New arts groups were forming every year, and they
were producing an explosion in the number of concerts and other performing arts events. The fact that audience growth did not keep pace
with this frenzied expansion had little impact on the growth in this
nonprofit sector. Most performing arts groups were subsidized by unearned donated income, as well as tax incentives, and therefore did not
always have to link revenue to the quantity, quality, or type of product
they offered.

The Ford Foundation was largely responsible for the rapid growth
in cultural philanthropy, providing $400 million between 1956 and
1976. Ford's strategy was rooted in granting seed money, not long-term
support. Their awards required arts groups to raise up to four times the
grant amount, ideally broadening the base of funding—and audiences—
indefinitely. This base, wrote San Francisco Foundation director John
Kreidler in an *In Motion* magazine article, resembled a pyramid scheme,
in which a business venture crumbles when the pool of new investors
whose cash had supported the company disappears.

Any student of biological, physical or economic systems would
immediately recognize the flaw in the logic of funding leverage,
as it has been practiced not only in the arts but also throughout
the nonprofit sector. One of the fundamental tenets of systems

studies is the "free lunch" principle: no system can depend on the unlimited growth of resources. The leveraged funding strategy of the Ford era can be likened to a chain letter, a Ponzi scheme, or any other pyramidal growth system. The initiators of chain letters and Ponzi schemes often claim that, for a small effort or investment, a virtually limitless return will be realized, and though initially this prophecy may appear to be feasible, inevitably all such arrangements must fail because resources are finite. In other words, there is no perpetual free lunch. Ultimately, funding leverage will become unsustainable.[1]

These pyramid schemes paralleled arts rhetoric from the sixties, an idealism that promised to lift spirits, create new opportunity, and teach a better way to live and prosper. The plan relied on two factors: an expanding population of philanthropists and a stable stock market to provide predictable interest income from endowment investments.

Even before the Ford grants were first awarded, some arts groups tended to spend more than they took in and to perform more concerts than the public wanted to hear. In 1956, *New York Times* critic Howard Taubman questioned the glut of performances in his article "The Philharmonic—What's Wrong with It and Why."

It is beyond dispute that the Philharmonic's subscriptions have been diminishing . . . the staggering final deficit of $245,463 tells its own story. . . . As far as this observer could make out this season, the only Thursday night concerts that looked absolutely sold out were those at which Heifetz and Oistrakh were the soloists. . . . On most other occasions, there were stretches of gaping, empty seats.

Needless to say, there are external factors beyond the quality of programs and performances to explain the Philharmonic's attendance record. The ubiquitous television set has made deep inroads on attendance at all public entertainments. The spread of the high-fidelity vogue and the vast expansion of the repertory on records have had their impact. The inflationary pinch has caused some concertgoers to think twice about paying out high prices for concert tickets. The competition in opera house and concert hall for the music lover's dollar is intense in New York. Furthermore, the Philharmonic assumes an ambitious schedule. It plays for twenty-eight weeks during the regular season. . . . Is it possible that there is no market in New York for so many concerts? That may well be.[2]

Foundation, corporate, and federal support were expected to fill the financial void, and a Ford Foundation program began training the first generation of arts administrators in 1962 to handle the increasingly complex budgets. The Rockefeller Brothers Fund recommended that the Philharmonic and other orchestras, struggling to fill their part-time schedules, extend those seasons to satisfy the surge of interest in culture that was expected to sweep America in the 1960s.

Orchestras acted on the recommendation to lengthen their schedules, and the number of orchestra concerts in the United States increased 80 percent between 1966 and 1974.[3] New orchestras were formed as well, growing from 58 in 1965 to 225 in 1988.[4] Yet while musical events were becoming more numerous, ticket buyers were not. A 1968 *New York Times* article stated that impresarios estimated that concert attendance had decreased between 7 and 40 percent from the year before, with even Leonard Bernstein and Dietrich Fischer-Dieskau failing to sell out Carnegie Hall.[5]

"It's the same old tired people doing things in the same tired old way," 1960s publicist Alix Williamson lamented. Others complained concerts had lost their zip, with performers losing rapport with their audience. The postwar immigrants who had been a loyal audience began aging out of the picture. "Every day I look at the obituaries, and every time I see a Russian or Jewish name, I say, There goes another customer," moaned Ukrainian-born impresario Sol Hurok.

At the New York Philharmonic, the minimum number of weeks called for by the musicians' contract had crept from thirty-five in 1961 to forty-two in 1963. In the following year, the schedule expanded by ten weeks to fifty-two weeks. Because nine weeks of paid vacation were also added to the contract, the Philharmonic musicians were only working one additional week. "Players had as much free time as they'd had twenty years earlier, but now they were being paid for it," wrote Alice Goldfarb Marquis, in *Art Lessons*.[6]

Managers raided new endowments to pay for quantum leaps in expenses caused by the longer seasons and full-time employee benefits. The strategy was shortsighted, since endowments are meant to generate interest income rather than pay directly for higher operating expenses. Since orchestras weren't selling out the greater quantity of concerts being produced, they relied heavily on donations and other unearned income.[7]

The Chicago Symphony had promised its musicians full-time employment by 1968, but the cost of doing so shot up quickly. The orchestra's endowment shrank from $6.2 million to $1 million between 1964 and 1968, and its deficit tripled. During the same period, operating expenses grew 50 percent, outpacing a 30 percent growth in operating income.[8]

Cultural expansion continued even during the 1970s economic crisis, the "stagflation" of low growth and high inflation. The Atlanta Symphony's budget mushroomed from $300,000 to $3 million between 1965 and 1975, as the organization expanded and added events, staff, and services. The syndrome highlighted a chronic problem with arts funding, which nonprofit analyst Waldemar A. Nielsen noted in his 1980 *New York Times* story "Where Have All the Arts Patrons Gone?"

> Whatever happens, funding for the high arts will never be "adequate." The more the money available, the more troupes and theaters and companies will be formed. This Malthusian, or rabbits-and-lettuce, phenomenon is a considerable element in the putative present crisis of the arts.[9]

Even former Ford Foundation chair McNeil Lowry, inventor of the foundation's matching grant, denounced the maniacal growth. He blamed elitist motivations and predicted a regression to "ritual circuses of the lowest sort." In desperation to raise income from ticket sales, groups turned away from their artistic mission and instead employed pop stars, crossover artists, and programs of hackneyed classical warhorses.

As the concept of culture as a public good became more accepted, arts organizations received—and spent—more money than ever before. In 1970, symphonies collectively took in $30 million but spent $76.4 million. By 1990, they took in $290.4 million but spent $688.9 million. More fund-raising resulted in more spending, even for debt-ridden organizations. The initial 1960s funding boom was meant to stabilize struggling groups, but monies were funneled into new expenses that were related to supporting additional performances instead of paying for existing needs.[10]

Full-service marketing departments in the 1980s were employed to sell all those extra performances, where orchestras in the fifties had simply announced concerts by sending a postcard to existing subscribers. Famous soloists and conductors, and their rising fees, were soon considered a necessary lure. Starting a relentless cycle, orchestras hired expensive development executives to pay for it all.

The business of classical music grew exponentially with this expansion of arts management, analysis, and lobbying. Some thirty colleges offered arts management degrees by the 1980s. Before long, arts funding struggled to finance not only performers but also a widening field of cultural scholars, consultants, and analysts, who pored over ways to increase the efficiency of artists and musicians.

Arts funding kept pace with spending growth during the phenomenal economy of the mid-1980s. Over twenty-five thousand leveraged mergers had driven the stock market to spectacular heights. The net worth of the Forbes 400 richest Americans tripled, and the new multimillionaires sought both tax exemptions with cultural donations and the instant elitism that comes with arts patronage. However, the age of excess came to an end one Monday afternoon, just two months after the Philharmonic returned from its 1987 tour. On October 19, the Dow fell 508 points, nearly 23 percent, marking the largest one-day drop on the New York Stock Exchange.

Fortunes shrank overnight. The country was already weakened by a 1982 recession and by the dual crises of farm debt and savings-and-loan deregulation—which cost thousands of Americans their life savings as well as $166 billion in government bailouts. Additional public resources were limited, since taxes, which had been cut by Ronald Reagan in 1981, brought in no additional revenue.[11]

Backstage, a small number of the busiest musicians with money to invest rued individual losses, yet few saw how Black Monday would affect the performing arts world as a whole. Foundations had given 14 percent of their grant money to the arts through the mid-1980s, but now began turning their attention toward poverty and other social issues. By 1990, only the Getty Trust, the Pew Trust, and the Wallace Readers' Digest Fund still significantly supported the arts.[12] Federal arts spending had decreased 24 percent between 1980 and 1988, while states slashed appropriations for their arts councils. In the private arena, the 1986 Tax Reform Act had decreased philanthropic incentives by lowering the maximum tax rate from 70 percent to 28 percent.[13]

Ten to 12 percent of all corporate gifts in the mid-1980s had gone to cultural causes, but the flood of corporate mergers reduced the number of actual donors. Companies that had once sponsored the arts (in order to soften a harsh corporate profile) wanted, after a decade of excess, to support universally acceptable causes like health and education.[14] Oil companies that had cashed in during the 1970s had less to spend after petroleum prices plummeted in 1986. In 1987, Exxon withdrew its $1.5 million sponsorship of the New York Philharmonic's weekly radio broadcasts, which had been on the air since 1922 with only an eight-year break. In 1989, Exxon also ended its thirteen-year sponsorship of the television series *Live from Lincoln Center* and stopped funding the orchestra's free summer parks concerts.

Corporate America was downsizing, but arts organizations, isolated from the financial reality of earned income, stuck to their growth model. Only a month before Black Monday, Donal Henahan described the malaise in a *New York Times* story:

The irony is that arts administrators, orchestra trustees, critics and others in influential positions have worked hard for generations to help bring about the current state of doubt and confusion. Driven by economic winds and, in some cases, fearsome ambition, they have sold the American public on the need for quantity in music rather than quality, on the necessity for glamour at the podium and on the crippling belief that music is a product that must be promoted, advertised and devoured like so much fast food.[15]

By 1990, twenty-seven of America's forty largest orchestras reported deficits, nine of them over $1 million. Washington's National Symphony was running a $17 million annual budget on its $13 million endowment.[16] Managers blamed musicians' salaries, which exceeded inflation by 6 percent in the late 1980s. At the best orchestras, musicians were taking home increasing salaries (their raises almost always outpaced inflation), but they weren't the only ones. Frantic board members turned to orchestra executives and conductors to serve as figureheads and potential saviors of their organizations. In return, the executives and music directors used the symphonies' financial woes to exact even higher salaries. Conductors topped the list of earners by averaging $700,000 at America's top five orchestras in 1990. By jetting to multiple directorships around the world, they grossed hundreds of thousands more. Both Ricardo Muti and André Previn made $2 million a year.

Newspaper arts critics rang the death knell, reporting that audiences had fled. To the contrary, classical audiences had grown slightly over the 1980s and would continue increasing up to the millennium. With 21.3 million attendees in 1982, that number reached 23.8 million by 2002, according to the National Endowment for the Arts (NEA). Because the audience was now spread more thinly over so many more performances, attendance at each event appeared more sparse as a result.

The music industry not only produced more concerts but more musicians as well. Starting music education in kindergarten and elementary grades, Suzuki string classes and grade school bands across America encouraged bright young people to develop skills for which there was little demand. Though only 250 orchestra jobs were advertised each year—many paying under $20,000—music conservatories in New York, Boston, Cleveland, Cincinnati, Philadelphia, San Francisco, Rochester, and Hartford churned out thousands of graduates each May.

Musicians became increasingly isolated from cultural economics, as nonprofit organizations provided a buffer between performer and patron. Sequestered in specialized arts schools and full-time symphony employment, musicians could avoid the very people who attended and paid for their concerts. This, as sociologist Paul DiMaggio has noted, further mystified the artists and gave them the illusion of sanctity. The mission of art as public service was forgotten, and many in the arts community came to believe that they were entitled to federal funding, as Joseph W. Zeigler pointed out in his book *Arts in Crisis:*

You, the United States, should be paying for me to create, because I'm here and I'm creating. As an artist, I'm an important member of the society—and so the society should be supporting me.[17]

Orchestra musicians demanded to be compensated just like employees in the private sector, even as the symphonies in the late 1980s failed across the country. Their musicians compared their conservatory training and twenty-hour weeks to those of professionals with advanced degrees who sometimes worked round-the-clock shifts. "Doctors make the same salary here as they do in other cities. So do lawyers. Why should musicians be the only ones to subsidize music?" said one Buffalo musician. The director of the American Symphony Orchestra League echoed that musician's protest, saying, "The arts, unfortunately, don't remain a high priority when budget deficits strike."[18]

At a time when artists had come to expect government entitlements, citizens and politicians began questioning the need for a federal arts agency. Even choreographer Agnes de Mille, an initial supporter of the bureau, lamented the disappearance of a mission to help the best and brightest. "The whole tendency today is to help the unknowns and the unproven, but all that does is encourage mediocrity," de Mille said.

The agency had granted money to controversial projects from the beginning. There had been the $500 grant for the seven-letter poem "Lighght," $5,000 for Erica Jong to revise her zipless fuck in *Fear of Flying,* and $6,000 for a "space-sculpting" artist to throw party streamers

157

from a plane. NEA funds helped create a film in which a dog was killed and a Mafia-themed opera production of Verdi's *Rigoletto*.

Finally, two NEA-affiliated exhibitions ignited a firestorm of controversy in 1989. Artist Richard Serrano, who received a $15,000 grant from an NEA-funded organization, was targeted by the American Family Association for his *Piss Christ*, a plastic crucifix suspended in cow's blood and the artist's urine. The Corcoran Museum in Washington, D.C., canceled *The Perfect Moment*, an exhibition of Robert Mapplethorpe's gay-themed photography, because uproar over the show threatened the Corcoran's federal funding. As NEA opponents hurled charges of obscenity, artists countered with accusations of censorship.

Marketed as a panacea to enlighten and unify, American culture had mushroomed into an industry far removed from its initial mission. The NEA episode provoked outrage among writers, actors, dancers, artists, and musicians, and I was among them. Believing that society would and should support culture even if its citizens showed little interest in attending arts events, I forged ahead with my "career." I was thirty years old, and it seemed too late to change course.

Danse Macabre

13

AVERY FISHER HALL was dark, with only center stage lights shining on a solitary music stand. Toward the back of the auditorium, a long screen hid the audition committee. I took a deep breath to prepare myself for the next fifteen minutes. I had been practicing and making reeds at least eight hours a day for a month. I was well prepared in terms of the music, but the best of my reeds was awful. Its tone was harsh. It didn't always articulate clearly, and its intonation was funky.

I crossed the strip of carpeting (laid to muffle women's shoes), as if I were walking the plank. Personnel manager Carl Schiebler adjusted the stand for me and then sat twenty feet away. The familiar gold and wood panels flanking the stage suddenly looked like a phantasmagorical maze. Shadows threatened from every corner. Usually, a hundred other musicians sat onstage. Now, every sound I made boomed through the hall.

I had discovered the stage fright drug Inderal, or propanolol, which blocks the receptor site for adrenaline. Unlike anxiety medication like Valium, Inderal lessens physical symptoms without affecting the brain. I'd gotten mine over the counter in Ecuador, but Inderal is best prescribed by a doctor. Too much sends people with low blood pressure or asthma into a tailspin. But at least my nerves wouldn't flare up.

The orchestra had automatically advanced me to the semifinals, since I had substituted with the Philharmonic for a decade. As I blew into my reed to make a crowing sound, I imagined my teacher behind the screen, screwing his face into the lemon-sucking scowl he used whenever I played. A good reed should have sounded two octaves of the note C, but this one squawked a nasty C-sharp. Sliding it into my oboe, I tooted a few notes and began.

Missing the Mozart Concerto's very first note, a low C, I stopped and took a deep breath. I had to blow harder to make this terrible reed respond. Behind me, I sensed Carl flinching. Beginning again, the phrase came out just as I'd practiced, my tone soaring across the cavernous hall. Good. On to the excerpts.

I could tongue unusually fast, but today my reed wasn't cooperating. My articulation sputtered in Rossini's Overture to *La Scala di Seta*. I missed another low C in Stravinsky's *Pulcinella*. The intervals in the *Don Juan* were woefully out of tune.

No orchestra hires more than four regular oboists, who at the top orchestras will then usually stay until retirement. I'd been preparing for these fifteen minutes for ten years now, and there wouldn't be another opening for ages.

Concentrate. Breathe. Show this stupid reed who's boss.

Next, Samuel Barber's dark, brooding First Symphony. My low B woofed, bouncing around the live hall with the memory of every imperfect note I'd played here. I couldn't control my vibrato with this reed, either. On the way offstage, Carl patted my back. He knew. And I knew that not only would I not get the job but that I had just plummeted to the bottom of the Philharmonic's sub list.

I treated myself to a taxi home and arrived just as Sydney was leaving the Allendale to play her Saturday matinee on Broadway. She had been hired a couple of years ago for a musical that promised to run for a decade or more. Sydney consoled me, mentioning that she hadn't taken an audition in ages herself. She had done well with orchestra tryouts in the past, almost always advancing to the final round. I was surprised that she'd taken the Broadway show job, since most successful classical music freelancers like Sydney thought musical theater wasn't serious art.

"It's so awful," Sydney said, when I asked how her show was going. She explained she was playing all eight shows this week, and not calling a substitute to fill in for her at all, since she didn't have any other gigs. Classical freelance work had really fallen off lately, she said. She checked her watch and headed to the subway. I went upstairs.

I unlocked my apartment door and started to play my answering machine messages, feeling at loose ends. After spending ten years fantasizing about winning the Philharmonic job, and more recently devoting my days to preparing for it, I didn't know what to do next. Automatically, I went over to the reed desk, but I couldn't bring myself to sit there. I took the audition music off my music stand to put it away. The stand looked strange with nothing on it.

Suddenly there was a crash in the bathroom. I ran to see if the shelving I'd tried to install myself had fallen, but instead there was a two-foot hole in the ceiling where the brown stain used to be. Wet plaster was everywhere, and water gushed into the tub and onto the floor. Turning off the water in the apartment had no effect, since the water was coming from upstairs, so I put a pail under the leak and went to find Angelo.

When I returned with the superintendent a few minutes later, the pail had overflowed onto the floor and water continued to pour from the ceiling. Angelo didn't look alarmed. "Don't worry, that's not a leak," he said. I looked at him incredulously, and he promised to return and fix the problem once he found some duct tape to patch it up.

In the days following my Philharmonic audition, I was paralyzed by a musical form of postpartum depression. Now that it was over, I had no direction. Although I loved classical music, I had never honestly been interested enough in the field to make it my career. I simply got hooked as a teenager because it earned me attention. Knowing I'd have to make the best of it, I felt stuck in a life that was wrong for me.

Musical groups had started to founder nationwide in 1990, and employment possibilities for orchestral musicians didn't look good anymore. The Buffalo Philharmonic went on the auction block, advertising itself to be bought by another city as if it were a sports team. Smaller symphonies in Hartford, New Haven, and Bridgeport all posted huge deficits. I couldn't have afforded to travel to any more auditions anyway, even if the orchestras had been thriving.

Sydney wasn't imagining that work was drying up. Freelance groups cut back and disappeared in the early 1990s as well. The 92nd Street Y pulled its Schubert series over a $1.5 million deficit. The New York Gilbert and Sullivan Players canceled their schedule for the first time since 1977. The Opera Ensemble of New York called off half its season, and deficits mounted elsewhere: Queens Symphony, $120,000; Long Island Philharmonic, $130,000; Orchestra of St. Luke's, $80,000.[1]

The New York City Opera, a populist company with a history of municipal support that enabled low ticket prices, struggled back after a sixty-six-day strike by the orchestra in 1989, in the wake of which the company's entire season was canceled. Its pit musicians demanded a 20 percent raise over three years for parity with companies in San Francisco and Chicago, despite those groups' far higher ticket prices.

Unlike the City Opera musicians, I felt like an antique, painfully aware of my irrelevance. CD players were rapidly replacing turntables in the early 1990s. Computers were being used for jingles, replacing musicians with synthesized tracks. And MTV had become an entertainment staple, adding a visual element to rock that made classical music look even more archaic.

Without many options, I started subbing in a Broadway show. *Les Miserables* was one of the few musicals that included a straight oboe chair, meaning that the oboist didn't double on flute, sax, or clarinet. The pop opera had taken Broadway by storm and promised to last for years.

I met the show's regular oboist, who led me to the Broadway Theater pit. In my black silk blouse and billowing skirt, I was overdressed next to musicians in faded black jeans and sneakers. The audience couldn't see in, anyway. The pit was deep and covered with netting, to catch props, scenery, and even actors that sometimes flew off the set's revolving turntable.

This was the typical scenario for Broadway subbing. Watch the show go by, and play it the next night without a rehearsal. The music was lyrical, and a long tuneful oboe solo provided the mood for much of a scene in the Paris sewers. Recording the show on my cassette Walkman, I watched attentively and marked my part.

The next night my performance went off perfectly, and the oboist called me once or twice a month from then on. Once I knew the show, it was easy money. A three-hour performance paid $160 in 1990 dollars. It would only be for a while, I told myself, just until I won a gig of my own playing "real" music. The best classical musicians looked down on those of us who worked in for-profit venues playing these crowd-pleasing tunes, instead of what we were trained to do.

I didn't want to go sour like some of these Broadway pit musicians. Two of the fiddle players who shared a stand didn't talk, turning away from each other all night. It felt like toiling in the salt mines. I wondered if the audience even realized they were hearing live musicians piped through the speakers.

My fall from glory was a little depressing, but I was more concerned about Sam, whose health was quickly deteriorating. He and I had ended any romantic relationship, but I still loved him like a member of my family. Since we both lived under the Allendale's roof, it wasn't hard to maintain our new status as near relatives.

Sam told me he was in trouble early in 1990. Backstage at a recital with Itzhak in Cleveland, his fingers hadn't worked right. He couldn't fasten his tie. His toothbrush slipped into the sink. Bartók's fiendish First Sonata began and ended as if someone else were playing. At the airport, presenters had bustled to bring Itzhak a wheelchair, while no one noticed when Sam fainted and slid down the wall.

At home in his apartment, Sam had eased his swollen feet from wide black sneakers and peeled off support socks. Diuretics had turned his ankles a shade of dark yellow. "Shit!" he shouted, as a prescription bottle he reached for clattered off his bedside table. "Sorry, sorry," he said sheepishly, scowling at hands that were swollen with uric acid. He pleaded with me to open the medicine vial, pulling out five more bottles. Pills were everywhere: on the floor, in his briefcase, sprayed across the bed. He threw back a handful and lay back, breathing hard. The ball bearings ricocheted inside his heart.

I put my hand on his shoulder, hoping to calm him. I felt guilty that I had rejected him as a lover. Sam was literally disintegrating. I wondered if his heart would explode, or if his imperfect arteries would leak slowly until he died. My eyes wandered to a spot where a brick was missing outside the windowsill. It was hard to see out, the building's windows were so sooty.

Across West End, I found the windows of the co-op where I once watched the couple having sex. The woman was bouncing a gurgling infant. Her eyes smiled as she twirled the baby overhead, cooing. In the next room, her husband leaned over a drafting table, their toddler playing beside him. Sam's eyes followed my gaze. His breathing had finally slowed, and he squeezed my hand.

"It's okay, honey," he said softly. "I understand, I really do."

In September, Sam's doctors checked him into the hospital. I learned that a few months ago he had found out the name of one of the world's leading cardiologists, Valentin Fuster, and simply showed up at his office. When he told the nurse he hadn't made an appointment because he didn't have time, she had misunderstood. "I mean, I won't live that long," said Sam. Dr. Fuster saw him immediately.

As dire as his situation was, Sam treated his hospital visit like any other performance. He folded tissue paper between his pajamas and robe as he packed, smoothing sleeves against lapels and folding more tissue paper on top. Shuffling to his Steinway, he centered piles of violin sonatas and straightened his toy soldiers. Some were from his former student Margo Garrett, a few rare ones from Alice Tully, and a goose-stepping Nazi from me. As always, he left his piano room in perfect order.

Once he was in the hospital for a few days, Sam seemed to recover with bed rest. His drawn face filled out, and he was calmer. Parts of him still had an alarming appearance, however. His ankle, now nearly black as fluid crystallized into gout, stuck out beneath stiff hospital sheets. Blood caked his lips. His heart monitor frequently skipped, tracing a mountain range of jagged peaks. Sam pointed at the lights blinking from the George Washington Bridge. They had given him hope on the ride to Baltimore back in 1947; they gave him hope now. Not expected to survive grade school, Sam had already made it to fifty-two.

Bringing over his mail one day, I handed him a bundle of cards, fliers, and bills. I had peeked inside his bank statement, which was already two thousand dollars overdrawn. Sam hadn't worked for a month and a half now. He owed rent and tuition for his daughter's freshman year in college. I could hardly fault his estranged wife, after years of separation, for trying to make their divorce formal before the hospital bills came. Perhaps they hadn't split legally because of child support or shared health insurance.

Sam's teaching job at the Peabody Institute provided health insurance but covered only part of the costs, which included an annual prescription bill of $30,000. He had little family left, but he knew he could count on his brother Martin for help, even though he desperately wanted to handle it himself.

The room was filled with cards, baseball trinkets, and other gifts from his circle of friends. Someone had brought him a Walkman. Sam didn't even have a stereo at home. "Listen," he said, more lively than I'd seen him in months. He passed me the headphones, looking uncharacteristically happy. I recognized the song, "An die Musik":

O sublime art,
In how many gray hours
When wild tumult of life ensnared me
Have you kindled my heart to warm love?

When the Schubert finished, Sam revealed his grim prognosis. With three open-heart surgeries behind him, his heart couldn't be patched any more than a shredded tire could. A transplant, though, might work.

Get on with it, Sam had told his doctors decisively, as if he were talking car repair. A heart with the right blood type could come today or never, but with his medications adjusted daily, Sam could hang on for a while longer. The view from his hospital window was better than the Allendale, too, he said, in an upbeat tone that almost sounded genuine.

He asked if I could run some errands. For days there hadn't been visitors, and he needed a little help: some good company, he said bashfully. Sitting in his cubicle, I brought the latest gossip from the Allendale, stories about my subbing gig at *Les Miz*, and the details of what was probably the last concert I'd play with the Philharmonic, which I was hired to play before bombing my audition.

It was planned as a week of Shostakovich, I told Sam, but changed suddenly when we learned that Leonard Bernstein had died. Tonight's concert, the orchestra manager had announced during the rehearsal, would start with an elegy, Mahler's "Adagietto" for strings and harp.

Mahler himself had served as the Philharmonic's music director from 1909 to 1911, during which time he wrote his final three symphonies.

Most listeners knew the Fifth Symphony's lush music, a paean of passion and remembrance that was featured on the soundtrack for Luchino Visconti's 1971 film, *Death in Venice*. Music fans also knew that Bernstein championed a renaissance of Mahler's music in the 1950s.

The death of Bernstein, America's only classical music superstar, signaled an onerous changing of the guard for a foundering music business. That night I sat onstage, ready to play the Shostakovich, while string players started the Mahler. The audience fell quiet as Leonard Slatkin conducted without a baton, shaping the music with his bare hands.

It had been a long and emotional day, and the musicians were tired. The Philharmonic usually played Mahler passionately, but not tonight. One cellist came in too early; another made a scratchy attack. The harp wasn't quite together with the strings. First violinists fell out of sync and others began weeping. In their moment to pay tribute to Bernstein, these musicians were blowing it colossally.

The mood turned tragic. Slatkin set his jaw, as if he could will the performers into submission. Just as the orchestra played another messy chord, Slatkin's cummerbund popped off. One hundred pairs of eyes watched as it hung in the air, along with a diminished seventh chord, before sliding to the floor. Slatkin's face froze as if he were about to burst. Musicians twitched with laughter. Bernstein was here somewhere, mocking us all.

Sam snorted over the story, doing overwrought Bernstein impersonations from his hospital bed. Yet isolated as he was with other critically ill patients, Bernstein's death depressed him, and he seemed desperately lonely.

Where was everyone? Where were Sam's friends? Sam wasn't at the parties anymore, not networking like he usually did. And with the severity of his health problem, his chances of ever coming back didn't look so good. He'd been forgotten by all but a few. Even though we were only friends now, I felt a responsibility to take care of him, since no one else was doing it. Part of me imagined how I'd feel in Sam's position. A more selfish part of me probably wanted to feel needed. I vowed to visit Sam every day.

During one of my visits, Sam told me about his debut recital in 1951, at the age of thirteen. With a rave from *The New York Times*, Columbia

Artists signed him to their roster of pianists, violinists, cellists, and singers—performers with the greatest and most versatile repertoire from Bach to Bartók. Listening to Sam, I decided to jump-start my career by giving a debut of my own.

I was just an oboist, without the solo career opportunities of a pianist, yet a debut would offset the Philharmonic audition, improve my playing, and maybe even heighten my image so I'd be offered better work. I wouldn't get a free ride like Sam had, after winning his all-expense-paid concert as a prize in a piano competition, but my parents, concerned about my stalled life, offered to help pay for a recital of my own. A debut could catapult me from freelance obscurity. I was sure of it!

Sam perked up, happy to be useful, and helped me plan a program that would attract a newspaper critic. Getting a review was the goal, I knew. We put together a set of oboe pieces about insects that included a short world premiere that would be composed for the recital, all accompanied by famous assisting artists, mostly from his network.

In daily contact with a familiar face like mine, Sam's buoyant personality returned, even though he still looked like a skeleton. I'd never seen anyone pull himself up by the bootstraps as strongly as Sam did. He started planning the chamber music programs for his summer festival, which was still nine months away, from his hospital bed. He invited me to play there and even let me pick a composer to write a piece just for us.

"How about George Tsontakis?" Sam asked. He suggested composers who were his friends. A new work by mainstream names like these would become standard. Look at Bert Lucarelli, he said, who traveled the circuit playing an oboe concerto commissioned from John Corigliano, his name forever associated with the work. It was also a good political move, as I'd be welcome in the composer's network too. Corigliano was part of Sam's crowd and had not only written classical compositions but also the Oscar-nominated score for the 1980 film *Altered States*. He'd also finished his *AIDS Symphony* on a commission from the Chicago Symphony.

"But I want *her*," I said, naming the composer who was writing "Boll Weevil" for my recital. She was virtually unknown, without any connections in the academic world that most composers inhabited.

"You're absolutely sure?" Sam gave me a quizzical look. "Your call," he said, shrugging. He paused, then jotted her name down, along with our composition idea, a work based on Thoreau's walking tours of Cape Cod. Despite his cheerful outlook, Sam looked so physically frail, I doubted we would ever play the piece together.

I told Sam how much I was looking forward to my recital, since life had been less than glamorous lately. Driving nightly to Poughkeepsie for a gig with the Hudson Valley Philharmonic this week, I also had to fit in a wedding, a kiddy concert with the Brooklyn Philharmonic, and a contemporary music recording in Albany.

Today was Saturday, and I'd already taught a private lesson at eleven and subbed in *Les Misérables* from two to five before racing to the convenience store at 96th and West End to meet my Poughkeepsie carpool. By five-thirty, fifteen people milled in front of the bodega, which was a sort of a Grand Central Station for freelance musicians because its location gave easy access to several subways and the West Side Highway. The cast of characters waiting for rides here didn't vary; only the venue did. These freelance classical musicians pieced together employment with part-time orchestras like the Stamford Symphony, Greenwich Philharmonic, Northeastern Pennsylvania Philharmonic, and New Jersey Symphony. Sometimes, musicians got in the wrong car, ending up in Springfield instead of Scranton.

Transportation could become more complicated than playing the oboe. Sometimes public transit worked, but if you only had two hours, say, to leave a gig in Newark, travel through Manhattan, and out to the Tilles Center for the Long Island Philharmonic, a car was required. Musicians phoned each other to arrange multiple carpools. "Are you doing Jersey next week? Long Island too? Oh, then never mind."

All the driving posed an occupational hazard for freelancers. One friend, French hornist Maureen Snyder, died en route to the Long Island Pops. The family of a flutist who was also killed collected $3.75 million in damages, part of it from the musician who'd been driving. Another flutist died in a pileup on I-95, and a French hornist lost an eye while driving drunk. One carpool of musicians never showed up for a Hudson Valley concert after they were broadsided on the Taconic. No one was seriously hurt, but one musician passenger successfully sued the driver for $1 million.

I kept dashing around to gigs and squeezing in daily hospital visits. Sam had been in the hospital for weeks, and told me that Itzhak hadn't visited in all that time. Without connecting with the famous violinist, I guessed Sam was nothing to his circle of friends either. There was an unspoken feeling that he was abandoned. No one wanted to invest their time in visiting a dying man.

Somehow he kept his spirits up. Down by the river, the autumn leaves turned and fell. Sam said he saw the little red lighthouse beside the bridge's east pylon, but I couldn't make it out. I often thought about Sam's gift, the strength to see what no one else believed could be possible.

Coming home from *Les Miz* one night, I hustled by the crack house across from the Allendale's 96th Street entrance just before midnight, clutching my oboe. It was already Halloween. The wind blew a child's costume mask between cars, and dead leaves swirled in its wake.

Joan, one of the spinsters, was coming outside to walk her matted dogs as I hurried upstairs. The elevator stank of cat piss, because Angelo used the same mop for both the basement and the lobby. I fumbled with my lock as the phone rang, flinging open the door just in time to pick it up. Sam's voice squeaked on the other end as if he could barely speak.

"We're doing it now. The heart is coming," he said. His daughter's dorm phone was busy. He pleaded with me to help him. I told him I'd get the operator to interrupt. "Thanks, oh, thanks. I love her so much. . . ." He trailed off. I was beginning to realize that this could be our last conversation. "Blair," he said, "wherever I am, I'll always be there for you."

I held the phone receiver, reluctant to sever the connection. After a minute or so I hung up, got through to Sam's daughter, and puttered around my apartment. My most recent roommate, a pianist Sam had introduced me to, had moved out a few days before and left a dusty mess in her empty bedroom. Unaccustomed to the extra space, I felt restless and poured myself some cheap brandy, sitting on the radiator to watch the street.

Out on West End Avenue, Halloween revelers wobbled down the sidewalk. I saw a couple dressed as East and West Germany, a drunken bee, a Carmen Miranda shedding grapes and bananas on the ground. The street fell quiet for a moment. I felt utterly hopeless and empty: Sam would probably not survive this surgery.

14
Unfinished Symphony

AT THE HOSPITAL, Margo Garrett was waiting outside the cardiac recovery room. "They only let in immediate family," she whispered, pushing back her blond hair. "You're his fiancée. I'm his niece." Niece? Margo didn't in any way resemble Sam.

I hadn't seen Margo since she coached me on Bach cantatas in college. One of Sam's best students, she now traveled the world with sopranos Kathleen Battle and Dawn Upshaw, cellist Sharon Robinson, and violinist Jaime Laredo. Like any great collaborator, she had arrived at a crucial moment.

Sam's brother had finally left early that morning, after it was clear that Sam had survived the surgery. Around town I'd heard Sam's circle of friends grumbling that Martin should send Sam money. What would five or, better yet, ten thousand dollars be to Martin? I seemed to be the only one who saw how Martin privately took care of bills, attending to the financial burden of each of Sam's surgeries like Sisyphus eternally laboring uphill. I wasn't immediate family, but my daily visits had made Margo and me the next best thing, given the dearth of visitors otherwise.

I washed my hands, like Margo had, and donned a gauze mask to protect Sam's vulnerable immune system. His body would always identify the new heart as foreign matter and try to destroy it one cell at a time. For the rest of his life, Sam would take powerful antirejection drugs like cyclosporine that suppress the immune system's T-lymphocyte cells. The drugs, which were already being administered to him intravenously, also lowered his defenses to germs.

Flat on his back, Sam resembled a vibrating cadaver. A ventilator was rammed down his throat. Fluids, antibiotics, and the antirejection drugs snaked into his body through enough tubes to resemble a dish of spaghetti. The respirator shook his frail, inert body, and his eyes were taped open and coated with opaque gel. His head looked like the marble death masks I'd seen in Italian museums.

I sank helplessly into a chair. "I felt the same way," Margo said. "The nurses say if you talk to him he'll hear you."

Margo fussed with something outside the room in order to give us privacy. I covered Sam's limp hand with mine. Bandages were plastered across his chest. *Blip, ping, whir* went the machines. My own breathing sounded conspicuous, irregular, but Sam's heart monitor beat in strong peaks, instead of its old ragged pattern. His ball bearings were gone.

I stayed for about fifteen minutes. I babbled on about the weather and the Allendale, but it was as if I were talking to myself. I told him Bobby White said he'd come up later in the day. I didn't imagine anyone else would be visiting except Martin, since I hadn't seen anyone else at the hospital before. I needed to get home and ready myself for an afternoon rehearsal, so I slipped on my jacket, said goodbye to Margo, and went into the waiting room.

Outside the sterile area, a polished brunette dialed the pay phone. I recognized her from Sam's parties; she was an arts publicist and journalist. Sam had spoken often of her before going into the hospital, but he hadn't mentioned her in weeks.

"I'm just back from vacation. . . . Yes, the beach," the brunette said into the receiver, inspecting her manicure. "Of course I felt *justified* in telling the nurse I was family; how else could I get in?" As I left the waiting room, I heard her begin saying something about the healing properties of touch.

Two weeks after the operation, Sam was able to sit upright. He transferred his relentless practice discipline to recovery: setting up rehearsal schedules on the phone—"If I'm still around"; he guffawed—ordering ice, water, and Jell-O he couldn't yet have. He wanted the sports pages, his Walkman, a real shirt, and fewer male nurses.

"She can blow my shofar anytime," he whispered, as a young aide arrived. Sam unbuttoned his shirt as she readied a new dressing; I could see purple skin blooming around his incision. Sam explained that the new heart beat so strongly, it bruised him from the inside out. He pulled his shirt aside to show me a wire sprouting from the middle—standard procedure in case he needed a pacemaker.

I sat down once again, feeling faint.

"Tell Brunhilde I'm not dead yet," Sam said, with mock bravado. "You're coming tomorrow?"

I shook my head no. Between this week's visits, I'd driven two hours to Bard College every day, then two hours back, rehearsing as soloist for the American premiere of British composer Nicholas Maw's *Little Concert* with the Hudson Valley Philharmonic. With only three weeks to prepare, I'd used Sam's method of practicing first fast, then slow, then with different rhythms, and finally at half speed with a metronome. The boring routine programmed the virtuoso piece into my fingers.

"Sunday, then?" He looked meek and, suddenly, very small.

I nodded. Yes, Sunday. On Saturday, though, Sam called, his voice wavering. Divorce papers were being delivered to the Allendale. Couldn't I just drop them off for him to sign? Wasn't I driving right by? The envelope came late in the day, as afternoon edged into rush hour. I double-parked my Honda and ran into the hospital, my blue silk concert gown flapping around my ankles.

"Thanks for coming," Sam said, squeezing my hand and clutching the packet. "They're moving me to a regular room tomorrow." He paused, swallowing, as if he wasn't sure how to continue. "Without all this," he said, and gestured to the transplant unit's control center, where closed-circuit screens monitored each patient. His forehead furrowed. I held his hand tight, snatching glimpses as the wall clock. Its second hand circled relentlessly.

Nearly six o'clock. The concert's at eight, ninety miles away. Damn! Where are all his friends?

"You'll be fine. Promise," I said, kissing his cheek and rushing for the door. If I ever was to endure what he had, I thought, I hoped there would be more people around to help me.

My own heart pounded as traffic on the Saw Mill crawled. Finally, whipping around the curves near Cold Spring, I bit off a chip of Inderal, washing it down with yesterday's flat Diet Coke. Sam could never use Inderal like he once did; his heart's severed nerves would probably render beta-blocking drugs less effective.

Screeching into the Bard College parking lot, I was greeted by the stage manager. He parked the car while I ran backstage, where I heard the orchestra begin Joseph Joachim's *Elegiac Overture.* I was on in ten minutes.

The piece was so well-rehearsed, my notes spilled out precisely, fluidly. After all that preparation, it was over in ten minutes. I stayed at the reception for an hour, chatting with Bard professors and the conductor, Leon Botstein.

The trip home was far more arduous than the few minutes I'd spent onstage. I backed over something in the parking lot. Getting out of the car, I saw it was the principal trumpeter's straight mute, one of those conical fiberglass plugs that changes the instrument's timbre to a softer sound. I promised to replace it. Once I was on the road, snow started falling on the Taconic's curviest section. When I finally reached New York, a midnight squeegee man threatened to smash my windshield at 96th. A parking spot right outside the Allendale was a small yet welcome comfort.

My new neighbor, a Russian tenor named Slava Polozov who'd just sung at the Met for the first time, followed me into the elevator. He was still shaken up after a disaster at the opera house that afternoon. Standing in the wings during intermission, waiting to go on again as MacDuff in Verdi's *Macbeth,* he'd seen something falling eighty feet from the very top balcony; then he heard screams and a loud commotion. An old Bulgarian man, someone Slava had studied with as a vocal coach, had jumped to his death. The performance was canceled and a tape replaced the live nationwide radio broadcast in progress.

It wasn't the first recent tragedy at the Met. A stagehand had killed violinist Helen Hagnes back in 1980 and thrown her naked body down an air shaft. She'd been Sam's au pair, and the police hauled him to the station for questioning.

I said goodbye to Slava at the door and went inside to call Sydney. I'd seen her light on while I was parking. I invited her for a glass of wine, which was our code for at least a bottle's worth. I looked in my bare fridge, then scrounged Sam's keys from my collection. I hustled upstairs, borrowing a bottle of Far Niente.

What the hell. I took a bottle of Sonoma Cutrer too.

When I woke late the next morning, the anchovy pie Cheesy Pizza brought at 1 A.M. was congealing in my belly, with a layer of furry lint coating my tongue. I was so thirsty. Ugh, why did I drink so much again?

The phone jolted me awake.

"Who is this? Can you come now? I need help."

"Sam," I mumbled, "it's Blair. You called *me.*"

"Just come now," Sam said, his receiver clattering back into its cradle.

The phone rang again, and this time it was Bobby, calling from next door in the annex. He'd gotten the same strange call from Sam, just before mine. "Go ahead, Blairiekins, I'll meet you there."

I climbed out of bed, harvesting clothes from the floor. I tried brushing last night's wine smell off my teeth, then hurried to the elevator. In the lobby, Angelo squatted at the decorative Italianate arches beneath the balustrade. "Cats." He grinned, smearing mortar over the heating grille between the 1910 marble columns. The fetor of piss and rat carcasses permeated the foyer. Brunhilde supervised, leaning on the banister.

"Mr. Sanders had his operation?"

I guessed that Brunhilde wanted to know if Sam had survived or if perhaps his apartment would be available soon. I didn't answer her. Outside violin scales mixed with a grating flute on the second floor, which I could tell instantly was not Sydney. Her beautiful tone was distinctive and sweet, played on the valuable old Powell flute that was perfectly suited to her musical style.

An hour later, I stumbled into Sam's new hospital room. A strange man, Sam's new roommate, slept in the bed nearer the door. Without monitors, LEDs, blips, or pumps, stillness filled the space. A second bed, empty, faced the George Washington Bridge.

Sam slumped on a potty chair, the phone receiver dangling off his forearm. I touched his shoulder. He glanced up but looked right through me, as if his eyes were still coated with gel. I stared at him, paralyzed by the gravity of his situation.

Just then, Bobby White strode in, all business.

"Sam," he said, scolding. No response. "Sambo," Bobby said, more gently this time. Sam trembled, reaching up for Bobby like a lost toddler. These two had known each other longer than I'd been alive. Bobby's arms encircled Sam, pulling the hospital gown around his skeleton. I slipped into the hall.

Bobby edged out the door, and stood beside me.

"Blairiekins," he said. "He needs twenty-four-hour nurses. Go arrange it."

I'd seen Sam's November Chemical Bank statement, which dipped far into the minus side. I didn't even look at the medical bills, sending them to his lawyer unopened. I stared at Bobby incredulously. He knew there was no way Sam could pay.

"Dear heart, worry not," Bobby said theatrically, pointing my way down the corridor. He'd seen Sam recover twice over the last twenty-five years. "Survival first, bills second," said Bobby, with the same burst of upbeat energy I'd seen from Sam in his most difficult moments. I headed toward the nurses' station, grateful for Bobby's booming stage bluster and Sam's endless joking. They'd made an art of his illness and vastly improved on the reality of his situation.

A nurse dialed the extension, handing over the receiver before darting off to answer a patient's buzzer. I made the arrangements with a coordinator for the twenty-four-hour nurse service. Full-time care would cost thousands for the time he'd need.

"Call Martin," Bobby instructed when I told him the sum, but Sam's brother was unreachable for hours, aboard a flight to Tel Aviv. The nurse coordinator was on her way with a contract to sign, and we had no money for her.

I returned from the nurses' station to Sam's room and opened the door. Sam sat up in bed, wearing his Yankees cap and goofiest grin, basking in Bobby's attention. "Sambo's pitching next season," Bobby boasted, as if nothing were wrong. I beckoned Bobby to come into the hall, so I could tell him the bad news, but Bobby had already solved the money problem.

"It's all set," he said quietly. "Don't tell *anyone.* Alice Tully is sending up a check."

Sam improved quickly. Sitting with his nurse in the same hospital room a few days later, he barely seemed sick. The nurse sat quietly in the vinyl chair as Sam finished opening his mail and then flipped through cartoons in the *New Yorker* I'd brought him.

To pass the time, I'd brought a paper bag of more books, CDs, and magazines. I perched on the windowsill, holding a newspaper clipping. "Want a laugh, Sam?" I asked, reading aloud from my concerto review in the Kingston *Daily Freeman. "In addition to sounding serenity against string angst, and calling with the plaintive haunt of a passing wild goose, oboist Tindall sported one of the most appropriately revealing gowns—"*

"You're making that up," Sam accused, snatching at the paper. I held it out of reach and continued.

"Behind the prim jewel neckline of her floor-length royal blue satin sheath, Tindall flashed a fine back to the waist and great leg to the same point—"

"Stop, stop! It hurts!" Sam laughed, clutching the bruise on his chest. "Critics!"

That blue dress should take center stage, I thought. Even though a friend sewed it as a gift, the materials cost half my concert fee of $500. These solo gigs weren't financially rewarding. Once I added in a hundred hours of practicing, five hours of orchestra rehearsal, and twenty hours of commuting, the pay worked out to less than minimum wage.

Sam said he could relate. Itzhak earned $33,000 a night but paid Sam only $1,000 to accompany him. Still, Sam's price was double the highest mentioned in a *Wall Street Journal* story about accompanists, which estimated that most earned 5 to 10 percent of a soloist's fee. The star's manager got 20 percent for filling out a few forms. Sam said that at one point accompanists organized to set minimum fees, but agents threatened a Standard Oil–style antitrust suit.

"I would play your debut for free," Sam said. Suddenly, I noticed a tiny blonde standing in the door. Sam blushed, beckoning her in.

"Sue, meet Blair." Sue had first met Sam in the hospital a few weeks ago, through one of her doctor acquaintances. The two were clearly sweet on each other. My guilt over rejecting Sam as a lover eased as Sue bent over to kiss his forehead.

*   *   *

D-day had arrived.

My debut recital expenses mounted quickly. Because it was my project, I didn't receive a performance fee but, instead, paid to produce the event. Anyone can rent Carnegie Recital Hall by simply calling the booking office, and in 1991 the rental was $1,200. Fees for the quartet and pianist came to an additional $2,000. Bobby White wouldn't take payment, so I bought him a Barney's gift certificate. I found a tea-length dress, more appropriate for the late afternoon concert than the sexy blue number, at Fowad for $79. The recital manager, Lee Walter, whom Sam had recommended, charged $2,000 for recital management, worth every penny. With decades of contacts, he easily handled printing and designing the flyers, tickets, and programs, which were the recitalist's responsibility. Sydney, with her eye for detail, ordered reception platters from Fairway, bringing the total to $8,000.

Carnegie Recital Hall was in its final stages of a 1991 renovation. The changes were underwritten by Sanford Weill, chairman of Citigroup and of Carnegie Hall, and the recital auditorium had recently changed its name to Weill Recital Hall. The regular dressing room behind the hall was gutted, so I crowded into another one upstairs, near the Kaplan rehearsal space on the fourth floor. It was a standard dressing room with makeup lights and a private bathroom, and it overflowed with cards and flowers. The dozen red roses came from Sam, who wasn't well enough to attend.

I started soaking a few reeds in a film canister of water and unzipped my garment bag. The gown was a stunner, midnight-blue silk chiffon over a slip dress. I slipped it on and zipped up the back. It fit perfectly, the sheer bodice just skimming my body. A shirred satin sash cinched the waist, and the skirt fell to the ankle in the back, and draped asymmetrically like a theatrical curtain in the front. I inhaled sharply. It was the magic dress I'd been searching for! The whole day reminded me of Arleen's triumphant *Magic Flute* debut in Vienna.

Playing a few scales, I breathed deeply and tried a long tone. I'd taken twenty milligrams of Inderal, this batch from the apothecary in Bangkok, but still felt clammy and confused. I may have looked good, but I was scared to death. A friend, manning the box office downstairs, stuck his head in the door.

Debut recital flier. (Christian Steiner)

"*Times* picked up their ticket," he said, catching my eye in the mirror. My pale reflection stared back. Bombs away! I grabbed my reed case, oboe, and music and headed for the door. Together with Brian, the pianist Sam had recommended, I picked my way down another iron stairwell, past the audience entrance, to the recital hall, and down the narrow corridor to the stage door. A kind stagehand, who came as part of the rental package, wished us luck and switched on the hall's substandard recording system. We weren't allowed to bring in our own engineers and would have to take the tape recorded on this cassette deck as a memento.

Brian followed me onstage as applause filled the auditorium. Weill Hall glowed in three shades of ivory, its chandelier crystals shimmering in the silence. If only life could always be as lovely as this room, I thought, sliding the reed in my oboe and glancing over the audience. There was Sydney, my brother, Dad's editors, and lots of strangers, one of whom was a critic. Trembling from head to toe, I took a breath, giving Brian the upbeat to the Telemann Sonata.

At first, it felt like someone else was playing the concert. I concentrated on the difficult ornaments I'd written into the music, the extra notes that a performer is expected to add to simple phrases of Baroque music, much like a jazz player's improvisation. Still, my mind shot to every other subject but playing this concert I'd planned for so long.

People paid to hear me? Can you see through my dress? Did we order enough cheese for the party? I left the iron on. I left the iron on! I'm gonna miss this fast scale.

At last the Inderal kicked in. My mind had cleared and my hands calmed by the time we played the last chord of the Telemann. Next came the first bug piece, Antal Dorati's *The Grasshopper and the Ant.* We were relaxed, and the audience murmured at the musical joke. I'd gone from feeling as though I might die from fear to having fun communicating with my listeners. I was so well prepared, there wasn't a chance I would miss anything. That sense of security freed me to play more expressively than usual. Even if I did fluff a note here or there, this wasn't an orchestra audition that had to be note-perfect. People had come to be moved by an emotional performance, not a musical automaton.

The dressing room was a zoo at intermission, since the second half of the recital involved not only Brian but also Bobby White and three of the Colorado Quartet's string players, all of whom needed to dress in the small room. At the same time, Bobby wanted to go over some of the *Blake Songs* by Ralph Vaughan Williams that would open the second half of the recital. We didn't have time for much rehearsing and soon made our way down to the recital hall again.

The Vaughan Williams arrangement was unusual, as it called only for tenor and oboe without any other instrumental accompaniment. The text used poet William Blake's *Songs of Innocence and Experience.* Once onstage, Bobby and I arranged our music quickly and began. From the moment he began singing, I felt as though I'd been transported to a higher level of musicianship, where my phrasing flowed naturally, almost like an extension of my thoughts and emotions. Bobby and I started the second song, "Eternity," a work that had a surprisingly moving effect on the listener, given the composition's simplicity.

He who binds to himself a joy
Doth the winged life destroy;
But he who kisses the joy as it flies
Lives in eternity's sunrise.

I was still frightened to be onstage but, at the same time, filled with joy and enthusiasm. I felt a physical sensation that I'd only experienced a few times before, when everything was going right. I'd never known it to happen in any other situation and believed it might be specific to making music, or perhaps dancing or performing athletically. It combined elements of preparation, emotional expression, physical involvement, precise motor skills, and several different mental processes, all in real time. Anyone who has felt it knows it's as addictive as a drug.

The concert continued with the Mozart *Oboe Quartet,* and before I knew it, we ended with the flourishes of Saint-Saens's *Oboe Sonata.* I didn't want the recital to end, so I played an encore, repeating "The Wasp," from Benjamin Britten's *Insect Pieces.*

Afterward, people congratulated me in the back of the hall. My friend Lisa Monheit, a wonderful contralto with whom I'd played Bach cantatas while at Manhattan School, told me it was one of the most satisfying musical events she'd ever heard. Since Carnegie's reception room was under renovation, everyone set off for my apartment, where Sydney had set up food and drink for a celebration. Surrounded by friends and relatives, I felt like the toast of New York. The only sad note to the day was that my teacher, Joe Robinson, had not attended the concert, nor had he responded to the invitation and complimentary tickets I had mailed him.

Two nights later, I went out for the paper. Fine snow blanketed the Allendale's decrepit crevices. I stopped to admire the tree that was covered with pink flowers in the spring, the light from car headlights now dancing through the ice coating its branches. Skidding down to 96th, I handed over my dollar just as the *Times* bundles bounced off the truck.

In the glare of lights under the Red Apple's grocery awning, I held my glove between my teeth, pawing through the arts section until I came to the headline: OBOIST ALONE AND AIDED.

Blair Tindall . . . played a clever, stylistically varied debut program. . . . Her sound was narrowly focused and as sweet as an oboe timbre can be, and her phrasing in the finale was bright and playful. With Brian Zeger, a pianist, she played a Telemann Sonata in C Minor and applied ornamentation that was adventurous, sometimes unconventional, and consistently rich in character. . . . Ms. Tindall met those technical demands easily. She and Mr. Zeger also gave a graceful, vibrant performance of the Saint-Saens *Oboe Sonata.*

I bought five copies and hugged them to my chest as I hurried back up Broadway. My upstairs neighbor was just pulling down the metal security gate of the video store her family ran at the corner of 99th. I saw Betty up the street and slowed down. She was loading her elderly lover in a taxi, guiding him into the back as he gripped the car frame. It was hard to remember the opera star he'd once been.

Betty slammed the cab door, waving at the taxi until it turned out of sight. Stepping under the streetlight, she looked old, haggard, and sad. Her dejected posture could not have contrasted more sharply with my sense of joy and accomplishment at that moment, yet I was starting to understand more about how Betty had become so sad.

For one glorious afternoon, I had stepped out of the depressing ranks of freelance musicians and made some very special music. The debut qualified as my number-one life accomplishment, I thought proudly, but what came next? I could try to get a few solo gigs here and there. They wouldn't pay much. Watching Betty plod up 99th Street, I was overcome by a deep sense of dread. The glow from my recital would fade soon, and I'd be back where I started. Now that I was thirty-one, I could start to see how Betty got the way she was, her life slipping away upstairs in the Allendale. If I didn't take action, I could be heading in the same direction.

Soon after my debut, Sam was released from the hospital and almost immediately began teaching again at Juilliard. In the late spring, he and I took a long-planned vacation to Charleston, South Carolina, to visit with his pianist friend Charles Wadsworth and other musicians at the Spoleto Festival. He didn't know Sue well enough yet to travel with her, but he and I had agreed that we could be friends.

We rented an old carriage house with twin beds on Queen Street and related like brother and sister. Stumbling up the creaky, twisting steps in the dark carriage house one night, Sam dubbed the passageway the Itzhak Perlman Memorial Staircase, irreverently joking about Itzhak's disability. He and Itzhak relentlessly teased each other about their physical problems in the most politically incorrect routine imaginable.

By April, Sam hit the road with Itzhak, traveling to Dallas, Quebec, and across the Midwest. Squeezing in weekly cardiac appointments, Sam endured painful catheterization as a tube snaked through his groin and up into his heart, where the probe sampled tissue for early signs of rejection.

He took more pills than ever. Cyclosporine, a drug derived from Norwegian soil fungus, fought the body's response to Sam's new heart, which his system tried to reject as foreign matter. The drug dose constantly had to be adjusted. Imuran further reduced the white blood cells, compromising his immune system and giving him slight hand tremors. Prednisone, a steroid made from human adrenal-gland hormones, suppressed his immune system but came with side effects: Sam's face puffed out like a chipmunk, and fluid pooled in ankles already plagued with "flea bites," as he called his phlebitis. The drug also clouded his eyes with cataracts.

Sam had no time for cataract surgery. His Cape Cod festival started next week, and he had our new piece to learn. Weaving tales of shipwrecks and ghosts, the composer named her work *A Fragile Barrier*, depicting shifting sands, sailors' tombs, and the struggle between man and sea. She used contemporary techniques in her composition, such as strumming strings inside the piano and sounding eerie microtones between notes on the oboe.

Sam and I rehearsed in a hot Hyannis church. He squinted through his cataracts, patiently marking fingerings and notes in gargantuan scribbles. Checking the music, Sam bent inside the piano with a guitar pick. He strummed a dissonant chord, and his anger rose and overflowed in a fury that had probably been building during his recovery. He simply couldn't see well enough to play the piece.

Eva, a violinist playing the festival, rushed from the pews, where she'd been listening. She rubbed his back and, after a few minutes, found the right strings for Sam, color-coding them with bits of tape. Standing by as page turner, she rearranged the pages, whispering to Sam like an opera prompter.

Before the performance, I waited alone in the rectory of Wellfleet's First Congregational Church as Margo Garrett performed a four-hand piano piece with Sam. The chapel stood only a few blocks up the hill from Cape Cod Bay, and I could smell the salt water. I skimmed off my summer dress, pulling on a pink crepe gown whose fluid drape and low back eliminated any possibility of a bra. Inspecting my reflection, I rummaged in my purse and pasted Band-Aids over my nipples for modesty.

It was a sweltering night. As the applause died, Sam followed the Lark Quartet down the dark stairs and into the rectory. "I'm schvitzed," he declared, and splashed water on his pink face. With a hairbrush, he fluffed his damp curls, which were thicker than ever thanks to a positive side effect of the cyclosporine. He pursed his lips, posing for the mirror like a society matron.

"Ready, deeeaaar." He put on his best Alice Tully voice and prodded me onstage. Programs crackled as the audience fanned themselves. I gave Sam his cue, and we began the "Hymn" movement, an elegy for sailors who'd died nearby in the Atlantic Ocean. Sam, who'd memorized the piano's guts by feel, strummed ethereal chords on its strings; by the movement's end, sweat drenched my hair and dress. There was thunderous applause. In fact, a surprising amount of applause.

As I bowed, I could see why. My pink dress was dark with sweat, perfectly revealing the Band-Aids plastered on my breasts. The scenario was a new one in my annals of concert clothing mishaps, which most often

Backstage with Sam before performing at the Cape & Islands Festival, 1991.

included broken spaghetti straps, popped buttons, or busted zippers that revealed too much skin. I whipped my long hair in front of my chest for the remaining bows and changed clothes for the reception.

Over wine and cheese, I watched the composer accept congratulations for her beautiful music. She was happy the audience loved it so much, but I could see she knew to truly appreciate the moment. Given her relative obscurity compared to other composers, I feared the piece would never be played again.

Sam climbed in my old Honda for the trip back to Hyannis, and I complained that we'd probably heard *Fragile Barrier* for the last time. I buckled him into the passenger seat, since he was always bewildered by the mechanics of seat belts. He gave me a silent *told-you-so* look, since he'd originally suggested more well-known composers. We passed the Cape Cod National Seashore. Impulsively, I drove across the empty parking lot to a wooden boardwalk leading to stairs that zigzagged down the dunes to the beach. The surf churned in the night. I still felt a high from the performance.

I helped Sam out of the car, and we stood looking down the stairs. To me, a time like this was what made music worthwhile, this abstract emotional afterglow, but Sam's personal relationship with music was nothing like mine. To him, moments away from hard work were wasted minutes, and he didn't have many to spare. Salt misted his face. He was blind and vulnerable.

"Can we go now?" he asked softly. "I need to practice."

The air-conditioning hummed inside Nashville's performing arts center. In the warm-up room, one girl furiously scraped cane, squawking her reed fortissimo, to test whether it correctly sounded the note C. She was one of sixty oboists, about the usual number who showed up at each orchestra audition. I recognized people from other auditions; the second oboists from the Columbus Symphony and the Louisville Orchestra, as well as a San Francisco freelancer, were here. We had all met at these auditions many years ago and become friends.

I'd arrived early and had already warmed up and arranged my instrument and music. As I waited for my audition time, I unfolded the clipping of a review from *The Cape Codder* that I'd brought along to bolster my confidence.

> Blair Tindall made an indelible impression as a creative musician, totally in command of her instrument . . . pure tone quality, impeccable technique and phrasing. . . . Tindall and Sanders remained well-composed and undaunted by the technical and musical demands of this piece.

I hoped the Nashville Symphony would like me this much too. The second oboe job only paid $18,000, but Nashville's recording scene was America's third largest after LA and New York. I could rent a nice apartment, pay off my credit cards, and buy a new car. From here, I'd climb to a bigger orchestra.

Adopting Sam's practice discipline, I'd drilled every excerpt. Setting aside three hours each day, I played through some excerpts one hundred times each, moving up the metronome beat bit by bit, then playing the entire list twice at half tempo. Not the creative bliss many audience members might imagine as the working life of a musician, that's for sure, but together with the Inderal there wasn't a chance I'd miss anything.

I sat quietly until the personnel manager led me to the usual audition setup. I knew exactly what to expect, and despite a harsh-sounding reed the audition went well. Afterward, I waited with ten others for the personnel manager to return. As he flipped to a page in his notebook, I felt I was watching a familiar old film clip. "Number nine and number eleven will advance to the finals," the personnel manager said. "The rest may go." I had grown so accustomed to failing at these auditions, the rejection didn't bother me this time.

My flight didn't leave for a while, so I took a cab down to Printers Row. In a dive beside the Pink Poodle bar, a man in a redneck cap slumped over his whiskey. A woman took a long draw on her cigarette, giving me a suspicious look. Willie Nelson's "Heartaches of a Fool" played on the jukebox.

I traced my Bud's weak froth with a bar straw, catching my reflection in the mirror. Dressed in a white blouse and pleated pants, I looked like a secretary. My hands were crosshatched with reed knife nicks and greasy with honing oil. A few cane splinters stuck in the fabric of my pants.

I was tired of pretending I wanted this. Tired of my hopeless reed-making. Sick of the same old excerpts. Sick of spending every cent trying to win a job with an orchestra that offered only a minimal salary. After twenty-five auditions, I had spent $30,000 on flights, hotels, private oboe lessons, and missed work, most of it accumulating on a credit card. Even if I had won this gig, I'd never get out of debt.

I signaled the bartender and ordered a double Dewar's. He wiped down the bar. I swallowed the burning whiskey and cleared my throat.

"I tried out for the Nashville Symphony today," I told the bartender. He didn't know Nashville had an orchestra. He loved music though, played a little guitar himself. What was my instrument?

"Oboe," I said simply. "I play the oboe."

"*Oh*-boe?" he asked, and stopped wiping, rag suspended over the bar. "What the heck's an *oh*-boe?"

Thunk! Like mine, Betty's doorbell didn't work. Given Betty's often-grouchy personality I imagined that her apartment was a pack-rat's mess, stuffed with double basses, out-of-style clothing, and 1960s magazines. I wondered how many empty wine bottles lined the closet. I scolded myself, remembering that I had started to accumulate quite a few myself.

I dreaded visiting Betty, because I feared I might do something to antagonize her. So far, I'd navigated through Betty's personal minefield, but she and nearly every other musician in the building were at war. Between laundry room spats and elevator squabbles, Sydney and I were the only Allendale musicians still playing in Basically Baroque.

However, I'd been called just that afternoon to go on tour with a Broadway musical and had mixed feelings about whether to accept it. The money would be fantastic. I was dying to discuss it but was Betty a good choice? I was at a crossroads. Would going on the Broadway tour shut the door on my classical music career? Playing for Broadway didn't exactly feel like a life's work; besides, the gig was only temporary employment. Finally, I had called Betty to ask if I could stop by.

She slid open the mechanical peephole, then flung open her door.

"Wel-come," she sang, radiant in a peach silk top and flowing taupe pants. Pearl earrings set off her tasteful makeup and freshly styled hair. Recovering from Betty's surprisingly polished appearance, I took in her tidy apartment, which looked nothing like what I expected.

Sparsely furnished, the place was painted in pastel shades that had not been applied by Hippolito or his sloppy co-workers. She'd arranged an assortment of olives, pâté, and goat cheese on a glass table. A brilliant white fur rug filled the space between her leather sofa and loveseat. She'd added her own cabinets and flooring in the kitchen, and bookshelves lined an entire wall. An original lithograph, a framed festival poster, and an oil painting hung on another wall.

"Red or white," Betty trilled from the kitchen.

"Red," I called. Glancing at the white rug, I changed my mind. "No, white. Definitely white."

Betty returned with two etched glasses and a slim bottle of Pinot Blanc. Striking a match, she lit a painted oil lamp beside the cheese and sank into her Scandinavian chair, cradling the glass.

I told Betty about Nashville, my twenty-fifth unsuccessful audition. I paused, wondering if I should be admitting my failures to an orchestra contractor like Betty, who was in a position to hire me. Despite her volatile behavior, though, I sensed that she was supportive of other women. I continued, telling her that someone on the plane asked what I wanted to be doing in five years. I didn't know. There was a nagging sense that I was supposed to head somewhere. Where?

Betty nodded, swirling her wine. She felt the same way. She had almost no money saved, with only a small pension from her part-time job at the ballet. She'd do something else in a heartbeat but didn't know what that something else could be. She didn't know anything about computers and didn't have a college degree.

"I saw your name in the Marlboro programs," I said, trying to steer to a more positive subject by describing my night with Sam at the Whetstone Inn. In the soft light of Betty's apartment I could almost see her, twenty years and forty pounds lighter, smiling with the same musical joy I'd felt at my debut, as she played Schubert's *Trout Quintet*.

In the late 1950s, in the first wave of women to win orchestra jobs, Betty joined the Houston Symphony part-time. It was all exciting and new for her. She moved up to the New York City Ballet Orchestra, which performed in one of Lincoln Center's shining new theaters. It was literally a jewel box—the prisms of faceted lamps lined the balcony.

As she talked, I pictured what the ballet orchestra was like today. I'd substituted in it during my romance with Randy, who played principal oboe there. I couldn't see the stage from my chair in the pit but had strained to make out the dancers in a reflection, either in the jeweled lights or in an audience member's glasses. Now veiled with dust, the lights and their design dated the theater. Outside, Lincoln Center's marble had cracked with neglect, and rust stains dripped down the white stone. The scene no longer looked the idyll it had been when Betty began playing there two decades before.

"I can get my pension soon," she said, but she couldn't afford to leave the Allendale. "I'm going to be working until I die." Betty looked glum.

"I got offered a Broadway tour," I blurted out. The forty-week tour paid $1,200 a week. In addition, my $600 weekly per diem to pay for hotel and food was cash, therefore nontaxable. I could pay off my audition debts and schmooze a big contractor who might move me to a real Broadway show back here in New York if I did well.

Betty brightened. Why was I hesitating?

"It would be a fantastic job if it were permanent," I said. There was no guarantee I'd ever be offered a show back in New York. "I could come home to nothing. If you're out of town for weeks, no one will be offering you work when you return."

There were other considerations. It would be hard to be viewed as a serious classical musician after taking this kind of work, and I could lose the gigs I had right now. The groups and musicians I had been playing with described musicians who turned to Broadway as *selling out*. I'd also be playing exactly the same music every night. If I took this tour, my life and career would change. Was this what I wanted for my future? I hadn't even mentioned the job offer to Sam, because I was afraid he'd lose respect for me as a musician.

"It's not, you know, real music," I said, summing up my thoughts. Betty shrugged, drinking more wine. I might have to give up the two solo concerts I'd booked this season, which ended up costing more than I would make playing them. In addition, the rest of freelancing looked bad for me, since the oboists in a position to hire me were either my ex-boyfriends or oboe rivals who hated my ex-boyfriends.

Betty set down her glass, sloshing wine over the rim. "How much does it pay again?" she asked. In Betty's day, union benefits weren't much, but now I'd get insurance, pension, and $72,000 per year, a third of it nontaxable money for food and hotels. If I moved to a long-running Broadway show, I might have that for years.

As Betty ticked off the list of good reasons for me to go on tour, I looked around. Beneath the decorating, her kitchen had the same tin cabinets as mine. Water damage stained her ceiling and the windows were rotting at the same rate.

Sounds like a great thing, Betty concluded, refilling and then quickly draining her glass. There was a *ping* as the crystal glanced off her pretty stone coaster and shattered on the floor.

"Damn it!" Betty's face twisted, her voice prickly. It was time to go. I had decided to join the Broadway tour.

15

The Pits

THE WHOLE BAND was in the hot tub. As water frothed over my bare breasts in the moonlight, I considered how quickly my life had changed. Well into a forty-week tour with *The Music of Andrew Lloyd Webber in Concert*, we were playing two weeks at Costa Mesa's Orange County Performing Arts Center across the street from the hotel. My fellow New York musicians had all acquired a California glow and lost their inhibitions.

This tour was different from the business of classical music in nearly every way. Audiences flooded in to hear Andrew's popular tunes, sung by his wife, soprano Sarah Brightman. Unlike symphonies, these for-profit productions were paid for by investors and audiences, not charity. With steady employment, I'd already paid off a sizable chunk of my credit card debt.

I was surprised to find that I enjoyed playing Andrew's pop tunes, even throwing myself into making reeds each morning so I could produce a more beautiful sound. After I got over my initial snootiness about pop music, I came to prefer the more casual concert presentation and being around the fun cast of actors. However, I did miss being part of the primary attraction, as I would have been at an orchestra concert. My magic dress was now in mothballs.

The musicians on tour hardly resembled the classical prima donnas I knew. No one pretended they liked starving for art but squirreled away their steady paychecks for a rainy day. The road life of upscale hotels seemed a world away from the grit of New York, and although many of us were strangers, others had traveled together for years. The tour felt almost like a family vacation.

Mike perched on a chaise beside the Jacuzzi. A percussionist, he'd lived out of a suitcase for ten years straight, using his tour savings to buy a house in upstate New York. Saving his per diem by bunking with friends in nearly every city, Mike had nearly paid off his mortgage.

Touring offered more opportunities than just money. Vinny, a bass trombonist, wanted to move up the food chain to become a conductor in order to better support his family. This was exactly how most Broadway conductors got their start, although the majority were keyboard players who could make themselves even more versatile by accompanying the singers during piano rehearsals. Vinny had taken a leave of absence from *A Chorus Line* to be our assistant conductor, leaving his Tony-winning actress wife, young son, and infant daughter behind.

No one was more determined than Dale, who would do nearly anything to keep playing his trombone. Though classically trained at the Eastman School of Music, he had crossed over into jazz and pop, working first with the Buddy Rich and Woody Herman bands, then with Blood, Sweat, and Tears. Sometimes the gigs were months apart, so Dale ran a construction contracting business, getting up before six to remodel kitchens. To fill the gaps in his income, he drove trucks at 2 A.M., delivering *The New York Times* to distribution centers.

By 1987, Dale was still driving trucks, even though he'd landed his first New York show. His future looked promising; Broadway had seen a 12 percent box office increase the previous year, and he hoped that meant his show would enjoy a long run. He could use the extra cash to make Christmas special for his daughter. Changing out of his tux at the Minskoff Theater, Dale had skipped the opening-night party for a short nap and then taken off to deliver his papers. Alone in a dark newspaper warehouse a few hours later, he ripped open a stack of newspapers, quickly finding Frank Rich's review of his show:

> For those who worried that Broadway might be nothing more than a carnival fairway offering mindless fun, along comes *Teddy and Alice*, a show that fearlessly puts pedagogy back into the American musical. The result is an evening that combines the educational mission of *My Weekly Reader* with the entertainment agenda of a halftime show at a high-school football game . . . This

exorcism, unfortunately, takes considerably longer to accomplish than the charge up San Juan Hill.

Dale took a long look at the truck, stuffed with thousands of copies of the review. He was delivering his own show's death sentence.

There were more stories like Dale's on this tour. Each of the thirty-five musicians, twelve actors, one conductor, several company managers, a handful of stagehands, and a sound designer had one. The orchestra's large size, augmented by thirty-five more players in large towns, was unusual at a time when producers wanted more synthesizers and fewer acoustic musicians.

What our large orchestra represented in this show was a visual metaphor for luxury. Unfortunately, the artistry of our musicians was obliterated by excessive amplification. Critic Robert Commanday of the *San Francisco Chronicle* described the result:

A symphony of sixty players was made to sound, through the magic of electronics, like an orchestra of sixteen. But the image was preserved—a whole symphony with full wire choir (string section to you) was sitting there playing. With each instrument miked, you were spared having to listen to the real uptown thing, in natural aural perspective.

Reduced to being an oversized stage prop, we had plenty of free time for reading, socializing, and sightseeing. There was Alcatraz in San Francisco, botanical gardens in Milwaukee, and the St. Louis golden arch. Christmas Day in Los Angeles we shared candy canes with a heavy-metal band that was also staying on our floor at Hollywood's Le Parc Suites. Living in the alternate reality of hotels, all the usual tour misbehavior had started in earnest by the third week.

"Did you hear?" A violinist in the band room was spreading the gossip before a matinee.

"Percy and Connie were naked in the outdoor swimming pool last night. No mistaking them," another violinist said, describing our conductor's midnight grope with a stunning actress.

It must have been very, very dark outside, because I didn't look a thing like Connie. Percy and I had returned from an evening stroll at Corona del Mar, the temperate California air exotic to his British senses. Soothed by low tide lapping over the tide pools, we'd sprawled on the rocks, enjoying the stars. Percy had a girlfriend in England, but tours being tours, I knew we'd sleep together that night.

I followed Percy into the hotel's pool. The air felt good against our skin, and we kissed and embraced in the warm water. Being around him was easy, and with his British accent and repertoire of jokes, everything he said sounded new. He was also a fine musician. I loved playing for him, and he was more appreciative of my efforts than most conductors. We dried off and then made our way upstairs to his suite. Percy made love as exuberantly as he conducted.

A few hours later, the early morning light hit the Barolo remaining in my glass. I didn't feel so good, but the lack of sleep and overindulgence during the entire tour had yet to affect Percy. We lay in bed, listening to Madonna's new CD on Percy's Walkman. He lit a cigarette.

"You're quite extraordinary," he said. "Do you want to do *Aspects* in New York?" He stubbed his cigarette in the bedside ashtray and looked expectant. *Aspects of Love* was Andrew Lloyd Webber's latest, going into the Broadhurst Theater in a few months.

Why, I thought, did I bother with an answering machine? Between Sam and my former oboist boyfriends, I got hired for most of my gigs in bed.

As I dressed, I totaled up the jobs I'd acquired this way. Jayson got me onto the hiring lists at Philharmonia Virtuosi and for several studio contractors. Although I'd originally been hired for St. Luke's and Orpheus through recommendations, Jimmy had kept requesting me as long as he and I were intimate. The New York City Ballet came through Randy, though that was short-lived and my absence there had been permanent so far. When the relationships ended, my spot on each group's hiring list dropped. Some would never call me, others would do so only occasionally, and only for second oboe. I would love to play a show. I had just about run out of classical gigs in New York.

* * *

The Hudson Valley Philharmonic had a concert almost as soon as I returned from the Andrew Lloyd Webber tour. I was surprised that Sydney had taken off from her show to sub Hudson Valley, which paid substantially less—about $100 a concert and $70 per rehearsal. The show would have brought in about $150 a night, which was paid to Sydney's own substitute whenever she was absent. "I need to play something else to break up the boredom," she explained. When the van returned to New York around eleven-thirty after the final performance of the week, Sydney and I joined two Hudson Valley violinists for nachos at the Border Café on Broadway.

"No, no, no," Sydney mumbled, pushing my hand away when the check came, then squinting to read it. "Imagine, *me* needing glasses," she said.

Sydney reached for her wallet, lurching to the right. She spun around, scrambling under the table. "My bag! My flute!" Her voice rose. Didn't she hang it on her chair? After two killer margaritas, I wasn't sure myself.

"Maybe you left it in the ladies' room," I suggested, although I knew she had not. She returned, frantic. The violinists clutched their own instruments as the bartender, Angel, called 911. Angel said he'd seen a woman leave with a bag that looked like the one Sydney described.

A few minutes later, two cops took out their notebooks under the punched-tin bar lamps. "You say there was some kind of flute in it?" The officer sighed. He didn't appear very interested in the theft, suggesting that the department gave grand-larceny cases, which meant thefts exceeding $10,000, precedence over petty crime.

"No, no! It *is* grand larceny. The flute's silver. And gold. Solid silver and gold!" Sydney said, her voice shaking. The instrument was quite rare. She'd last had it appraised for $10,000, and it was insured for that amount.

As Sydney and I headed around the corner to the Allendale, we met Sam, coming home with his conductor friend Joel, who stayed in Sam's apartment whenever he visited from Minnesota. They offered to help us look through the neighborhood trash, our last chance before the garbage trucks came. Joel, whom I didn't know too well, glued himself against me, his arm locked around my waist. He could probably tell that I was a little tipsy. I felt violated but was too distracted by the flute to do much about it.

"I think we've looked hard enough," Joel said half a block later. We returned to the Allendale's lobby. The thief had probably hopped on the subway to points unknown.

Joan and her two smelly dogs were resting on the lobby sofa. She smiled pleasantly, unaware of what had happened. The elevator door opened. Betty emerged, gripping her lover's elbow as he shuffled out of the lift. I squirmed away from Joel, although he kept edging closer as the four of us stood aside to let Betty and her boyfriend pass.

Joel offered to come and hang out with us, but I said no. Once Sydney and I were alone, I began replacing her lock, since her keys and address had also been in the bag. Fortunately, I had an old lock in my apartment.

In the morning, Sydney called 1-800-VIVALDI to file her claim with Clarion Insurance. A friend plastered bus stops from Lincoln Center to Columbia with homemade signs that eventually turned up as fodder for a *New Yorker* illustration. Sydney and I checked pawnshops for days, but the flute didn't surface.

Sydney fell into a funk, as if she'd lost a lover or family member. She thought she'd found her musical mate for life in that old Powell flute. It was hard for me to imagine, since wooden oboes tended to wear out after a few years. But instruments like flutes or violins can be an extension of the player's soul. Sydney's had been stolen.

Aspects premiered with an eight-hundred-guest party at the Rainbow Room on opening night. In my strapless dress, I vamped it up on the revolving dance floor near Liza Minnelli, bumped into Dan Rather near the tarot cards, and heard a reporter grilling Prince Edward about a rumor some tabloid had started that romantically linked him to our leading man, Michael Ball. I loved these dress-up events.

Compared to performing onstage, though, pit life was mundane. Here, the audience came for the actors, not the musicians. My view of the audience took a different angle as well, as I watched the front row fill up each night at my eye level. The sights were fairly predictable. A man's hand inched up his date's skirt. Shoes came off, and bare toes invaded our space. An old lady crinkled through her shopping bag for minutes at a time.

Tonight, though, two middle-aged men in kilts plopped down in the front row. One demurely crossed his legs, tucking the skirt underneath them. His companion sat splay-legged, as if he were watching television at home. Doughy flesh flowed over his theater seat. What *do* they wear underneath? I wondered.

As I stole glances at the men in kilts, concertmaster Sanford Allen called for silence by rapping a pencil against his stand, signaling me to play the tuning note, A, as the oboist always does. Also the house contractor, Sanford earned 50 percent over scale to keep track of orchestra issues, payroll, and decorum. He looked disapproving as I craned my neck at the men in kilts.

As Paul Bogaev, our conductor, started the overture, I spread *The New Yorker* across my stand. At first I read only during rests, like everyone else, but soon I discovered an unusual skill possessed by about 10 percent of Broadway musicians. I could read a magazine while playing my part simultaneously.

Those without the gift passed time in other ways, plugging in transistors, knitting, making lists, or doing crosswords. One trumpeter studied maps. The lucky ones with several minutes off left the pit, bringing back falafel sandwiches from Natureworks across the street. Sometimes the conductor even left the pit for a few moments.

At intermission came audience contact. Most of the visitors at the pit railing were simply interested in the instruments, asking questions about the size of the orchestra or offering an appreciated compliment. Others were annoying. "I used to play the flute," a young woman hanging over the railing said vacantly. At least one ex-flutist visited each week. This one stared at us like zoo animals, which made me self-conscious.

I considered escaping the pit altogether, maybe checking out that heavy door in the north side of the basement. It led to a tunnel that connected all the Shubert-owned theaters on 44th and 45th: the Broadhurst, Shubert, Majestic, Golden, several others.

"Miss Oboist! Oh, Miss Oboe, Miss *O-boe!*" A paunchy man waved his Playbill over the railing. I raised my eyebrows and smiled at him, hoping for a compliment.

"Danny Kaye—he was a comedian before your time—said, 'Oboe's an ill wind that no one blows good!'" He stood there, beaming. Beside him, the fat Scot laughed, shifting his butt.

Bingo! Tartan boxers.

The top classical freelance musicians looked down on Broadway work, but I no longer cared. It paid $1,100 per week in the early 1990s, with three weeks' vacation, eight sick days, and a pension based on healthy revenues. (I'd signed up for my first physical since junior high, along with an eye exam and a visit to the dermatologist, just in case the show closed right away.)

We could even hire a substitute for half the performances (pay was docked) and had tenure for the run of the show. Like most classical musicians playing Broadway, I continued playing freelance concerts by taking off nights at the show. I quickly learned the ropes. Subs came in two basic varieties: available or good. Available ones bailed you out at busy times, like the last Saturday before Christmas, but never seemed to understand that's why they got called. The most desirable players repaid the Broadway musician by hiring him for outside work like City Ballet or American Symphony, which not only broke up the show's monotony but often carried over to provide employment after a show closed.

In addition to base salary, musicians like me got an extra 12.5 percent for doubling on a second instrument, which justified the expense of instrument purchase, maintenance, and time spent making reeds and practicing. Two doubles earned more, and three instruments—or playing the synthesizer, regarded as a musician-replacing device to be discouraged—got 25 percent. Costumed musicians, like the onstage violinist in *Fiddler on the Roof* or the guitarist in *Man of La Mancha*, cost producers an extra five bucks a night, and wearing body paint brought an additional eight dollars in pay.

*　*　*

Like 69 percent of the Broadway shows running in 1990, *Aspects* didn't earn back its investment, qualifying it as a flop.[1] It closed eleven months after opening. Frank Rich—*The New York Times* "Butcher of Broadway" who had panned Dale's show—had flung his cleaver, with a reference to the roller-skating actors in Lloyd Webber's *Starlight Express:*

> Andrew Lloyd Webber, the composer who is second to none when writing musicals about cats, roller-skating trains and falling chandeliers, has made an earnest but bizarre career decision. . . . While *Aspects of Love*, with its references to Huxley and Turgenev, may be the most high-minded of Lloyd Webber musicals, isn't it also the one in most desperate need of roller skates?

Closing in March of 1991, *Aspects'* $8 million loss rivaled the five-show run of *Carrie* as Broadway's biggest flop ever.[2] The failure didn't bother me, since I had a blockbuster show waiting; the same contractor who had hired me for *Aspects* was also picking musicians for the next big musical, *Miss Saigon*. I'd accepted, planning to quit *Aspects* anyway, along with the French horn player in my pit band, to join the new show. Even though I wasn't playing as much classical music as I once had, and I was hidden in an orchestra pit, I still felt there was something important in playing for these hit shows.

Unlike *Aspects*, the new show promised to be a spectacle in the *Phantom* tradition, with an onstage Cadillac, a two-story Ho Chi Minh statue, and a real helicopter landing onstage. Young Asian girls in tiny bikinis were almost an afterthought.

On *Miss Saigon*'s opening night, Sardi's waiters bore silver platters of the *Times* review. "This musical is a gripping entertainment of the old school," penned a kinder, gentler Frank Rich. The Butcher's blade jabbed only once, in noting the Broadway trend to opulent staging. "The helicopter stunt, which will most impress devotees of sub-Disney theme parks, is presented . . . for no good reason other than to throw Andrew Lloyd Webber fans a pseudo-chandelier or levitating tire."[3]

I had a hit, and a job for years.

Settled into *Saigon*, life became more stable. No longer did I worry about gaps in my income. Within weeks, however, I began experiencing the Broadway musician's nightmare of repetitive work. Four hundred sixteen times a year I would be playing the same notes, accompanying a story that always ended the same way. Broadway musicians who'd worked for years were bored out of their minds but endured the work because it paid decently and offered a flexible schedule. I noticed, with horror, that the repetition paralleled a boring consistency in my personal life, which had lacked anything in the boyfriend department for some time now.

Hoping to meet some new men, I signed up for a wine class at Windows on the World, the restaurant atop the World Trade Center. "Business attire required," the brochure said. Probably not the pit musicians' duds of faded black jeans, sneakers, and T-shirts. I owned only fancy formal wear and knocking-around clothes, but nothing in between. I bought a tight corporate-style suit with my new gold card. And since I could also afford a Paris Health Club membership, my body fit into the size-zero miniskirt.

I had swooped in on Doug by the third class, on Côte d'Or wines. We tossed back our Bienvenue-Bâtard-Montrachet like seasoned oenophiles. Dark and gorgeous, he'd just started at a big Wall Street law firm, and he asked me out for Saturday night.

I worked on Saturday night. Doug was one of those day-job types. He'd need training that my work was every bit as valuable as his, even though it happened to be at night. Doug would learn the three-show rule. He'd accommodate to my schedule until the third date. Only then would I forfeit a night's income to accommodate his.

Date one went well. I played a concert at Carnegie, a job one of my subs had tossed me as a thank-you in return for work, while Doug sat in the audience. Impressive, I thought! Tonight was date two. He'd meet me at the stage door for a late drink, which I thought might sound glamorous to an outsider.

First came the show, though. I walked through the stage door, down a narrow set of stairs to the labyrinth of basement lockers, and into a sea of gay actors in their briefs, waiting to dress in show costumes. Outside the orchestra pit, the sound man tucked body mikes in between nubile bodies and their G-string costumes. I stole glances at a burly stagehand, wearing a dress, who was halfway through his series of sex-change operations.

It was a typical night backstage. Male musicians in faded black jeans and T-shirts lounged on the sofa, draped by beautiful Asian actresses in bikinis who massaged shoulders and cooed in their ears. I poured myself some coffee.

"Places! Orchestra to the pit!"

The only woman among winds, brass, and percussion, I slid into my seat behind our saxophonist, poking at the dismal selection of reeds soaking on a shelf beneath my stand. Someone slid the heavy steel pit door shut with a crash. Now, only a slice of light connected us to the outside world, a space where the stage extended nearly to the front row. Netting to catch flying props and actors covered the rest. Since our music was piped through a sound system—completely inaudible for the three minutes while the helicopter landed—our playing didn't matter much more than our scruffy looks.

The door creaked open again, and Timmy, the large flutist, heaved into the pit bathed in sweat. He was lugging a large bag of new CDs from Tower and two books on the futures market. Timmy complained nightly about his wife, a "ball and chain" who played in another Broadway pit, and he acted out with a toy box that included a fart machine, three different electronic screaming balls, a toy gun with a BANG! banner, plastic vomit, rubber dog shit, mooing cow toys, and an actual condom that he produced in conjunction with dirty jokes to intimidate female subs.

Timmy also collected a fee as first-call substitute on the bamboo flute book. Though he refused to learn the difficult instruments, his fee was set in stone with his initial union contract, and the dollar amount could not be reduced after the show opened. Despite his pay, Timmy was always broke, complaining about the mortgage on his expensive new house.

Timmy put his flute together as our loud pit conversation commenced. Those wearing earplugs shouted because they couldn't hear; those who refused to wear earplugs shouted because they were practically deaf. Hearing loss was a serious workplace issue in the music business, whether in a symphony, rock band, or orchestra pit. The musicians' union provided free annual hearing tests and a voucher for custom-fitted earplugs.

Our conductor, Dale Rieling, entered the pit, barging through the woodwind section to reach the podium. He picked up the phone attached to the pit railing to communicate with the stage manager, then hung up to start the show. As Rieling raised his baton, I tried evaluating his mood, which changed from sweet to nasty by the hour.

A size 14 foot poked through the fabric hung overhead. Its mate appeared, and a clod of something ricocheted off my ponytail. I rooted around in my tray for the Wite-Out I kept for the occasional changes we were asked to make in our parts, painting a big *L* on his right sole, an *R* on the left.

Clang! An aluminum trombone mute, the conical plug that goes in the instrument's bell to change its timbre, slipped from its owner's fingers, hit a metal music stand, and crashed to the floor. The sound woke Jack, the trombonist who dropped it, five bars before his solo in "I Still Believe." He scooped up the device, inserted it in his horn, and played beautifully. A Broadway presence since 1957, Jack had played with Maynard Ferguson, Woody Herman, and Buddy Rich and arranged music for Garrison Keillor's radio show, all while teaching at Manhattan School. A polymath, he stayed up all night calculating pension-related actuarial tables, composing music, scheduling lessons, planning union agenda, and learning music software.

During a soft passage we suddenly heard a retching sound, followed by a toilet flush, booming over the music. Some actor, I supposed, had forgotten to turn off his body mike between scenes.

I couldn't see the percussionists behind their 165 Asian gongs, rain sticks, and other drums. Before he started this job, percussionist Michael Hinton had landed a yearlong gig as Jefferson Airplane's drummer, moving on to Buddy Rich's band and appearing with the Grateful Dead. He and his Japanese violinist wife had migrated to *Saigon* from *Les Miz.*

As we started "Sun and Moon," two synth players hammered away at their silent keyboards, the tinny sounds blaring from speakers aimed at the 1,700 theatergoers above. Mysterious digital readouts ran across their control panels, the ones and zeroes of digital audio simulating a larger string section.

Lino, the clarinetist, was lost in thought during a rest in his part. As a little boy sailing from Cuba twenty years back, Lino had dreamed of his career as a successful reed player. *Saigon* filled in the rare free spots in his busy and diverse schedule. Not only was Lino a fine classical clarinetist, he doubled on flute and saxes in a variety of musical styles. His dreams had come true, and he played as a substitute musician with the Philharmonic and the Metropolitan Opera, performed with a saxophone quartet, and played jingles. He'd recently won a regular spot as the baritone sax player in the *Saturday Night Live* band, but the television show asked him to tint his beautiful salt-and pepper hair dark with Fanci-Full temporary dye, which was part of the deal to make seasoned musicians look young enough for their viewers.

Miriam, another clarinet sub, played a solo, and Timmy whipped around.

"Pretty good," he hissed, "for a *girl.*"

Suddenly, Rieling motioned for us to play softly. Whoever played Kim right now had a bad body mike. Without amplification, she was almost inaudible. Why could opera singers project to the top of the Met's 3,800-seat house, while these performers couldn't be heard in a theater half that size? The band responded immediately, playing in subtones to let the actress's tiny voice project.

Playing *Saigon* was old hat by now; we'd been at it for ten months. Down the street, *Cats* was in its fourteenth season and *Phantom* its seventh. Musicians watched their kids grow up during long runs like this. Yet what happened onstage was a mystery. Except for a few musician-actress liaisons, we didn't know many of the cast members—or the stagehands, who ran computerized sets as complex as our instruments were simple.

The theater suddenly shook with a bomblike *kaboom.* David Letterman's staff had warned our company managers that he'd blow up a taxi in the street between his stage door and ours. He waited until showtime to perform his outdoor tricks, when the tourists were safely inside.

Rieling started a tantrum, flailing wildly with his right hand and picking up the phone with his left. What now? Looking up through the slit, I could see the chain-link fence which dropped near the stage lip to protect the audience from the helicopter's whirring rotors. In this scene, actors boarded a helicopter's hollow body and exited out the back before it ascended. I followed Rieling's eyes up to the fly space, where the chopper had snagged on a bank of lights. For the rest of Act II, few of the computerized cues worked, and glare bathed the musical's tragic ending.

After the show, I put away my instruments, hauling the case onto my back. Outside, couples snuggled under the marquee, sheltering themselves from a driving rain. Others crowded the stage door.

"She's one of the chorus girls!" cried one teenager, pointing at me as I exited. Her friend snorted contempt.

"Nah, that's nobody," she said, straining to see if there might be a real actress behind me. Exiting past the fans and onto the sidewalk, I glimpsed Letterman ducking into a car at his stage door across 53rd, where bits of taxicab chassis spilled out from a Dumpster. His crew was always neat, cleaning up the mess made by the show's stunts, which could involve anything from explosions to high-diving acts.

Searching the crowd, I found Doug standing in a tiny dry patch beneath the theater's fire escape. We stopped in at Joe Allen's for a drink, but Doug didn't stay long. Adjusting to my three-show rule, he'd worked late at the office. His alarm would buzz at sunrise, and then he'd cab it to work, tired from the late night, to write briefs, attend meetings, and search old cases until dinner. Just when he was ready to slow down, I'd be leaving for my two and a half hours of work.

For some reason, there wasn't a third date. I was frustrated and didn't understand why Doug didn't call. On the second date, we had talked about his cases and trials. I dismissed it all as boring, yet I had an uncomfortable sense that I was missing some larger picture.

16
Beggar's Opera

SCHLEPPING BACK FROM a church gig in Jersey, I held my instruments tightly while passing through Port Authority. The bus station had long been known as a magnet for crime. However, today it felt safe, even bucolic, as Mozart's *Eine Kleine Nachtmusik* echoed down empty corridors. New York had discovered "musical bug spray," a term coined by Northwestern University professor Robert Gjerdingen. The technique was first used in 1985 to chase away loiterers at a Canadian 7-Eleven. The trend spread as Pavarotti cleared out Denver parking lots, Chopin thwarted Toronto thugs, and an endless loop of Mozart blared from bullhorns across a Florida slum. Fort Lupton, Colorado, even punished its noise violators by forcing them to listen to Barry Manilow, songs from the kids' show *Barney*, and excepts from Beethoven's Fifth.

I thought about the message of Port Authority's Mozart. It was 1994, and the sound of classical music had become offensive enough to be used as an effective weapon against crime. How could we, the industry producing the stuff, demand that our fans pay top dollar for the same treatment? Ironically, the public's distaste for classical music opened up a new market for repackaging symphonies and sonatas as cultural spinach. Mozart may be yucky and boring, went the reasoning, but it's good for you.

Author Don Campbell trademarked what he called "The Mozart Effect," capitalizing on research performed in 1993 by Frances Rauscher, a conservatory classmate of mine who'd turned psychologist. Rauscher had observed only a brief improvement in spatial reasoning after listening to classical music. However, Campbell expanded Rauscher's theory to meet the needs of America's quick-fix culture by claiming that listening to classical music could increase intelligence.

Anthologies of classical favorites soon appeared with titles like *Baby Loves Bach, Mozart for Mothers-to-Be, The Most Relaxing Classical Album,* and *Classical Music for People Who Hate Classical Music.* Georgia and Tennessee would later jump on the bandwagon, providing each of the states' newborns with a classical CD in 1998. The popularity of these Top Forty classical music albums wasn't surprising. The layman, bewildered by a confusing array of classical music in the record stores, had little idea of where to start listening. Unfortunately, the quality of many of these recordings often reinforced preconceptions of classical music as a boring genre, as labels recycled old monophonic cuts onto undistinguished remixes.

Orchestras also dumbed down their marketing strategy while trying to appeal to a younger audience. Baltimore's symphony sold itself as that city's Other Major League Team, while Philadelphia rocked Gen X (to sleep) with its "ClassiX Live: No sex. No drugs. No rock 'n' roll. Come anyway." Juilliard professor Greg Sandow critiqued Lincoln Center's view of youth in the *Village Voice:*

"The New York Philharmonic Proudly Presents Life Beyond MTV," the poster scrawled, in wavy green type superimposed on a blurred image of an ear.

But the text that followed was the real showstopper: "Become a Young Friend of the New York Philharmonic, and discover how live classical music can be as much a part of your musical life as classic rock!"

Now, this was a blunder. The Young Friends program aims at kids 12 to 17. Classic rock (which MTV doesn't play) isn't part of their lives. It's music of the '60s and '70s, music their parents listened to, which means (a) that they're likely to hate it, and (b) that the Philharmonic has made itself foolish, linking itself to the one musical style teens might find stuffier than Beethoven.[1]

These advertising formats were created in response to spiraling deficits, sparse attendance, and rising costs, as documented in the *Wolf*

Report, an exhaustive 1992 study of statistics and data analysis that evaluated the industry's financial future. The American Symphony Orchestra League (ASOL), which commissioned the work, rejected the Report's dire findings and countered at its 1993 convention with a guide for selling dead white European men's music called *Americanizing the American Orchestra.* This volume was skimpy on data but heavy on anecdotal and emotional description, which revealed the industry's conceit in the guide's opening statement: "Our greatest challenge is Americanizing the American orchestra. What are we about, if not continuing the great experiment that is these United States, through our symphony orchestras?"

At two hundred pages, the guide hit on multiple hurdles: a video generation, lack of ethnic diversity, pricey tickets, disappearing arts education, busy schedules, and working women (but not, apparently, working men). Aging audiences, measured by the average age of concertgoers, provided a particularly ominous sign for the end of classical music, the *Americanizing* report warned. The terror about older listeners was misplaced, ignoring the fact that average audience age had hovered in the late forties for some time. It was logical for people to wait until midlife to begin attending the symphony. With children grown, tuition paid, and more leisure time, concerts fit well with mature baby boomers' rich lifestyles, tastes, and income. In addition, half the classical music audience was younger than the average, with 29 percent under thirty-five in 1992, according to the National Endowment for the Arts.

Older people will always be there, rationalized the orchestras, which alienated this loyal army by appealing to a more diverse group with the "extras" recommended in *Americanizing the American Orchestra.* Orchestras tried incorporating the suggested frills into performances, including giant video screens and vaguely multicultural pops concerts that diluted several musical styles. In doing so, musical integrity was compromised, driving off both core audience and newcomers.

The problem also extended to the administrators, who were isolated from the music itself. Orchestra executives wanted to increase earned income by selling more tickets, but they did not do so by examining the music and programming and perhaps offering fewer concerts of higher quality. (To them, music was known as the *product* and the particular orchestra the *brand*.) Instead, they overspent on marketing and advertising, office facilities, cosmetic concert hall extras (interior decorators and multiple renovations of the same hall for acoustic purposes), excessive vacation time for musicians, astronomical salaries for conductors and soloists, and, finally, high-priced fund-raising services to raise enough money to pay for it all. The mounting expenses were justified by the insistence that classical music was a cultural necessity at any cost. Curiously, the salaries of these administrators surpassed those with commensurate jobs in nearly every other type of public endeavor except for university endowments and public hospitals.

Shortfalls began appearing with such regularity that executives coined the phrase *structural deficit* to explain away chronic debt. Just when the situation looked dire, economic salvation swept across the United States when the tech boom arrived to boost the stock market. Orchestras and other charities benefited as their existing assets grew in value. In 1995 alone, the average endowment increased among the nation's fifty largest orchestras by 76 percent.

Although the gain dropped substantially the following year, average increases in U.S. orchestras' endowments bounced between 7 and 19 percent through 2000, peaking with an average annual increase of 8.7 percent in 1997. Blessed with sudden wealth, orchestra boards lavished money on administrators, conductors, programs, and facilities, each of which was considered more relevant to increasing audiences than the music itself.

By 2003, at least seven orchestras paid their music directors (the primary conductor, who also makes programming and music personnel decisions) more than $1 million, with two earning over $2 million. Ten paid their executives over $300,000, with three paying more than $700,000. Player pay, which steadily averages around 43 percent of an orchestra's budget, saw raises of 3.2 to 5 percent between 1994 and 1999.

These increases surpassed the same period's rate of inflation by as much as three times. As money poured in, a hierarchy formed as leadership became removed from the musicians. In turn, a class structure emerged even among the musicians, as principal players earned two to four times the minimum salary earned by the rank and file.

The annual base pay of a New York Philharmonic musician in 2003 was $103,000. Glenn Dicterow, the Philharmonic's concertmaster, made $366,000; Carter Brey, the principal cellist, $255,000, Philip Smith, the principal trumpeter, $243,000; Philip Myers, the principal hornist, $227,000; and Cynthia Phelps, the principal violist, $216,000. The have-nots in this scheme were primarily section string players, who had to pay for instruments costing significantly more than woodwinds or brasses, worth five or even six figures.

The hierarchy widened, not only among members of the same orchestra but also between the largest orchestras and the smallest. Minimum pay was much lower in symphonies of cities like Baltimore ($73,000), Milwaukee ($56,000), Nashville ($35,000), and Charlotte, North Carolina ($27,000). Another division became clearer as well, between contracted members of these orchestras and freelance musicians like me, who competed over a diminishing market of per-service performance work.

Like nearly all Broadway musicians, I accepted outside work and took advantage of our generous contract, which allowed us to hire substitutes for up to half of our 416 annual shows. I performed the occasional recording gig or played in a few of the freelance orchestras, like the *Encores!* series at City Center, the New York Pops, Basically Bach, and the Metropolitan Opera Guild, which produced operas for children. Some of the old groups where I was once first-call still hired me when the latest hot oboe player was unavailable.

The Philharmonic called me to play after a two-year absence. Avery Fisher's backstage was expansive, almost like an office complex within the building. The area was in need of renovation. The hallway's concrete floor was cracking, sofas in the central lounge were fraying, and the washroom's tissue dispenser was filled with scratchy brown paper towels. Vertical blinds were missing, and the coat rack was held together with rubber bands.

Most of my time at Avery Fisher had been spent on the ground floor of this backstage maze, where the locker rooms were located. I'd never gone downstairs to the basement, where the Philharmonic stored its tour trunks and unusual instruments, like the bass flute used in Ravel's *Daphnis and Chloe* and a hand-cranked wind machine, the size of a bass drum, used in Richard Strauss's *Don Quixote* to make the whooshing sound of windmills. I'd rarely visited the higher floors, which housed the music library, soloists' dressing rooms, the executive offices, and the green-room where soloists greeted well-wishers.

In a backstage washroom in Avery Fisher, I tugged on the nylons the Philharmonic required in its dress code, whacking my elbow on the broken toilet paper dispenser. Subs had long ago been ejected from the ladies' locker room by the orchestra's regular members. When I finished dressing, it was almost time to warm up. I took my reeds out of the film canister where they'd been soaking by the sink, gathered my music, oboe, and garment bag, and looked around the bathroom to make sure I'd collected everything.

Outside in the corridor, the associate principal oboist Sherry Sylar handed me a copy of my debut review. She said she'd been saving it all year. At that moment, my former teacher, Joe Robinson, came around the corner from the locker room used by the men in the woodwind section. He hadn't responded to the invitation I'd sent for my recital and never even asked about it. I tried to show him the clipping, but he waved it aside.

On my way upstairs to the stage, a violist friend asked me to go with her to a before-concert Singles at Symphony mixer, one of the Philharmonic's new audience-building experiments. The administration had asked a few musicians to mingle with the guests. I accepted gladly, thinking the party would give us both the rare opportunity to meet concert-going men who were, by default, our admirers. Working six nights a week, I could never figure how to meet people outside my own world of classical music. Now that my friend, an adorable blonde, was divorced, she found herself in the same boat. Visualizing a room full of bow-tied daddies, I primped in the elevator's reflective brass, feeling like Cinderella on her way to the ball,

We exited on the fourth floor, where the event had already started. I opened the greenroom door. Inside, a sea of floral polyester dresses clustered into two pods around not one but both men who had come. The room was quiet and sedate, without the usual chatter of a party.

What was I thinking? If regular singles events marked desperation, a classical-music singles event meant utter hopelessness.

I tried to start conversations without much success, then met the violist back at the elevator, disappointed. At least tonight's upbeat concert would thrill the lonely hearts. We were playing Vaughan Williams's familiar *Fantasia on Greensleeves* and Bill Bolcom's new clarinet concerto, a jazzy splash of rock chords, Broadway, and blues that was almost like popular music.

"Onstage!" Personnel manager Carl Schiebler's voice crackled over the intercom. The violist headed for the crossover corridor behind the stage that doubled as the cellists' locker room, in order to reach the door nearest her seat on stage left. I stashed my bags under the offstage piano and headed toward the oboe section.

I sat in the second oboe chair and started arranging my accessories: the usual cigarette paper for leaky keys, my swab to clean spit out of the instrument, and a pencil for marking anything in the music I wanted to remember when we repeated the program tomorrow night. The Bolcom was far more accessible than most contemporary music the Philharmonic played, I thought. It was nothing like Anton von Webern's *Concerto for Nine Instruments* that I performed here years ago. Though my conservatory professors venerated that 1930 work for its twelve-tone serialism, I secretly filed it under *H* for *honk-beep-squeak*. Perhaps it was no accident that an American soldier shot and killed the composer during World War II.

Still, I had been nervous about doing a good job on the Webern, especially in placing my delicate entrances precisely. The sparsely orchestrated piece was transparent and challenging, and Avery Fisher's unforgiving acoustics would emphasize any flaws in my tone and articulation. The hall's properties also amplified the sounds of a fidgeting audience, and before long I could barely hear the other eight musicians over the coughing in the house. The cacophony had grown. At last, conductor Zubin Mehta was straining to hear as well. We finished the first movement, and the audience applauded prematurely, then cleared their throats en masse. Reddening with anger, Zubin waited for silence before starting the next movement. Someone giggled loudly. A nose trumpeted.

We waited for nearly a minute—which felt like an eternity onstage with audience and orchestra staring at each other—and began again, to the accompaniment of another wave of coughing. Now enraged, Zubin signaled a mid-movement cutoff. I was shocked. Conductors stopped concerts rarely, and then only if the musicians were irretrievably lost. Zubin swiveled toward the audience, steaming with fury.

"The orchestra has played only five measures when nobody coughed." He spoke deliberately, as if lecturing a room full of toddlers. "The last movement is a minute long. Would it be possible to get through it without interruption?"

A few days later, a concertgoer from Hoboken had written to the *New York Times* in defense of the audience's behavior:

Perhaps Mr. Mehta should have realized he was inflicting on the audience not one but several compositions by Anton von Webern. Since many concertgoers regard performances of Webern as the musical equivalent of a visit to the dentist, audience unrest should not have been a surprise.

It is no accident that selections by Webern are generally programmed before, not after, intermission. Otherwise, few would return for the second half.

Happy that we weren't playing Webern tonight, I opened the Bolcom concerto's second oboe part while my violist friend tightened her bow hair and tuned. As the Philharmonic fell silent, conductor Leonard Slatkin, on loan again from the St. Louis Symphony, ushered the orchestra's principal clarinetist, Stanley Drucker, ahead of him. Applause thundered, and a young couple sitting front row center hooted as Stanley bounded downstage.

Stanley had something of an underground following as father to Lee Rocker, bass player of the Stray Cats rockabilly band. In fact, Stanley and his wife were the only parents who'd let the band practice in their garage. Later, when the band had become successful, the couple proudly followed them around the country like groupies.

A virtuoso showman nearing seventy, Stanley bobbed and danced, one moment a klezmer player, the next, ragtime. Today, though he didn't miss a beat, I could see he was distracted by something in the audience. During a rest, he glanced at the front row. Once, twice more. After the

Cantabile movement, Slatkin shot an icy look over his shoulder. Even the outside string players were grinning, which was a rare sight. Was there a babe? The cellos blocked my view. Finally, the first-chair cellist adjusted his chair and I could see clearly.

The Philharmonic marketers had won their quarry. The young couple sitting front row center were sipping cans of beer.

Paying audiences often attended Thursday morning open rehearsals. It was an opportunity to observe Philharmonic musicians at work. Many regular concertgoers were curious about how the conductor and orchestra prepared their performances, and seeing the musicians onstage in casual clothing served to humanize them.

At one of these dress rehearsals in 1996, on the morning of a performance of Hector Berlioz's opium-driven *Symphonie Fantastique,* an audience of two hundred took their seats in the back two-thirds of the hall that was reserved for them. Was the audience too far away from the stage to understand what they saw that morning? Two violinists, bored and frustrated from playing the same musical work many times over during their careers, started behaving like children. It was a scenario unimaginable to audiences paying high ticket prices, who expect that classical musicians live cultured, erudite, and fulfilling professional lives.

The listeners provided a smattering of applause as Czech conductor Zdenek Macal walked onstage and arranged his large score, the conductor's sheet music that includes every instrument's part in the symphony, printed one beneath the next. The second violins began rumbling, however, as soon as the Z-man, as some musicians called Macal, began the "March to the Scaffold" movement. Violinist Nathan Goldstein leaned to turn the page of his part, but his stand partner, Mark Schmoockler, whipped it back.

"Too early!" Schmoockler hissed.

Goldstein shrugged, returning to his fiddle. He reached for the next page, Schmoockler whacked his bow against the music, locking it to the stand.

Goldstein snorted. "If you're not happy with my page turning, turn them yourself!" Schmoockler stormed offstage, with Goldstein in pursuit.

It wasn't unusual for musicians to leave the stage during rehearsal—for earplugs from the backstage dispenser or a replacement string. My oboe teacher, plagued by intestinal problems, had even fled during concerts. The orchestra would wait quietly for his return, which was at least once accompanied by an audible flush from the offstage commode.

Today, these fiddlers ended up before personnel manager Carl Schiebler, who subsequently issued a written reprimand to both men, stating that their behavior was unacceptable, "absolutely unprofessional," and would not be tolerated in future. The letter warned of unspecified but "most serious consequences" for any future offense. Goldstein countered with a two-page letter to the personnel manager, which made the rounds backstage after some musician obtained a copy. The text mentioned many of the Philharmonic's members who routinely left the stage during concerts:

> *The deceitful skulduggery on Schmoockler's part enables you to cite "unprofessional behavior". . . . now let me review some history relevant to leaving the stage during rehearsals: I recall a musician, whose name I'd rather not mention and that you certainly must know, who has a physical problem, which has forced him to leave the stage several times. This colleague at one point left the stage during a concert of the subscription series. The whole orchestra and conductor waited on stage for nearly ten minutes, until he returned to his seat, and then we resumed the concert. . . .*
>
> *I also remember that [a violinist] some years ago left the stage because I dared criticize her rudeness toward me at the previous rehearsal. And what about the incredibly infantile attitude of [another violinist], leaving the stage also during a rehearsal because I asked him to turn a page now and then, in the spirit of good fellowship and collegial cooperation!*

The Goldstein case finally reached Local 802's trial board, a union version of the Supreme Court. Since the most extreme trial board penalties include expulsion from the union or prohibition from holding union office, it was unlikely that the two Philharmonic fiddlers would suffer serious consequences from Local 802. However, the case was mentioned in the union paper and therefore may have provided some sense of justice over a page poorly turned.

Just as the Goldstein case finished, another argument from across the Lincoln Center plaza came before the trial board. New York City Opera clarinetist Charlie Russo had accused French hornist Stewart Rose of yelling "You haven't played one note in tune here in two years!" The incident was sparked when Russo warmed his instrument by blowing loudly through it.

Exhibits included a letter from one City Opera violist certified as a social worker, confirming that Russo routinely annoyed the orchestra with abusive comments and ostentatious noise. He testified that this "unpleasant and hostile work environment" had momentarily driven Rose over the edge.

We were sensitive artistes indeed. Or perhaps we were just miserable employees caught in a version of cartoon character Dilbert's cubicle but with union protocol available to vent our frustrations. Why weren't we blissfully fiddling and tooting our evenings away? "All of this may come as a shock to the average concertgoer, who, from the perspective of the second balcony, sees only the 'glamorous' side of concert life," noted composer Gunther Schuller, who had also played as a New York Philharmonic French horn substitute.

Indeed, a full-time symphonic job evolves into monotony for many players. Orchestra musicians saw away like factory workers, repeating the same pieces year after year. Once a player is employed by a desirable orchestra, career advancement is severely limited. Perfectionism and injuries wear musicians down. Nighttime and holiday work disconnect them from mainstream life. Players complain they forfeit autonomy to an omnipotent conductor who works a third of their schedule, is paid as much as twenty musicians, and gets credit for the music they make.

The orchestra musician's plight caught the interest of Harvard researcher Richard Hackman, who was studying the job satisfaction of workers employed in a variety of industries. Orchestral musicians were near the bottom, scoring lower in job satisfaction and overall happiness than airline flight attendants, mental health treatment teams, beer salesmen, government economic analysts, and even federal prison guards.

Only operating room nurses and semiconductor fabrication teams scored lower than these musicians.

"All in all, membership in an orchestra is now seen as a dead-end street—a well-paid job, to be sure, but nevertheless a dead end," summed up pianist and critic Samuel Lipman.[2] Many such musicians feel a low-grade depression, sensing their professional lives are beyond their control. Seymour and Robert Levine, a father-son duo (Seymour was a Stanford psychiatrist, his son Robert a Milwaukee Symphony violist), described the syndrome in *Harmony*, the Symphony Orchestra Institute's forum:

> Subject to enough uncontrollable stress, we learn to be help-less—we lack the motivation to try to live because we assume the worst, we lack the cognitive clarity to perceive when things are actually going fine, and we feel an aching lack of pleasure in everything.

The resulting frustration would overflow during contract negotiations, the musicians' grand moment of leverage to spell out the limits of a conductor's authority, restrict rehearsal hours, control time elapsed between performances, and establish protocol regarding employment and termination. The musicians' seeming pettiness, as seen in the New York musicians' trial board complaints, represents the only power available to intelligent, educated performers who are dissatisfied with creative and professional stagnation after a lifetime of hard work and sacrifice.

The triteness of their demands, however, can lead orchestra administrators to devalue the musicians' training and commitment.

> Some orchestra managements, for example, treat their players almost as if they were a class of schoolchildren always at risk of unruliness [said Hackman]. Research findings show clearly that when you treat people like children they act like children—which, of course, then provides justification for continuing to treat them that way.[3]

The complaints of highly paid orchestra musicians looked absurd to the outside world during a rash of 1996 orchestra strikes in Philadelphia,

San Francisco, and Atlanta. Already earning $100,000 and enjoying up to ten weeks of paid vacation, these musicians parading with picket signs outside their deluxe concert halls seemed a far cry from industrial union strikes at textile and auto mills. The strikes drove away public support for what were perceived as coddled artistes, since raises demanded by the musicians would not be paid from earned revenue but by gifts from their audiences, patrons, and the volunteer board.

Many of the demands illustrated the entitlements orchestral musicians had come to expect, earned or not. During the 1996 strikes, Philadelphia Orchestra musicians demanded an annual $6,000 apiece for recording, even if the orchestra made no recordings at all. Atlanta Symphony members struck for ten weeks in the same season, when asked to reduce their orchestra size. San Francisco Symphony members walked out for nine weeks, complaining about their "grueling" twenty-three-hour weekly schedule and a change in health coverage.

It was shocking to hear the spokesman for the San Francisco musicians say that health benefits are the chief issue that put the players on the street [wrote the *Orange County Register*]. Where have they been? Nearly every American worker has had to accept a reduction in the quality of health benefits as health costs spiral higher.[4]

Where *had* they been? As the American Symphony Orchestra League's *Wolf Report* had predicted in 1992, orchestras began separating into two groups: somewhat stable big-city organiations and foundering mid-size ones, orchestras that insisted on playing year-round schedules to half-empty houses instead of shorter seasons that might sell out. Yet ASOL conferences buzzed with talk of growth, though smaller symphonies were costing their communities far more than they returned in alleged public service.

Orchestras began failing between 1991 and 1996. The San Diego, New Orleans, Denver, and Sacramento symphonies all declared bankruptcy; musicians likened their demise to the end of Western civilization. "Our orchestras are the canaries [in the coal mine]—not there to sing, just to provide a milepost on the march to barbarism," said a Sacramento

Symphony clarinetist after his paycheck disappeared. Yet almost without exception these same orchestras rose from the ashes, only to extract more money from donors before overspending their way into the same straits.

The Phoenix Symphony epitomized the small-town inferiority complex. Founded as an amateur orchestra in 1947, the group began to covet international status and expanded into a full-time orchestra between 1978 and 1982, under the direction of conductor Theo Alcantara. The longer season lured musicians, who turned down higher-paying orchestra jobs elsewhere in favor of Alcantara's promises of future tours and recordings. By 1984, however, the symphony had to beg the city of Phoenix for $650,000 to plug its $1.5 million deficit. Alcantara left in 1989, leaving Phoenix to pay for the mirage he'd built and his musicians to accept a collective $800,000 pay cut.

According to 1960s cultural theory, a community like Phoenix should maintain a holy trinity of opera, ballet, and symphony in the belief that these organizations would transform their region into a cultural mecca. The arts were expected to attract new dollars from tourism and business relocation and therefore spark local economic development. When the expansion failed in Phoenix, the symphony board was puzzled over what went wrong. "Part of the answer may be that Phoenix ain't ready for culture," explained the local paper, noting that citizens weren't interested in going to concerts every night.

The mid-nineties strikes and bankruptcies signaled a new trend, as orchestra schedules and expenses, set in motion over thirty years ago, spiraled out of control. A generation of classical musicians had become dependent on fiscal indulgence, relying on elite audiences, foundations, and government money to bail them out without questioning the value of their existence. *Orange County Register* critic Scott Duncan noted that the operation of even the most established orchestras, blessed with sizable endowments, was slowly bleeding them to death. Hearst *San Francisco Examiner* critic Allan Ulrich concurred:

> American orchestras in 1997 aren't exactly a growth industry. It's like watching the life go out of the last specimen of a nearly extinct species.[5]

* * *

I was going to the newsstand one Saturday morning when I ran into Sam in the Allendale lobby. He and Sue had rented a larger apartment across the street in 777 West End, and now he only used the Allendale place for teaching and practicing. It had been weeks since I'd seen him, and he invited me for breakfast at the Broadway Restaurant, a diner near 102nd Street.

It was about eleven o'clock, the hour when the Allendale came alive with practicing. A violinist was playing the Tchaikovsky Concerto loudly in a first-floor apartment. Some string players used heavy-metal practice mutes that muffled their sounds out of consideration for neighbors, but not this one. She was not only playing loudly and with a strident tone, but also rushing the tempo.

"Un-*speak*-ably sloppy," said Sam, gesturing with his head toward the violinist's window and mumbling something about a metronome. "Let's get out of here." As we headed down 99th, I could hear at least two cellists practicing Schubert's *Arpeggione* Sonata, Jorge's contrabassoon, and a new pianist who was playing the Grieg concerto. I listened for Sydney but didn't hear any flute at all.

We passed Marni, the Allendale spinster who ran the record label for women composers. She was wheeling a shopping cart full of boxed CDs to the Cathedral Station post office on 104th Street. As we turned the corner onto Broadway, the pharmacist at Unity Drug, who knew Sam well because of filling his eight standard prescriptions weekly, waved at us. The homeless crackhead to whom passersby gave spare change and food slept against the drugstore's 99th Street wall.

As we walked up Broadway, I told Sam about the couple drinking beer during the Philharmonic concert. He laughed and asked if I was back on the Philharmonic's list. I replied that the gig had been a onetime thing, and he quickly asked instead about my personal life.

We sat down at the Formica table inside the diner. An enormous man who always sat wedged in a window booth was murmuring to himself more loudly than ever. Sam had been not only understanding but helpful, after the romance between us fizzled. He'd fixed up a blind date for me with a male artist who was my age. I had liked Michael and his red-headed good looks, but the finances of his bohemian lifestyle had frightened me.

I told Sam that I'd given up on the orchestral audition scene and didn't even look at the ads in *International Musician* anymore. I said I wouldn't want an orchestra position even if I could win one. Orchestral music now looked to me like a dying profession, tainted with misery and greed.

We sat in silence for a few moments after giving the waiter our order. A violist I knew passed the diner window wearing a shapeless black dress and laden down with several bags plus her instrument case, heading for the 103rd Sreet subway. Her face was pinched and she was in her own world. I probably look just like that on my way to the show each night, I thought.

"Do you have enough money?" Sam asked at last, with a concerned expression. Cash flow, at least, was fine because of *Miss Saigon*. I felt ridiculous, complaining to someone in Sam's physical state, especially since he'd accomplished so much. Sam and I were growing apart. I was stuck in a dead-end career while he was immensely successful.

The waiter brought Sam's grilled cheese sandwich and my huevos rancheros, which I sprinkled liberally with Tabasco to try and cut through the wine hangover from drinking with Sydney in my apartment last night. Sam and I watched Marni pass the restaurant on her way home, now dragging her empty cart. Strands of dyed red hair fell over her face as she trudged along. Sam looked back to me and reached for my hand.

"I'm worried about you," Sam said. "What are you going to do now?"

17
The Age of Anxiety

SYDNEY AND I drove past the rusty carcass of the 1964 World's Fair as planes bound for LaGuardia roared overhead. Sydney reached for the radio, tuning to Friday afternoon traffic news. We didn't want to waste a minute after taking off work for a weekend in the Hamptons. I would have to interrupt my night and weekend work schedule if I wanted to meet more men, and we'd set aside forty-eight hours to do it.

"Music?" Sydney asked. She twirled the dial to 96.3, the *New York Times*-owned classical music station WQXR. Karl Haas droned on in a tone of voice usually reserved for misbehaving children.

"Ugh." I reached absently to punch a preset button and the pompous voice gave way to shrieking electric guitars.

I'd forgotten: WNCN had officially "rocked out." Despite archives that included treasures like Vladimir Horowitz's last interview and over fifty episodes of a show hosted by composer Aaron Copland, the station had announced that New York had one too many classical frequencies and then broadcast Haydn's *Farewell* Symphony. Ten minutes passed with the sound of a ticking time bomb before AC/DC crashed on air with "Ain't No Fun (Waiting Around to Be a Millionaire)."

News radio audiences had grown by a half million per year during the 1980s, but classical figures hadn't budged. After WNCN's demise in 1993, the FM frequency of WQXR had remained New York's only commercial classical music station. Its operations director, Loren Toolajian, had a suggestion for the producers of other classical radio shows around the country: "Lighten up! Establish a relationship. Don't act as though it's a sacred, holy, mystical thing."

WNCN had done just that at first, with inventive and casual classical programming, and as a result had increased its total audience. The station's average-listener age was getting younger as well. However, these gains weren't enough to satisfy the station owner, who changed format to cash in on the male eighteen-to-thirty-four demographic. The station had gone under once before in 1974, when it launched a new quadraphonic rock station with "Roll Over Beethoven," but the FCC had forced it back to classical for another two decades after listener complaints.

I grabbed the knob again and tuned to Top Forty WPLJ. Sydney stiffened. So did I, but in order to make conversation with the non-classical-music crowd, we should learn some modern cultural references, I thought. It was our version of Campell's Mozart Effect, only with pop music instead of classical. We settled in for the three-hour drive.

Last month, the musicians' booking service had called me to record karaoke music. The studio turned out to be the size of a tiny closet, and I squeezed behind boxes of moving blankets to the microphone. Two men in the recording booth had fiddled with their computer. Since some studios weren't yet equipped for digital music, engineers had been toting their Mac-plus computers to sessions since the 1980s, along with an electronic piano and the MIDI interface necessary for the keyboard. Loaded with samples that real instruments had recorded, these machines were making arrangers and multiple musicians virtually obsolete.

An eight-bar solo from "Penny Lane" sat on the music stand. I put on the headphones but heard nothing. "No click?" I asked, referring to the metronomic beat that usually played through the headphones so that the musician could play precisely with prerecorded tracks. "How fast does this go?"

"Oh, just the usual tempo," Ron called from the booth. I didn't know "Penny Lane," but the tune was pretty. I played the solo on the page with lyrical phrasing. The two men in the booth stared at each other. From their expressions, I thought they must have really liked my interpretation.

"'Penny Lane,' man," Ron said, irritated. "It's a lot faster. Let's try another."

I riffled through the Beatles standards, now completely lost. Ron cocked his head, then turned off my headphones while the two men conferred. I felt humiliated. They sent their assistant, a teenage boy who didn't read music, to sit beside me and give the tempos. I must seem like a geezer to this kid, I thought. I was only thirty-four.

It hadn't gone much better at my other nonclassical gig the week before, at the Blue Note jazz club. "It's the Charlie Watts Quintet," said the contractor, a violinist friend of Sydney's who was making a few extra dollars by hiring her colleagues as backup musicians. I'd been to the Blue Note when an old boyfriend took me to meet Chick Corea. But who was Charlie Watts? Soon enough, I discovered he was the drummer for the Rolling Stones. When Keith Richards showed up for the first eleven o'clock show, I discovered who he was too.

At the sound check, Watts strode to the drum kit, dapper in a suit and perfectly groomed gray hair. "Are you comfortable?" he asked. "Need anything?" Playing with Charlie's quintet was more fun than I'd ever had on the oboe, playing the solos in "Relaxing at Camarillo," "Dewey's Square," and the other tunes taken from the Charlie Parker with Strings set that Watts's alto sax player, Peter King, had arranged. I was surprised at how much I liked playing the music.

Upon discovering that the Blue Note management banished backup musicians to a cellar hallway between sets, Watts insisted we join him in his dressing room. The ten string players and I made friends easily with singer Bernard Fowler and the jazz musicians of Charlie's quintet: bassist Dave Green, pianist Brian Lemon, and the nineteen-year-old trumpeter, Gerard Presencer.

Charlie seemed more like a country gentleman than a rocker. He spoke with pride about his daughter, Seraphina, and told us about the English Tudor he shared with his sculptor wife and their twenty-seven dogs. Except for two rough collies from Elton John, the rest were former racing greyhounds, saved from postcareer euthanasia. Charlie slept with them on the bed, sometimes up to ten at once. He mentioned his obsessions, like color-coding socks to match his Savile Row suits and handmade shoes and a sketchbook filled with drawings of empty hotel beds.

I stayed late after the week's final 1 A.M. set, when Charlie threw us all a special party. At four-thirty I was ready to leave. "Careful," the Blue

Note's bouncer warned, unlocking the front door. I had expected the street to be desolate, but hundreds of people were outside, an hour before dawn. I pushed west along 3rd Street.

"Who are you?" someone asked.

"How'd *you* get in?" another asked.

"Charlie still in there? Keith?" someone else had shouted.

Listening to my Blue Note story in the car, Sydney agreed that whenever classical, pop, jazz, and rock musicians ended up together on a gig it was surprising how much we had in common. She peered at the highway signs and pointed out our exit to the Hamptons.

It was nearly sunset, so I suggested we try happy hour at a new club the restaurateur Jerry Della Femina had just opened. I'd read about it in both the *Times* and *New York* magazine. Turning onto Three Mile Harbor Road, we idled on the shoulder for a moment and watched as Jaguars, Mercedeses, and a Lamborghini drove to the restaurant's front door.

I couldn't pull up to the parking valet in this car, which fluttered with duct tape and corroding metal. Sydney pointed toward the Dumpster, which had a comforting familiarity; it resembled the ones that stood by my Broadway theater's stage door and Sydney's too. I jammed The Club on my steering wheel and beeped the car alarm. Sydney looked out over the water view as I primped a bit. It took several tries to apply my lipstick, since I never wore it when it would clog up my reeds. Perfume was another guilty pleasure, strictly forbidden in the close confines of pits and orchestras.

"The air feels so good," said Sydney, throwing her arms wide. She glanced at her watch, noting that it was show time on Broadway. What a relief to shed black pit clothes on a hot summer night.

Our arrival on foot flustered the parking valet, who ushered us inside to a loud happy-hour crowd. Sydney and I exchanged glances and ordered chardonnay at the bar. "Oops, sorry," I said, bumping into a dark-haired man who looked like a model from *GQ* magazine. He was an analyst at Lazard Freres, whatever that was.

"We're *musicians*," I said proudly.

His eyes narrowed. Musicians?

"Yes," Sydney chimed in, "classical musicians."

His eyes drifted over the crowd, toward a gaggle of blond gazelles. He must not believe us, I thought.

"No, honest," I said. "New York Philharmonic, American Symphony, Orpheus Chamber Orchestra, that sort of thing."

He turned back to us with a confused expression. "But what do you *really* do?" he said with a sneer, and then immediately made eye contact with someone across the room. Indignant, I tried to answer, but towering blondes were closing in on him, teetering in strappy high-heeled sandals, with designer logos emblazoned on their sunglasses, purses, baby Ts. I looked down at my two-year-old Keds and the fraying crochet of an $18 outlet sweater.

I suddenly felt dowdy, outfitted head to toe in cheap clothing that didn't quite match. The beautiful women in this restaurant understood this high-class social scene and had money to dress for it. I glimpsed my reflection in a sliding-glass door and suddenly saw myself as hopelessly unfashionable and out of touch.

Sydney got me another drink, and we wove through the smoky bar out onto the deck. At the railing, a model-perfect redhead played with her balding companion's ponytail, cooing in his ear. Watching them, I tapped absently on my glass.

One happy hour down, one show's income wasted. Sydney gazed distantly over the water at the sky's pink embers. In disappointing situations like this she was always attracted by something in the distance. I squinted to make it out what she saw, but the horizon looked empty to me.

The ocean view, however, was familiar, as I had watched the sun set over Gardiner's Bay near here once. I was visiting my recital manager, Lee, at the time, and I remembered that he lived nearby. Lee came from a different era in East Hampton's history, when the hamlet was still an outpost for maverick artists after the 1940s. Before Jerry Della Femina, Jaguars, and astronomical summer rentals, Lee and his lover, a painter, had joined these people in an artists' community named Springs after the Accabonac Creek's source.

Sydney and I found a pay phone, called Lee, and were soon relaxing by the swimming pool in his backyard with yet another glass of wine. It was a relief to be away from the glitzy crowd and in the company of an old friend. Lee's lover had died and I suspected he was lonely. The conversation quickly turned to talk of dating. Why weren't two beautiful classical musicians like Sydney and me married? Lee asked. Were we too picky?

No, I assured him. I liked bald men, short men, men without college degrees. I wasn't prejudiced. It was just hard for classical musicians to meet anyone eligible, I said.

Sydney shot me a look.

"Well, yeah, the married ones weren't so smart," I admitted. Back in my early twenties, men my age lived in squalor, and the ones I met in orchestras were either geriatric or already spoken for. By their thirties, though, responsible guys had jumped ship for a career that could support a family. That left people outside the business, who were difficult to meet and had peculiar notions about us anyway. Outsiders were forever intimidated by musicians, whom they imagined as erudite superintellects.

"Ha! Musicians are more like blue-collar workers than PhDs," Sydney joked. She had a point. Music performance was a specific craft that was perfected more by practice than analysis. Our colleagues' narrow focus sometimes made for dull conversation too, centering around dirty jokes, shop talk, and expensive wining and dining that everyone pretended they could afford.

I'd already dated almost every classical musician around my age. Working six nights a week, I didn't run into the after-work crowd, and even when I found a date, my share of dinner and perhaps show tickets, plus lost income from sending a sub to *Miss Saigon,* would approach $300.

I had met some nice men in the past, like Peter, a Harvard alum and commercial composer. In trying to tone down my sexual exuberance, I went too far and we never really connected. Tom, the trombonist, was sweet, but I feared being asked to produce ten children as his Catholic mother had done. Fred, the cellist, had been too old and too conservative. He also fell asleep once during sex, pinning me to the brass bed with its bass- and treble-clef signs that he'd once shared with his violinist ex-wife.

For a brief period, my debut recital gave me a more exotic image than the average freelance musician. A dynamic Broadway conductor took me out to dinner but quickly married a beautiful dark-haired composer who wrote a light opera that later made it to Broadway.

Next came a clarinetist old enough to be my father. Then a classical composer who asked me to return a birthday present when no relationship materialized between us. I tried my old boyfriends again, just in case, and then became more aggressive, pouncing on a cute guy in the Raleigh-Durham airport while visiting my parents. I accepted his first-date invitation to drink wine in his apartment, but he was forty-five minutes late. I waited. We drank. I went home. He never called again.

Then there were dating services. Paunchy nerds populated the Classical Music Lovers' Exchange. The service for bookworms turned up a handwritten note on Harvard letterhead from an insect-studying Indiana Jones character; I chalked up his eccentricity to his fascination with bugs, though there was also that troublesome childhood head injury. We traveled between my place in New York and his townhouse in Boston. Finally, we spent four weeks together on a trip to Central America, where I discovered he rocked and chanted and had a temper that bordered on violence. I ditched him.

Next came a fling with *National Geographic's* "Afghan Girl" photographer Steve McCurry. Personal ads turned up a handsome doctor who treated terminal patients with nutritional therapy borrowed from a Texas orthodontist. He didn't much like the preshow treatment. I didn't like reading his entry on Quackwatch, which mentioned coffee enemas and two malpractice suits.

I dined alone at bars before the show, but no one was in the pickup mode that early. Post-theater, the crowd was too drunk. Recently, Boston Pops conductor Keith Lockhart had been asking me out for late-night drinks when he was in town, even though he had recently married. I went and drank in his hotel room, cuddled, and returned home without having sex.

As a final insult after all this lackluster dating, the Hudson Valley Philharmonic had asked me to pose in a wedding dress for our annual calendar, parodying Smetana's *Bartered Bride* overture. I stood in the display window of Poughkeepsie's downtown bridal shop, offering my oboe to passersby. The elderly ladies who worked there swarmed around, pinning back the size twelve gown on my small frame. "Dear, you look so beautiful as a bride, why don't you get married?" she asked. Hung over, I was too tired to reply.

Sydney and I stayed beside Lee's pool until late, drinking red wine and enjoying the ocean air and chirping crickets. After saying good-bye the next morning, we drove out to the Hotel Montauket, an old boardinghouse near Montauk Point. We'd try a more downscale approach tonight. After dressing, we went downstairs and ordered plastic cups of white wine from the bar, carrying them outside to watch the sun set over Gardiner's Bay. I'd heard that Billy Joel hung out here, but we didn't see any single men. I regretted taking off from all those shows.

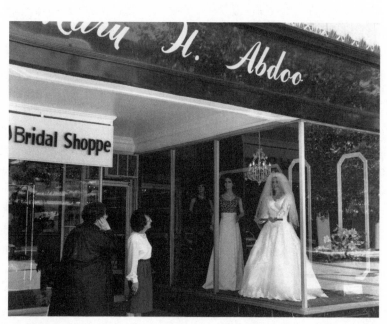

Playing "The Bartered Bride" in a publicity photograph for the Hudson Valley Philharmonic, Poughkeepsie, New York. (Michele Muir)

"I don't know what younger musicians are going to do," lamented Sydney, as we watched the water turn dark. "With my show, I can play out my career, I guess." Sydney's hit had already run for six years and was expected to last for many more.

The sun was low enough to cast a flattering light on Sydney's skin. She patted her cheeks with both hands, mumbling something about getting her face fixed. She looked exhausted, with a recent weight gain hinting at Betty's middle-aged figure. She was sliding toward Allendale spinsterhood, and I was right behind her. Between the Chinese Cottage restaurant's free wine before the show and microwaved nachos after, my mind and belly were growing soft. No amount of effort ever paid off, so what the hell, I thought. I stepped inside the Montauket's bar for another plastic cup of white wine.

I dropped by Sam's apartment in the Allendale one afternoon to lend him a little money until he could get to the bank. He often borrowed small amounts from me but always repaid it promptly. I mentioned that Sydney had asked about him.

"Oh, really," Sam said, in a disbelieving tone I'd rarely heard him use. He picked up the goose-stepping Nazi toy soldier I'd given him as a joke. "Sydney's cold. She acts like I should treat her like a princess." I'd already heard the same from other men.

Sydney's attitude had gotten to me as well. Since she did me favors, some of them substantial, I felt guilty for thinking of her in a bad light. Still, I could no longer ignore the feeling that she expected superior treatment, more because of her appearance than her accomplishments. She was no longer the woman I'd worshiped ten years ago. Now she represented the culture of entitlement I was coming to despise. I wanted to tear away from her but did not know where to start. My habits, after all, were just as destructive as hers.

Meanwhile, Sam had remained enthusiastic about music and worked hard for recognition. His new heart was holding up well, and he looked healthier than I'd ever seen him. Itzhak was finally embracing him on a personal level too, he said, telling me that he'd been invited to bring

Sue for a casual dinner at Itzhak's new brownstone, just the two couples. I already knew the dinner was just a ruse for a surprise party Itzhak was planning.

Grabbing my keys the evening of the party, I took a last glance in the mirror. I'd taken extra care to iron my silk pantsuit from Fowad. With my hair carefully blow-dried and makeup applied, I almost looked like I belonged with Sam's upscale friends.

I found a cab and gave the address of the brownstone Itzhak had just bought on 70th Street. When I arrived, I joined the other guests on a tour our host was leading. His place was at least four floors, with intricate woodwork and detail worked into every room. He showed off their remodeled wheelchair-accessible kitchen, which looked out over a garden. An elevator connected all the floors, including the basement lap pool. Itzhak's wife, Toby, must have an eye for design, I thought, since the fabrics and colors worked together seamlessly.

After the tour, I chatted in the living room with Judy LeClair, the Philharmonic's principal bassoonist. Her husband, Jonathan Feldman, taught in Juilliard's accompanying department with Sam. John Corigliano noodled on the piano, while composers, musicians, journalists, and a few philanthropic friends mingled.

One of Itzhak's kids called from the corner pay phone: Sam was coming. In the darkened room, I wondered how Sam would take this party. He didn't need to cultivate Itzhak, since the two spent days traveling together. What was special about his expectations tonight was that he believed Itzhak wanted to establish a genuine social connection instead of their professional relationship of musical superstar and supporting artist. I heard Sam's doddering Alice Tully imitation outside, as he climbed the steps with Sue.

"Surprise!" the crowd shouted. The room flooded with light. People jumped from behind the furniture. Sam frowned, glancing down at his special Yankees jersey that Martin had gotten him as a gift from the team, but he quickly forced a broad smile. Trays of hors d'oeurves and champagne flutes appeared. Sam rapped on a crystal glass with a tiny silver pencil from the piano for our attention.

"This is incredible!" he said. "I want to thank the people who were there for me, who helped me through the transplant," he continued, his voice rising. I flushed as several faces turned toward me. Everyone knew I'd played the martyr role, going by the hospital daily when many of them didn't visit him once. Margo Garrett, who'd also nursed him, would have liked this celebration, but she wasn't invited. Neither was Sam's brother.

"Thank you, all of you who visited me in the hospital," he said, his voice stronger now. Then Sam ticked off a list of names. People who gave him work. People he hoped would give him work. The very people who had abandoned him.

He did not mention me.

After a round of applause, someone started roasting Sam with songs at the piano. I slipped through Itzhak's fancy kitchen, out into the humid summer night, and walked toward Columbus Avenue. It hurt like hell.

When I got home, I put on a recording of Mahler's Sixth Symphony and blasted it. The work was sometimes called his "Tragic" symphony, and although it was written during one of the happiest times in the composer's life, its dark, brooding melodies and dissonant chords presaged the anguish Mahler would feel only two years later when his young daughter died. This music soothed me, because listening to its emotional depth was far more painful than anything I was feeling tonight.

After the first two movements of the symphony, I opened a bottle of wine and called Sydney, out of habit. She'd just gotten home from her show and came downstairs. She listened to my story of Itzhak's party with empathy. I felt even more guilty to be considering Sydney so scornfully when she could also be this kind. I wasn't happy, I told her. I wanted to do something else for a living. Maybe I could go to law school, although I wasn't sure what lawyers did. Two musicians I knew had done this. However, one Juilliard grad I knew said that Harvard Law had turned her down because they didn't accept candidates with "trade school" degrees. I didn't think I was smart enough anyway.

"Why don't you get an MBA then?" Sydney asked. "It should be a piece of cake after music," she said, suggesting I look into one of those courses at Kaplan Test Prep. I wondered why she didn't follow her own advice. She'd been an academic star in high school, and her music career wasn't exactly front-page news either. But she was encouraging and made me feel a spark of hope.

Sydney and I rode the 1 train, clutching the overhead handles. Tonight we had drunk nearly two liters of the free white wine at the Cottage Chinese restaurant. As the train screeched to a halt in the 96th Street station, I offered her a Breath Asure, a gelatin capsule filled with peppermint and parsley that was advertised to clean your breath from the inside out. Sydney refused.

"Everybody else does drinks before the show," Sydney said, waving the mints away. "I mean, it's the only way to get through it." I knew it was wrong to play inebriated when people were paying $100 to hear you, but here I was, blotto. I'd smelled other boozy musicians in the pit too. At *Les Miz*, a trumpeter stepped across to McHale's at intermission, and one of the horn subs frequently took a mid-show "botanical walk."

We both got off at Times Square, as I'd missed the 50th Street stop in my stupor. We fought a wall of people upstairs, surging through tourists at the turnstiles. My oboe backpack walloped people left and right as we battled north on Broadway. Sydney rolled her eyes and groaned as she stepped into the bike lane. She turned onto 45th at her theater and I staggered uptown. Lurching into my chair at 7:59 P.M., I jammed my instruments together, gave the tuning note, and swallowed a dab of minty toothpaste. I folded the *Times* crossword on my music stand.

I was too drunk to read. The letters blurred together. I stuffed the crossword in the trash and stared at the empty stand. I'd played this music so many times, my fingers moved on automatic pilot. This was no way for an intelligent person to be spending her thirties, I thought vaguely. Tomorrow I'd find out about this MBA thing.

The following week I waited in a classroom, three sharp pencils ready. Sydney was right, Kaplan was just what I needed to get up to speed. This afternoon I was about to take their free trial exam to analyze my weaknesses for the Graduate Management Admission Test, which was required to apply to business school. An instructor passed out the materials, and I opened my booklet eagerly. Pencils scratched furiously around me.

If it is 250 miles from New York to Boston and 120 miles from New York to Harford, what percentage of the distance from New York to Boston is the distance from New York to Hartford?

Percentages. We didn't cover that in music school. Next?

It costs x dollars each to make the first thousand copies of a compact disk and y dollars to make each subsequent copy. If z is greater than 1,000, how many dollars will it cost to make z copies of the compact disk?

Too hard for me. Next? My optimism was draining quickly. I really was too stupid to do anything but play the oboe. I lingered as the room emptied and the instructor tucked the papers into her bag. When she looked expectantly at me, I bit my lip, the booklet dangling from my fingers.

"I didn't know the math—" I started. I'd earned a D-minus in algebra twenty years ago, my last quantitative course. The instructor glanced at my blank answer sheet, asking my background. As I answered, I imagined her thoughts dancing in a cartoon bubble over her head.

Musicians are good at math. Why wouldn't you want to be a musician anyway? You do what you love all day long. Know the one about Danny Kaye?

I turned and ran down the steps before she had a chance to answer. Heading west on 56th, I blubbered past the City Center stage door, Carnegie Hall, Patelson's House of Music. I was already thirty-five. I could never even get into a community college. I'd languish in the pit every night until the show closed. Then I'd be in my forties, unemployed, uneducated, unmarried.

I cried as I barged down Seventh Avenue, my messy path weaving to 53rd, past the elegant theatergoers and their $100 *Miss Saigon* tickets. Nobody noticed me. Nobody ever noticed any of us. The stage doorman reading his *New York Post* didn't even bother to look up.

At thirty-five, I felt even more washed-up than I had at twenty-six, when I'd burned my best freelance connections. Back then there were rays of hope. I thought I'd get married. Surely I'd win an orchestra audition if I just kept at it. I'd had an unconscious belief that other careers would be open to me if I wanted them. Now every one of those doors appeared to be firmly shut.

Third Movement
Symphonic
Metamorphoses

One of the Allendale's stone lions, a remnant from the building's days as a luxury residence.

18
Airlift from Saigon

TWO DEEPLY TANNED men loaded nets into their dinghy as the sun sank between Inner and Outer Brass, steep rocky islands dropped into the azure sea off northern St. Thomas. I hung my wetsuit across the concrete balcony railing to dry.

The Virgin Islands house-sitting invitation couldn't have come at a better time. I would live here, and scuba dive for free, for two months just for taking care of Shivaya, the black Lab snoozing at my feet. I'd have time and solitude to consider my life and what I would do next.

I'd first visited St. Thomas on a short trip with my parents a few months earlier, in the winter after Sydney and I had gone man-hunting in the Hamptons. That was when I'd seen Shivaya's owner, Homer, loading scuba tanks near a resort's private beach. His muscles rippled beneath his tank top. When he caught me staring, I hurried into the dive shop and claimed the last spot on the beginner's dive.

Homer fitted my weight belt with extra care, cinching it tightly around my waist before leading me into the surf. Terrified, I concentrated on breathing, hardly seeing the colorful fish or Caribbean lobster peeking out from the rocks. Suddenly I felt dizzy, as if I'd gotten out of bed too fast. Suspended underwater, I swirled round and round inside a kaleidoscope of soft corals, then fuzzy whiteness, then black. Gradually, blue light shimmered and Homer's mask came into focus. He held me tight with one arm, signaling "Okay?"

Up, up! I pointed. He shook his blond head no, folding a hand around mine to lead me across the sandy bottom, past conch trails, clownfish, a green moray gaping from its cave. Feeling safe at last, I began to enjoy the strange underwater sights. After we surfaced, I thanked Homer, and he invited me over for a barbecue that night.

Homer had a routine for lady tourists like me, at his cement hurricane-proof bunker far from the island's glitzy hotels. He put his big arms around me as we looked at the horizon through the glass louvers of his windows that faced the sea. His hard body glistened like nothing I'd seen back in New York. He reminded me of Walter, the Argentine tour guide I'd met in the jungle years before. Homer slid his huge hand around me and unbuttoned my cutoffs. I was thirty-five and turned on for the first time in my life.

On this return trip, Homer and I had been sharing the house for two weeks until he left to visit family in Tennessee. He took one afternoon to show me the details of homeowning. Here's the cistern's water level. It has to last all summer. Be careful after dark; cops don't come to the north side of St. Thomas. Frenchies take the law into their own hands, just like in their French Huguenot village back on St. Bart's. Homer turned to a side table, reaching under a pile of cloth napkins. In one motion, he pulled out a Glock semiautomatic pistol and released its cartridge, snapping it back into place. There was a .38 special under the bed too.

Now I was alone in the house with the guns. It was eight o'clock. In New York, *Miss Saigon*'s curtain was rising now in its fourth year. My misery over such a good job seemed absurd, when everyone here on St. Thomas earned far less and worked harder, if they found work at all. Despondent, I stared at the Glock's muzzle, poking out from the napkins.

I hadn't told anyone I was seriously contemplating suicide. After failing the business school test so thoroughly, I was convinced I would be unable to support myself once the show closed. My plan was to give myself at least six weeks to try to sort out where I might fit in to the mainstream world I'd never known. If I could not find my way, I planned to use this gun.

After two weeks, though, I had calmed down enough to relax. For several years I had spent the evenings honking away in a dusty pit. Now I wanted to learn what other people did at night. Read? Cook a full dinner? I didn't even know when to go to bed. Reggae pulsed from the Frenchies' beach bar. Maybe I'd go there for a beer and tell everyone I was a rock star, a Romanian contessa, a real-estate mogul. The clouds turned pink as I headed down to Hull Bay. Shivaya bounded over to a blond man across the beach as if she knew him, and I never made it to the bar. Minutes later, the man and I walked back up the hill together to his tiny cottage right below mine.

Pete owned one of the dive concessions on St. Thomas. His one-room house was perched on a cliff just above the lobster holes in Hull Bay. "You're a nice little package," he said, rubbing my shoulders. We made love to the pounding surf below.

Soon, flowers showed up on my doorstep, then gifts from his dive shop—a swimsuit and funky flip-flops. Tall, handsome, and successful, Peter wouldn't have stayed single for an instant in New York. Here on St. Thomas, the bars were full of virile men, desperate for female companions. Homer had pointed out that he knew most of these men from AA meetings, but I didn't care. For two months I'd behave like they did, without thought of a permanent relationship.

My daily routine started each morning when I met the boat from Homer's diving company for their group trip underwater. As long as I tipped twenty dollars, the divemasters welcomed me aboard for free, especially if I tipped theatrically, which encouraged customers to tip generously too.

Today's group included a doctor from Boston, a London media exec, and a pair of fit construction workers from Texas, their wives and girl-friends left to lounge beside the Hyatt's pool in pricey resort clothes. Usually, I was the only woman aboard.

I stole a glance at Eric, who was helping customers suit up. He was a scuba instructor straight from central casting: yellow hair, hard muscles, and a macramé necklace of bleached seashells and leather. I chatted with the construction workers, who were fascinating to a late-night Broadway vampire like me. The conversation between the tourists and me on the dive boat was always the same.

"Where's your husband?"

"How long have you lived here?"

"How do you get two months off from work?"

Eric gave me a sidelong smirk. He knew all about glamorous jobs. Strapping on my tank, I splashed backward into the water to wait. Down thirty feet to the bottom, I lay on the sand, looking up at clouds through the clear water's surface. My hair drifted in a halo turned honey-colored by the sun.

I wasn't scared to dive anymore, after swimming against currents a hundred feet deep and stroking the sandpaper skin of a nurse shark. I earned a divemaster certification, addicted to the idea that I could move ahead at anything after the inertia of the classical music business. I listened to strange underwater sounds and could barely remember myself onstage, nervously fretting over a tiny piece of bamboo.

I became more attracted to Eric each day as I watched him help divers down the anchor line, his calf flexing with each fin stroke. I could tell the interest was mutual, and on his day off we made a date to dive together. Eric brought the equipment, and we swam underwater near Coki Beach, past the snorkelers' baby reef and out to the sand flats fifty feet deep. Conchs peeked from their shells, leaving long trails on the ocean floor as the sunlight dappled the sand. A diver's playground lay beyond the sand flats, with square, round, and triangular hula hoops for certification tests tethered to cinder blocks, the ocean's depth diffusing their neon colors. Eric and I played tag, twisting in and out of the narrow openings. I'd never felt so weightless and free. We hung suspended halfway between the surface and bottom in an embrace, until our air was nearly gone. On the beach, we ditched our gear in Eric's car and then headed for Homer's.

I flipped on the stereo to whatever I'd left in the CD changer. French horns and violas wailed as Mahler's Sixth Symphony started, its lush chords and complex rhythm rising over the reggae coming from the beach. When Eric's body froze, I rushed back to switch off the music, but stopped when Eric turned from the sunset, his expression earnest and intense.

"I never heard anything like that before," Eric said, setting down his Red Stripe beer.

"You're faking it," I teased. His hurt look convinced me he wasn't lying. I picked out the "Adagietto" from Mahler's Fifth, Bernstein's favorite. I slid back beside him in the hammock, and the string harmonies sailed through the house and out over the Caribbean.

"This music. Why haven't I heard it before?" he asked.

The next morning, I phoned Sydney, asking her for more CDs from my apartment. I was eager to tell her why, but I first had to endure the latest pit report.

"It's sooo awful," she wailed. "I give up! I quit!"

She was exhausted from all her jobs. If only someone would let her have a moment to herself. "The show conductor is terrible! Why does he hate me so much anyway?" she cried. No one would let her play first flute anymore on freelance gigs. Even Jersey Symphony called someone else before calling her.

"Why would you care?" I asked. She'd voluntarily quit her full-time position there more than fifteen years ago.

Before she could answer, my news bubbled out of me. Sunshine and blue ocean, scuba divers, and Mahler. Dating three men at once with no strings! Life seemed a pleasure here, not the repetitive, pointless drudgery of practicing and playing for audiences who only came for the "star" soloist. I was learning to smell the roses, savor the simple things. I had made chutney from the mangoes in Homer's yard . . .

From Sydney's complaints, I realized how far I'd come in only six weeks from feeling so miserable. I was enjoying the smallest moments of each day. As I relaxed, I was even starting to love classical music again. My turnabout reminded me of Sam's beatific expression as he listened to Schubert in his hospital room after a monthlong respite from the relentless work schedule that was required to earn a good living in freelance classical music.

As Sydney and I hung up, I caught a glimpse of the gun under Homer's cloth napkins. I had forgotten it was there.

The stage doorman at *Miss Saigon* tried to stop me from entering; he hadn't recognized me with my nut-brown skin and light blond hair. I looked very different; New York was the same. The conductor, Rieling, was just as nasty and the show was repetitive as ever.

The Allendale hadn't changed either. Jorge growled away on his contrabassoon downstairs. Slava Polozov vocalized next door, and I could faintly hear a flute playing Brahms's Fourth, maybe Brian, who moved in last year. Or even Sydney. I couldn't identify her sound anymore, now that she was trying different instruments to replace the stolen Powell flute.

Sam practiced violently and was more robust than ever. Returning from his first-ever Caribbean vacation with Sue, he was filled with the energy of a man in love. The humiliation I remembered from Itzhak's party was still upsetting, though. I had confronted Sam the day after, bursting into tears. He apologized weakly and urged me to understand that he was in the unexpected situation of a surprise party. Grudgingly I had accepted his words, but I believed he never valued the intense time I had devoted to looking after him during his illness.

Back from the Caribbean, I decided to put my bad feelings behind me and accept our now-distant friendship. I was looking forward to turning pages for him later this afternoon, when he and Itzhak would perform for the David Letterman show. I followed Sam into the Ed Sullivan Theater where Letterman taped the show, across the street from *Saigon*'s stage door. An assistant led us upstairs to the dressing rooms, where the other guest, political commentator Cokie Roberts, talked with Itzhak.

When it was time for their performance, I placed the Sarasate showpiece on the piano and sat quietly as Itzhak and Sam began playing. I hadn't heard them in a while. Tonight their emotional energy was stronger and more poignant than ever.

Letterman finished taping at six-thirty, and the *Saigon* stagehands had heard of my minor celebrity by showtime. I returned to obscurity soon enough, though, and *Saigon* continued on repetitiously eight times a week. Playing, reading, and ignoring Rieling, my mind wandered off to friends on St. Thomas, and especially to Eric. I realized I had fallen in love with him but had no way to tell him so. Hurricane Marilyn had battered the island of St. Thomas, destroying 90 percent of its buildings. No one came or went. The phones didn't work. Three weeks passed before Eric finally called.

"Come right away," I urged, the words a surprise even to me as I invited him to ship his belongings and move in with me permanently. Soft snow fell the morning he arrived. Living in Hawaii, American Samoa, and the Caribbean, Eric hadn't visited the mainland in seven years. He'd never seen the World Trade Center, the Empire State Building, or Brooklyn Bridge. He didn't have winter clothes.

At the Allendale, he searched his suitcases but found only one pair of long pants. Rob Fisher lent us a sweater, and my large *Saigon* show jacket just fit around Eric's solid torso. Socks and sneakers came from Sam, who regarded my island boy with curiosity.

"Your friend Sam doesn't look so good," whispered Eric, as Sam closed his door.

"You should've seen him before," I replied.

The snow accumulated, and at twenty inches the city declared a curfew. For the first time in years, Broadway went dark. With my unexpected night off, we bundled up and headed to Broadway and 105th. Eric caught flakes on his tongue and kicked up drifts with Sam's shoes.

Eric held open the door of Birdland, letting jazz music, smoke, and heat drift out. We ordered a bottle of Pinot Noir, and he leaned backward against the bar, wrapping his arms around my waist to watch the blizzard. "Hey, get a room," a woman chided. Eric gave her a long look and buried his face in my hair.

In the next few weeks, Eric adjusted to city life easily. He did the grocery shopping and filled my refrigerator with spinach lasagna, casseroles, and exotic chicken dishes. When I came home at eleven each night, Eric set an elegant table with my hodgepodge of dishes and played Vivaldi, Bach, or some new favorite of his on the stereo. He drizzled arugula and red globe grapes with walnut oil, arranged pink lamb chops atop wild rice with blanched almonds, or served up some other delicious combinations that never would have occurred to me.

Eric found a minimum-wage job selling dive equipment at Paragon Sports on Union Square. He did our laundry, moved the car on alternate-side parking days, vacuumed, scrubbed the toilet, and fixed the leaky faucet Angelo couldn't.

While I played the show at night, he trained as a police auxiliary volunteer. This man, generous with his affection and household responsibilities, was also showing me a social awareness. The fact that his employment opportunities were limited by his lack of a college education didn't matter, I told myself. It had all been so easy, as if I'd just been looking for love in the wrong places.

*   *   *

Eric looked happy as he crossed the street to Lincoln Center. I'd bought him a late Christmas present, tickets to hear a live orchestra for the first time. The Philharmonic was performing his favorite, Mahler's Fifth. The price, $140 for two second-tier box seats, was shocking. I couldn't afford to hear the Philharmonic very often as an audience member. Although Philharmonic and freelance musicians sometimes got two free seats to bring guests to a concert they were playing in themselves, there was no other way to obtain cheaper seats, even for an insider like me.

Eric entered Avery Fisher Hall's lobby and spread his arms beneath Richard Lippold's dangling brass *Orpheus and Apollo* sculpture. He presented our tickets proudly and walked upstairs, where a surly usher pulled open the box's door and pointed to our seats. Inside, a fortyish couple studied their Stagebills. I recognized them from years back, when I played frequently at the Philharmonic. They always sat in this box. The wife pushed back her velvet headband, and an assortment of jeweled tennis bracelets on her right wrist made a tinkling sound.

"Pardon us," Eric said patiently, using his best manners. The woman pressed herself backward as we squeezed by, her eyes inspecting my scuffed boots, Levi's, and faded black pullover and Eric's cheap cotton shirt and chinos. Her upper lip curled.

Had I stepped in something?

I checked my boots as the musicians trickled onstage. Gary Levinson shifted his fiddle and bow to his right hand, slapping the back of a cellist's tailcoat as he passed.

"Isn't that funny! Almost like they're greeting each other at work," said the husband, chuckling.

"What are they playing again, Mahler? Do I know that one?" the wife asked. She waved enthusiastically to another couple in the balcony.

Eric studied the stage. "Which guy plays principal French horn?" he asked. "Is that the grand harp, the one with the pedals you told me about?" The woman snorted, crossing her legs away from us.

When trumpeter Philip Smith sounded the work's first triplets, Eric closed his Stagebill and sat up straight, hands folded neatly in his lap. The violins began their simple tragic lament, their phrasing precise yet rife with emotion, as if they were speaking an elegiac poem for a loved one who had died. As Sarah Bullen wove her harp chords through the string harmonies of the "Adagietto," the ethereal sound floating with a warmth recordings never quite captured, Eric closed his eyes and squeezed my hand contentedly.

The husband jiggled his foot irregularly, shaking our entire row of seats. He cleared his throat loudly, then stretched his arm out to check the time. As Sarah's harp grew delicate, the wife crinkled cellophane in her bag, its chain shoulder strap rattling. She popped a cough drop in her mouth and crunched. Flipping through the program, she studied a page of restaurant endorsements from actors. One of my show's stars had just been recruited to appear on the page. He didn't get to pick the restaurant or write the description of his dinner but he ate free in return for the quote.

"I think it's almost over," said the wife, tugging her husband's cuff thirty seconds into the eleven-minute Rondo. Gathering their shopping bags, they left noisily.

After the show I took Eric to Café des Artistes as a romantic finale to our night out. Seated in the casual bar area hidden in the back, we ordered martinis and split an order of steak tartare. After laughing over the stuffy couple, talk turned more serious as we discussed marriage, children, and a new career for me. Eric said he'd help me find my way.

Next morning I called City College to ask about remedial math courses. A grouchy man answered the math department's phone. He asked how old I was, and why I wanted to enroll. I wasn't sure if he was a graduate student doing work-study, a professor, or office staff. Upon hearing the answer, he said they didn't offer that elementary a course and told me I was lucky to be a musician.

"Please," I begged. If so many people wanted to be musicians, why did the National Endowment for the Arts say the number of people playing and performing classical music had dropped by half?

"Musicians are good at math," he replied. "If you need help at your age, there's nothing for you here." He slammed down the phone.

I wondered if I'd been the victim of a phone prank. Even so, maybe he was right, and adults couldn't learn math. As I kept searching, I didn't find a beginning course except at Columbia University, which cost $2,500 and carried no credit. Finally, Eric found a course at the New School: ten weeks for $500. I could go Saturday mornings before my matinee.

Filled with optimism, I climbed the stairs to a class of all women, every one Latina or African-American except for me. A rainbow of gaily colored notebooks and sharp pencils lay on the desks. A woman next to me tore the cellophane off a new calculator.

Here in the classroom, I felt I'd joined the world that existed outside classical music. I sat, pencil poised, as a little man strode to the blackboard and scratched aggressively in chalk. He turned to us with a sneer, and all the women tensed their faces to study his scribblings:

$$-4,928/249 - 217/1099 - x/91,043 = 1/31 + 8,007/x - 7,397/1,835$$

What was the x for again? I didn't remember which part of the fraction got divided or how to add negative numbers. A few women hunched over their desks, concentrating. Most stared forward vacantly. I could tell the woman next to me was about to cry.

After class, I dragged myself uptown for the matinee while planning how to maximize my dinnertime booze consumption. The show went slowly; I fought back tears, feeling like a spoiled brat to be upset while I had this high-paying job. When Eric picked me up for dinner, I whimpered about the teacher, the women, and my hopelessness.

"This is fucked," he said. Grabbing my wrist, he led me to Coliseum Books. Eric had rarely seen the inside of a bookstore, but he marched to the information desk and found the class's assigned book in no time. The text started with one plus one and included a toll-free homework help number.

After dinner, Eric went home to read, and I returned to *Miss Saigon* for the evening show. The night flew by as I started reading my new math book. By the final curtain calls, I could already solve some simple problems. Maybe there was hope after all.

I walked home to burn off my new energy. In the window of the 72nd Street HMV store, big cardboard cutouts of the Three Tenors posed corpulently next to a CD jacket photo of violinist Vanessa-Mae Nicholson, the sheer sleeve of her white blouse slipping off her bow arm's shoulder.

Pushing open the door, I took a break in the store's air-conditioning. I looked for the classical CDs and found they'd been crammed into a back corner. The area was nearly deserted, except for two college-age guys. One of them had rented *Amadeus* the previous night.

The pair cruised down a quiet aisle, passing Bach, Copland, and Mahler before finding Mozart, Mozart, and more Mozart covering the store's entire back wall. The *Jupiter* Symphony took up several rows, as nearly every orchestra in the world has recorded it at least three times. It was only one of over six hundred of the composer's works.

"Why are there all these CDs of the same piece? Are they really all that different?" asked one, sounding as if he felt stupid. The men stared at the vast selection for a moment. "And which ones were in the movie?"

"I dunno, man," said his friend, looking around nervously. "This classical stuff is over my head. Isn't there an *Amadeus* soundtrack or something?"

Overhearing their conversation, I felt both distressed and relieved. I was sad that classical music was so confusing to newcomers. At the same time, the two guys had articulated something I'd always wondered. Why *were* there all these recordings of the same old pieces if classical music sales were already so low? No pop star in her right mind would put out an album of the same songs as a competing artist.

It took a couple of strange men who didn't know anything about classical music to make me realize I wasn't nuts after all. I was in a narcissistic industry that was stuck in the nineteenth century. At that moment, I gave myself permission to escape.

19
Smoke and Mirrors

I OPENED THE Broadway Theatre's stage door for Eric, who had wanted to come and see what my job was really like. Just inside, an actor was rummaging through a large paper bag full of day-old bread, which was distributed weekly to all Broadway theaters by neighborhood restaurants. Eric flattened himself against the bulletin board as a dresser heaved his basket of costumes up the narrow stairs. I explained to him that the dresser was a wardrobe expert who organized costumes. He was assigned to one or more actors to make sure their clothing changes went smoothly, and also maintained a system of washing and mending costumes and sending them out for dry cleaning and dying.

The Broadway Theatre had been built in 1924 as a movie palace and converted to theatrical use in 1930. Although it was one of Broadway's largest houses, with 1,700 seats, the backstage was still cramped from the days when shows didn't need the extensive sets, electronics, and other items that were now crammed in every corner. The actors' dressing rooms were on the theater's upper floors, and the pit was one floor down.

When the dresser passed, Eric pointed at a poster for Broadway Bares, a fund-raising event for Broadway Cares/Equity Fights AIDS. "*Stripping for a sexually transmitted disease?*" Eric said. I shrugged. The stairwell had emptied, but he lingered, reading the actors' sign-in sheet, ads for massage therapists, and forms to order house seats. His eyes settled on a party invitation.

Celebrate Five Years at *Miss Saigon!*

INVITING ALL CAST AND CREW

"No musicians?" Eric asked. "Isn't it musical theater?" I shrugged again. Since synthesizers hit Broadway and technology developed, producers hid us more with each show that opened. First came sound systems, blaring in 1920s theaters built for acoustic instruments and natural voices. Pits had shrunk and been lowered, causing the musicians to drop out of the audience's sightlines, ever since the 1950s, when theaters added an extra row of seats and extended the stage until the opening, for the orchestra, allowed almost no sound to escape except through the sound system.

We had become so peripheral, the union required a photo of the orchestra to be posted in the lobby at some shows. *A Chorus Line* had completely covered the pit. At *Cats* the band played in dressing rooms upstairs and had to follow the conductor and band through video and sound monitors. Now that synthesizers could replace instruments, producers wanted to reduce the minimum number of musicians our union required them to hire, which varied with theater size. The days of "walkers," extra musicians hired because of the minimums and paid *not* to play, had ended. With a new "special situations" clause, several producers had already won the right to hire smaller bands, based on artistic concerns—which were shifting from live performers to the special effects that thrilled moviegoers.

Eric and I continued downstairs. In the band room, musicians sat around a long table littered with takeout from Mee Noodle Shop. Someone rustled through a locker marked COFFEE SUPPLIES AND SHIT, while a violinist folded her cot up after a nap. Four guys playing poker regarded Eric with mild interest, probably thinking he was a new sub.

I grabbed a big black shirt for Eric from my locker and led him to the dressing area beneath our stage. A washing machine was spinning costumes washed after this afternoon's matinee. Eric peeked into the hair room for a closer look at the Asian wigs on their disembodied Styrofoam heads. Huge electronic consoles, an insulated box for the dry ice used to produce fog, and the wardrobe staff's systems for storing the stockings, costumes, jewelry, headdresses, and shoes needed during split-second costume changes filled every space in the old theater. Eric did a double take as he ran into the burly transsexual stagehand, who was wearing a ruffled blouse and heels.

In the pit, I pulled Eric's chair close to mine to give Lino enough space. I played a few notes, turned on my tuning machine, and watched my A register 440 cycles per second. Perfect. I tucked the music under my chair, out of Rieling's sight, and placed my math book on the stand.

Timmy's last-call sub was yammering on about a sore finger, her lack of work, and why she didn't get called more often. I dreaded these bottom feeders who tormented the regulars with talk about their career failure. She started warming up full blast on piccolo.

I handed Eric a fresh pair of yellow foam earplugs, squashing another pair in my own ears. Clapping on gun mufflers, I set my calculator on the stand and opened the book. Ready for blastoff.

Rieling fumed onto the podium in a dark cloud, where he stood watching the red lightbulbs that the stage manager would switch off to indicate curtain time. The lights went out and Rieling gave the downbeat. Eric jumped, stuffing in his earplugs, his eyes bulging as if he he'd been caught in a powerful jet blast.

Loud, he mouthed, emphasizing the *ow*.

A union official had measured our pit with a sound meter, finding peaks around 130 decibels, about the same as a gunshot, though solo flute can equal levels of chain saws and dance clubs. In our enclosed space, the acoustic sound bounced around, as well as being augmented by sound monitors that piped in the actors' voices and instruments from the other side of the pit.

There must have been a producer in the audience tonight. Rieling bent over his stand, giving his players nasty looks. "Violins!" he shouted, and then hissed at the woodwinds and snapped his fingers in the beat pattern. The band jumped to satisfy him, half of them trying too hard and racing ahead until we were barely playing together. Musicians in this band had played in the Met orchestra, the Philharmonic, Carnegie Hall Jazz Band, and numerous legendary shows, some of them in an era preceding our conductor's birth. Yet the connection between respect and results had not dawned on our maestro. I opened my math book.

Suppose that an object is thrown with an initial velocity of 96 feet per second. . . .

Suppose a textbook was hurled at the podium. Would that be enough to kill a conductor? Eagerly, I turned on my calculator as the first wisp of fog curled around the stage lip, spilling over the synths. More fingers of fog seeped above the percussion and over the brass, until a gaseous waterfall poured into the pit. A pregnant violinist slid open the door and left. She'd already miscarried twice.

Stage fog had become a health issue for theatrical productions. At *Beauty and the Beast,* musicians had developed eye and lung irritation, sinusitis, nausea, flulike symptoms, rashes, and asthma attacks. Woodwind players' reeds tasted of smoke and chemicals the next day. Many musicians wore gas masks, as recommended by doctors at the Mt. Sinai School of Medicine who had studied their work environment.

Some of the glycols contained in stage fog were identical to those used in antifreeze. Other fog-bound irritants included palm and mineral oil and glycerin. The stage fog came in plastic jugs with printed warnings not to use the products in theatrical settings or around asthmatics. The sulfur dioxide gas used in the show's pyrotechnics was even worse, as masks couldn't filter it out.

After unproductive talks with producers, musicians had hired an engineering firm to devise an "air curtain"—a primitive set of pipes to blast fog into the audience rather than allow it to sink into the orchestra pit. Now the kiddies who made up much of *Beauty*'s audience were inhaling the stuff too.

Less than two feet away, Lino played a high passage on E-flat clarinet. Timmy's sub shrieked on piccolo, horrendously sharp. Music stands crowded against our chairs, and trumpets and trombones played loudly ten feet away.

As the air thickened, Eric shifted uncomfortably in his chair. He hyperventilated and, flushed with panic, fled. The door slammed shut behind him.

251

If a Broadway hit is starting its fifth year, how many shows have been performed? Answer: 1,664.

Soon I'd have a chance to start fresh: *Les Miserables* had run so long its oboist had retired. I'd replace her in two weeks, escaping Rieling forever.

Except for the show, life had improved dramatically since my Caribbean adventure. I was enjoying a terrific relationship for the first time, I had taken steps to learn enough basic math to go back to school, and for the first time in many years I was in control of my future.

I quickly felt at home in *Les Miz*, where I had first played as a substitute ten years before. As the show's music director, Bob Billig, coaxed sweet sounds from his bored players, I remembered what these pit musicians had looked like a decade before. Everyone was a lot younger then.

Since the show started, one trumpeter's hair had turned gray. His daughter had grown into a beautiful actress. A cellist's toddlers were now starting high school. Two violinists had paid off their houses, and another had started a family. The guitarist had logged years with Buster Poindexter's band. The flutist, Jackie, had raised her children and now spent the days teaching school before coming in to play *Les Miz*. Mitch, the clarinetist, had celebrated his sixtieth birthday but didn't slow down, subbing weekly at the Metropolitan Opera.

I was thankful to be here. My job at the Hudson Valley Philharmonic would disappear soon. The orchestra had once been regarded as a treasured community resource but had financed itself hand-to-mouth in recent years, just like many other small American symphonies with yearly budgets under $2 million. Instead of cutting costs, the orchestra gambled on a single investor, a disbarred lawyer who promised to fund a summer "Tanglewood on the Hudson." The orchestra's board bought the spiel, despite the fact that Frank Zarro's background included a personal bankruptcy, default judgments, lawsuits, an offshore Bermuda account, and eleven tax liens. Though Zarro refused to post money in advance, the board—including one banker—signed anyway. Euphoric local media people regurgitated press releases, suddenly declaring the depressed Poughkeepsie area a mecca for the arts.

The opening concert was disastrous. Like an omen, a violent thunderstorm ruined the outdoor performance. Patrons rushed to escape lightning on the exposed hillside. Buses collided on the muddy slope as someone set off *1812 Overture* fireworks as evacuation lighting. The ensuing stream of bad publicity repelled audiences and donors, leading to bankruptcy for the orchestra. The Hudson Valley Philharmonic finally settled its $600,000 lawsuit against Zarro for only $50,000.[1] Zarro himself faced thirty years for swindling $25 million from various investors.

Les Miz, I thought, was virtually the only employment I still had.

I straightened the new accessory shelf on my music stand with pride. I was going to start out on the right foot with this job. I'd gotten new swabs and even fresh instrument pegs that held my oboe and English horn when I wasn't playing them, erasing all memory of those years at *Saigon.* And I was finally rid of Rieling, the one uncontrollable factor that made me miserable.

At intermission, the personnel manager made a brief announcement. "We'll be getting a new conductor next month," he announced. "Dale Rieling will be moving over from *Miss Saigon.*"

My heart sank. I could be working with an insulting boss until *Les Miz* closed. The show had already been running for nine years and would probably last for as many more. Even though *Les Miz* would pay $10,000 more because of overtime pay, I wished I'd stayed at *Miss Saigon.*

Since Eric had seen Rieling in action, he knew I wasn't exaggerating my situation. Over the next few weeks he tried to comfort me, but our relationship began falling apart. I lost the momentum I'd built for changing my life. Within weeks I had reverted to my old dreary self. I was bitchy and awful to be around. I had ruined our relationship, allowing the misery to infect everything around me.

Broadway started to look inescapable again. Eric's low salary outlook suddenly frightened me; I might eventually have to support both of us. At the same time, Eric was saying he was very unhappy living in the big city. He became an insomniac, and I sensed he was planning to leave.

"Your world looked great from St. Thomas," he said, stuffing clothes in a duffel bag, "but you're out every night. You've turned into someone else."

My eyes welled with tears as he told me he needed to go away for a while to help a relative move cross-country. I knew he wouldn't be back.

Les Miserables

20

ANGELO HACKED AT the decorative cast iron outside my window, smiling proudly as he pulled off a large section. A brick crashed six floors down, bouncing off a car before shattering on the sidewalk. Joan, the former singer who lived on Twelve, waddled past below, hunched like Quasimodo, her matted dog sniffing the brick shards. Angelo jiggled my new air conditioner between the jagged metal pieces and slammed the window shut.

I tipped Angelo as he was leaving and returned to the bedroom. Jorge still blatted distantly on his contrabassoon. Across the street in the apartment I looked into on West End Avenue, the couple's baby, grown to adolescence, pecked on a computer.

The air conditioner unit hummed away, drowning out street noise as I lay across the bed, missing Eric. Sleepless last night, I'd watched an X of light spread across my peeling ceiling from headlights streaming down West End. I'd lived in the Allendale for eighteen years, half my life.

I sat up and opened my calculus book. After Eric left, I had distracted myself by finishing the 1,400-page math book he'd bought me. It allowed me to pass the test to enter Columbia University's algebra and trigonometry class. The course cost $2,500, but completing it was a prerequisite to calculus. I started sketching the solutions. I tried again, again, and again.

"Goddamm it!" I screamed in frustration, and hurled the text away. The spine collapsed, its pages scattering everywhere. I was old enough to be the mother of my classmates. So far, I'd spent $7,500 on Columbia tuition, much of it to study basic or remedial material, like the algebra and an introductory chemistry course that most people completed in high school.

I still didn't know where I was going, but I figured that taking a variety of courses might give me some ideas. At the same time, *Les Miz* was selling fewer tickets and looked as if it might close. Sydney suggested I start taking every gig I could find, as she did, no matter how much travel or how little money was involved.

Sam was up early, hailing a cab to Juilliard to teach a piano lesson. He stood on the corner of 99th with Sue, who was walking the fluffy American Eskimo dog they'd adopted. I thought they looked good together. Sue was sweet and patient with Sam's sometimes volatile temper and erratic schedule. With her MBA and law degree, I imagined she fit in much better with Sam's party crowd.

I greeted them, explaining that I was about to perform as part of a quintet for a children's concert. Sam looked irritated. He was probably late. Since I had finished the "up-and-coming young musician" part of my career trajectory and now just played Broadway, he was polite but no longer expressed much interest in my professional activities. Once his taxi sped away, Sue told me she had quit her law practice in order to stay home and make jewelry from the beads and pearls she liked collecting. She much preferred the creative life, she said.

I took off for the subway, wondering if this morning's gig counted as part of the "creative life." Settling in for the Z train's fifteen stops to Brooklyn's Cypress Hills station, I watched Manhattan-bound commuters creaking by in the opposite direction on rush-hour trains. These morning kiddy concerts were unpleasant for all involved. Few musicians took them seriously, spreading out newspapers during the performances, sloshing coffee over the stage. We rarely played anything I'd want to sit through, so my heart went out to the bored kids. The conductor often spoke to them as if they were either imbeciles or PhD musicologists.

These jobs paid only $70, financed by the Music Performance Trust Funds, which was a union program. The resource was established in 1948 as recording companies were required to contribute a percentage of their revenues to provide free live musical performances in parks, nursing homes, and other venues across the country where audiences rarely heard live music.

Leaving the subway, I found the public school only a few minutes before show time. I stopped at the water fountain and opened my cigarette-style reed case to wet a few reeds, in order to make them vibrate. A shadow loomed behind me. A security guard thought my reeds were reefer. When he released me at last, I joined the four other musicians warming up in the gym.

"You know the orange book?" David, the clarinetist, asked. He held up the standard quintet anthology.

"Sure," I lied. I was embarrassed by my lack of quintet experience. He picked the Barthe *Passacaglia*, and we began playing. I had a decent reed, for once, and concentrated on how wonderful my tone sounded. I did not realize I had played the entire piece at half-tempo until the other four musicians reached the end and I was still going. We faced a sea of unruly faces. David gave me a long scowl as punishment for my mistake and then turned to the audience.

"Well, kids, what did you think of that?"

"Sounded like *shit* to me," a voice boomed, as the gym roared.

"Good, good, good!" said David, as panic crossed his face. Still, I could see his mind working.

"Ships at sea! Ships . . . at . . . sea," he ad-libbed. The other musicians snorted with laughter. "What else?"

"Yo! How come she's better than all you?" the same boy asked, pointing at me. I couldn't imagine why the kid would say this, except that, as a well-paid Broadway player, my hair and concert outfit were considerably spiffier than those of the other four musicians. I remembered someone describing how visually oriented kids were because of TV.

"Let's let her tell you," David said, suggesting I choose the next piece. "Perhaps something you actually know this time?" he added. Riffling through the music, I found an arrangement by Aaron Copland. It was familiar, even wholesome.

"Okay, okay, settle down," I called. How did these public school teachers do it? "Next, we'll play an American piece," I said, shouting over the noise. "It's called 'Hoedown.'"

"Woo-hoo!" The gym erupted. "Get the 'ho *down!*"

Were these kids getting anything out of this? Was I? I'm not sure arts education was ever much better, even if there used to be more of it. Maybe big-city schoolchildren were once steeped in Bach and Brahms, but outside metro areas, music education meant fourth-grade fluto-phones and Sousa-style bands open only to those who could afford the instruments. Many schools' general music classes ran through sing-alongs of popular and folk tunes. All these resources let kids experience mak-ing music themselves, but few explored classical music in depth.

When schools began cutting even these bands and sing-along music classes, an army of researchers, performers, teachers, and administrators hustled to justify their existence. They rationalized arts education as a magic pill for achieving academic success, rather than teaching the arts solely for their intrinsic value.

In 2001, Harvard researchers would challenge this assertion, combing 188 studies published between 1950 and 1999 to evaluate the effect of arts education on general learning. Their results were shocking: No reliable causal relationship was found between music education and academic performance (except for spatial reasoning). Creative thinking, verbal scores, and math grades were all unaffected by studying music.[1]

Authors of the 2001 research urged educators to teach arts for their own sake instead of promoting them as a path to academic improvement. They warned that otherwise arts education would lose its status if the promised academic performance never materialized.

Arts teachers weren't the only workers struggling to preserve their jobs. Layoffs across all industries increased 14 percent during 1994. With so many Americans losing paychecks, it wasn't surprising that demand for classical musicians and their concerts waned. Some musicians patched together a professional life of teaching, a few classical gigs, Broadway subbing, and unemployment checks that could be kept current for years by working sporadically. Even when orchestras were still a growth in-dustry in 1980, 1,100 musicians applied for a total of 47 available full-time orchestral positions on all instruments in all professional orchestras across the country.

Switching careers was tough. Performing musicians resembled trades-
men with limited obsolete skills rather than academic intellects. In his
1989 book *Music Matters*, George Seltzer argued that conservatory degrees
aren't commensurate with, say, a philosophy major seeking work in an
outside profession:

> In most music programs, because the curriculum is filled with
> courses in music, the student rarely has the opportunity even
> to become acquainted with the core of courses usually associ-
> ated with a liberal arts education. In other words, unless the
> music performance graduate continues in music, he or she is for
> all practical purposes not college-educated.[2]

By 2001, some 11,000 music majors would graduate with a bachelor's
degree, 4,000 with a master's, and 800 with doctorates.[3] Some 5,600
of these graduates majored in music performance (with the rest concentrating on music education, music therapy, religious music, musi-
cology, music history, composition, or theory). A handful would rocket
to the top in solo careers. Around 250 a year would find a full-time
orchestra job. Many would scratch away as freelancers, while others
played only sporadically, supporting their "career" with menial jobs.
The rest had squandered their college educations and, like me, might
start from scratch in a new profession at thirty-five or else work in
unchallenging jobs.

The plight of young music performers intensifies as they age. In
younger years, they sought fame in the city, doubling up with roommates,
working a minimum-wage job, their finances perhaps sweetened by an
occasional check from Dad. Nonprofit analyst John Kreidler describes
their situation twenty years later:

> Today, these same arts workers are in their forties and fifties. At
> this point in their careers, they may be earning annual wages of
> $25–40,000, no longer living in shared housing, intolerant of peri-
> odic layoffs, and almost certainly receiving no help from their
> parents. Moreover, the open job market has far fewer opportuni-
> ties for their skills, and the time for developing the qualifications

to enter an alternative career is past or becoming short. For many of these veterans, the realities of acquiring equity in a house, saving for retirement, obtaining medical insurance, or helping their children through college have become grim. Given their levels of education, advanced skills, and seniority, these veterans feel entitled to incomes more in the range of $50–75,000, and yet only a small fraction of them, especially in small- and medium-size arts organizations, are able to reach this expectation.[4]

Fanning my black blouse against my chest, I went out of the subway into the brilliant April sun at Columbus Circle. Women and children in pastel hats filled the sidewalk, on their way to the Easter Parade on Fifth Avenue. Amid the spring colors, a man dressed in black walked past the Columbus statue in the center divider. It was Bob, a violinist I knew from City Ballet.

"Who else would be wearing shrouds on Easter?" he grumbled, gesturing to my outfit and to his. In our dark colors, we were conspicuous among the other pedestrians' Easter finery. Bob was headed to Smoky Mary's—the Church of St. Mary the Virgin in Times Square—for the incense-heavy Easter services.

Walking south on Broadway, I turned east on 55th, toward the Fifth Avenue church that hired Basically Baroque each Christmas and Easter. Up in the wooden choir loft, chorus members had already started gathering. Singers like these live even more unstable freelance lives than instrumentalists, often taking jobs at the largest synagogues and churches to sing during their services. They get rock-bottom rates for these gigs, without the union-mandated benefits attached to my check. Together with office temping during the week, they strive to make enough to pay for vocal coaching costing between $70 and $100 or more per hour. Except for the highest echelon of opera stars, even the most successful vocalists barely scraped by.

At rehearsal break, I started walking toward a nearby deli with my Sunday paper. Betty caught up with me, wearing an eighties-style outfit, even though it was 1998. Her blazer was fresh from the cleaners, and she wore sharply pleated black pants and a starched white shirt. I was never sure what mood Betty might be in, but this seemed to be one of her upbeat days.

As she stepped off the curb to cross the long block between Fifth and Sixth avenues, Betty talked happily about the passing Easter bonnets. She did not hear the beeping sound that commercial vehicles make as they go in reverse. I tried to grab her, but Betty stepped off the curb and a van backed into her and knocked her down. I banged frantically on the van's panels until it stopped. A Hispanic man leaped out of the driver's side, distress showing on his face.

"Lady, lady? I didn't see you, sorry sorry!" the driver said. Betty lay motionless in the gutter; I wasn't sure she was conscious until she finally stirred. The driver held out his hand to help her up.

"Don't you look behind you?" Betty spat, dazed and trying to straighten the knee that had helped break her fall. Tears welled in her eyes. A black woman wearing a yellow suit hurried up the street toward us. She'd seen it all, she said, and would serve as a witness for the driver. She pointed to a crosswalk at the end of the long block, so far away no real New Yorker would ever use it.

We must look like two rich Fifth Avenue ladies to her, wearing these dressy black outfits, I thought. I said nothing to the witness, and suggested to Betty that we go into the deli across 55th.

"I saw it all, I saw it all! People like you . . ." The woman's cries became muffled as the deli door closed behind us. Betty retreated to the far corner of the back room, applying fresh lipstick while I ordered coffee. I brought it over to her, asking if she was hurt. Should we see a doctor?

"I'm all right," she said, lips quivering as she took deep breaths. "I'm just, just . . ." Betty couldn't complete the sentence. The lines around her eyes creased as her body trembled. Her chest caved in and she sobbed uncontrollably. "I work so hard but nothing ever gets better, I can't get ahead, I don't have any savings, I want to do something else but I don't have a college degree, I'm so lonely and everybody in the pit hates me, I hate playing, and I'm going to have to work and live at the Allendale until I die!"

She choked, breathing in and out in little wet gasps. Mascara streamed down her face. I reached awkwardly for her hand, but she jerked it away, smearing eye makeup across her forehead into her bleached hair.

Betty was now in her early sixties, retirement age for most workers. With a shortage of single men her age, she'd stuck with someone who was married to another woman. Professionally, she'd done everything right, winning orchestra auditions, practicing hard, and trying to love music even though repetition had drained her passion long ago.

Relatives, teachers, mentors had praised her ability. Now no one cared that she had to scrounge for rent or needed medical attention.

This time, I tracked down her hand, squeezing it tightly. I did not know what to say. I would be Betty in twenty years if I didn't do something more constructive than taking a few classes and hoping for an epiphany. I'd watched her age, unhappy and unfulfilled. Some younger person in the Allendale was going to see me in the same way. Betty's life had so much more value than the miserable face sitting across from me. She'd lost all her best years. I was losing mine too.

The Johnson O'Connor Research Foundation/Human Engineering Laboratory was intimidating in appearance, from its marble staircase to a dusty nineteenth-century pipe organ and safe (not opened since 1941) in the mahogany-paneled dining room of the Beaux Arts mansion housing its offices. The house had been built in 1900 for one of the Vanderbilts and remained a time capsule that had not been renovated since. The bathrooms retained their two-inch-thick glass towel bars and enormous tubs, and although the elevator didn't work and the fireplaces were boarded up to prevent drafts, stepping into Johnson O'Connor's headquarters was like stepping into another era.

The organization provided tests to evaluate the natural aptitudes of teenagers and adults who were choosing career paths. When it was started by General Electric in the 1920s, Johnson O'Connor aimed to reassign the company's employees who had been displaced by technology. That described my situation perfectly as a classical musician in a modern society.

I'd already exhausted everything I could think of to find a new career. I asked Sydney, Sam, and other friends what they thought. I asked my parents to remember what I'd liked as a child. Their answers—writing, architecture, animals, nature—were too broad to narrow down. After accomplishing so much in one profession, it was difficult to imagine I could achieve the same level in a new one.

I read Richard Bolles's career-change manual, *What Color Is Your Parachute?* In the book's appendix, I noticed seminars and tests for evaluating your strengths. I'd tried Myers-Briggs and the Strong Campbell Interest Inventory, but they didn't help because I was answering questions about what I *thought* I did well. Years of practicing had steered me so far from my own wishes that my answers didn't add up to anything constructive. I tried a Work/Life Design course at the Crystal Barkley Corporation, a career counseling institute, but the week-long seminar was meant more for business executives. Johnson O'Connor was on the list too, but I'd avoided it until now because of the $500 price tag for seven hours of aptitude testing.

The Johnson O'Connor theory promoted the idea that by using as many of a person's natural aptitudes as possible in work and leisure activities, the subject would be happier than if the work used skills that he or she wasn't particularly good at. The Institute's staff wouldn't prescribe a specific job but would instead discuss the kinds of professions where my aptitudes were useful.

I told the man performing my tests that I knew all about my weaknesses. I had a terrible memory, poor language skills, and no talent for math, design, or spatial orientation. I was rigid, uncreative, and an introvert whose only strengths were logic and analysis. He told me to put my preconceptions aside and treat the tests like a game, even if I felt I was doing poorly. The tasks Johnson O'Connor's test included would evaluate my natural aptitudes, not what years of trying to adapt to a profession I wasn't suited for had told me.

The man showed me a page of drawings, representing a cocktail napkin folded in specific patterns. An imaginary hole was then punched through the resulting layers. If this were three-dimensional, where would the holes be located when the napkin was unfolded?

"I can't do this," I said immediately, shutting off my mind.

"Remember, it's just a game," said the man.

I labored over the first diagram but wasn't sure, so I chose the solution that seemed right. I went through all twenty examples and finished within the time limit, although I was reasonably sure most of them were wrong. My brother would be great at this, I thought. He got all the math genes.

"You got all but one right," said the man.

The tests went on through the day, exploring things I'd never considered, like design aptitude and memory for numbers. I was in the rare state of having so much fun I didn't want to quit. George Wyatt, the Johnson O'Connor associate who was counseling me, spread the computerized results across his desk. I had invited Sydney along, hoping she would be able to help me decipher his advice and perhaps get some ideas on finding fulfillment for herself as well.

"You're one of the lucky ones," George said, pointing out that most of the black bar diagram lines stretched well past the eightieth percentile mark, and many of them went into the nineties. "You're good at almost everything."

I was surprised to see scores in the ninety-ninth percentile for "Ideaphoria" (a creativity measure), musical abilities, and several memory skills. Other high scores included observation; memory for numbers, design, and language; "Graphoria"; and one of the spatial visualization tasks. I'd done reasonably well with manual dexterity and numbers and scored sky-high for extroversion. I'd bombed at logic and analysis.

"You're an extreme example of someone trying to fit a square peg in a round hole," George said. He explained that he'd counseled other musicians, some of them quite famous. The ones who were happy as performers possessed almost the opposite profile from mine. Introversion and low "Ideaphoria" enabled people like performers and researchers to work alone, concentrating for hours on perfecting a minute task.

My classical music training had squeezed me dry of spontaneity. I had no idea what I liked or where my true strengths lay. Locking myself away from others in a practice room, I had drilled on scales and phrases, reproducing someone else's music instead of creating something of my own.

George's analysis was encouraging. He told me I was strong in "people-influencing" skills, and listed professions that would maximize these aptitudes. If I stayed in music, George said, I'd be happier switching my focus to music composition or conducting, where I would be generating new ideas instead of refining someone else's work. Teaching, advertising, journalism, and international business (because of a foreign language aptitude) would all be careers where I might find satisfaction.

Sydney said she could see me doing all the jobs George mentioned, especially something like business or advertising. Those were the two that interested me too, and George and I discussed various business schools.

"Wow, you could really get out of here in style, going to Harvard or somewhere," Sydney said, as George handed me the results and invited me to come back for a complimentary follow-up. Sydney and I went out onto 62nd Street and headed to Madison Avenue for a cab. I asked her where she thought her own aptitudes lay. Sydney was intelligent. I could imagine her in some influential position, perhaps directing a nonprofit organization or a chamber music festival or becoming a business executive. We reached the corner and climbed in a taxi.

"Hey, thanks for coming with me. It really helped," I said. "Would you ever want to do this aptitude-testing thing?"

"Me? Oh, no." Sydney laughed artificially. "I'm just a gig slut."

I winced. Sydney could be so much more. If she were truly passionate about music and freelancing, I could understand staying in the business. However, she complained incessantly. It was clear that Sydney's window of opportunity had closed. Her career wouldn't improve much from here. I tried to imagine how despondent she must feel to describe herself with such words.

We rode through Central Park in silence. Sydney had met a wealthy entrepreneur on a blind date set up through friends. They'd dated for long enough that she was going to move into the million-dollar duplex he owned in Greenwich Village, where she would pay him rent. She didn't behave like someone in love. In fact, she was starting to act more like Betty in her acceptance of an unhappy life. Maybe she was still holding out for a magic dress of her own.

21
The Medieval Baebe

WHEN SANFORD ALLEN had called to hire me for a week of film sessions back 1991, when he was concertmaster of *Aspects of Love*, I turned him down. I told him I was planning to audition for the Denver Symphony. The Denver gig only paid $18,000, but at that time I had deemed it more serious than commercial work. Sanford hesitated. "The film," he said dramatically, "is *Malcolm X*." I canceled my airline ticket to Colorado.

I was excited to be hired for such a high-profile film, especially because the quantity of recording work had been shrinking with the evolution of computer audio. Almost every television commercial I recorded in the early 1980s had featured an orchestra larger than thirty pieces, but subsequent jingle dates often called for fewer musicians as digital technology improved enough to replicate our sounds. Everyone hoped they were just imagining the trend, and *Malcolm X*, a multisession recording employing a huge orchestra, bolstered our hopes for the future.

Spike Lee's film used fourteen three-hour sessions paying $250 each. Recording during the day, I still performed shows at night, which promised the most lucrative week I'd ever worked, at $4,550. Plus, royalty income would come in annually once the film was released in video and broadcast format. Despite the inroads of digital audio, recording was still pretty big business at the time, with our busiest jingle contractor estimating that his 1992 musicians made $2.5 million at RCA alone.[1]

I'd been to RCA Studios many times. I recorded a Pepsi jingle for the Super Bowl, an ad for Ritz Bits, the film soundtracks for *Mad Dog and Glory* and *Mr. and Mrs. Bridge,* and a St. Luke's recording of Stravinsky's *Rite of Spring.* Buried inside a seven-story structure attached to RCA's headquarters at 44th and Sixth, the gargantuan Studio A could fit Mahler's *Symphony of a Thousand* with room to spare.

Recording detritus hunkered in corners of the two-story room: booms, cables, foam-padded sonic dividers, chairs, stands, a drum kit, and a portable isolation booth to keep louder instruments from bleeding into the mix. The orchestra seating was set up lengthwise to accommodate a full string section.

Beside the podium, a video monitor crackled gray, the onscreen digital timer set to zero. Curved blond-wood panels lined the room's upper perimeter. The ceiling could go up and down in three pieces with the touch of a button, and a double-thick glass panel separated studio and recording booth. Inside, engineers ran the show from a sixteen-channel console. The studio was so extravagant that, when it opened in 1970, musicians stood up and applauded after the first session.

In 1975, Sam and Bobby had recorded the album *When You and I Were Young, Maggie* in Studio A. Pianist Vladimir Horowitz, trumpeter Wynton Marsalis, and crooner Harry Connick, Jr., used it too. Broadway cast albums of *West Side Story, Guys and Dolls, Crazy for You, La Cage aux Folles,* and every Stephen Sondheim show were made here. Film soundtracks for *Aladdin, Beauty and the Beast,* and *When Harry Met Sally* were done here as well. Recording continued even after Bertelsmann Music Group (BMG) bought RCA from General Electric in 1986. One engineer, Max Wilcox, rated the studio's acoustics second only to London's Abbey Road, and Broadway music director Paul Gemignani declared it first choice in New York.

When I walked into the 1991 *Malcolm X* session, a French hornist was warming up and string players were unpacking their fiddles, rubbing rosin (a processed tree sap that is sold in hardened cakes) on their bows for friction against the strings. Some thrived in the recording business, never bothering with performance gigs because studio work paid so much better. Broadway violinists, usually drab in graying jeans and sweaters, now sported Italian shoes, tight wool pants, and blouses with one neckline button undone too far.

Others filtered into the break room between the mixing booth and the studio, where RCA supplied bagels, sandwiches, pastries, coffee, a stocked fridge, and free phone. Musicians were talking about the news of RCA Studios' impending closure, saying that *Malcolm X* would be one of the last dates here. Two months earlier, BMG announced they'd consolidate their New York–based companies, abandoning their $250 million mortgage here for a modern $119 million building.

The studios would be razed, then filled with IRS auditors' desks at a cost of $30 million. Half the technicians and engineers would lose their jobs, but the city showered BMG with an $11 million tax break for the move, enabling a taxpayer-funded operation to replace the profitable business. "It's just stupid, dumb, and shortsighted," recording mogul David Geffen told *Newsday*. Wilcox called its closure "a disaster." Gemignani thought they must be joking.

There was almost no alternative in Manhattan for recording groups this large. Carnegie suffered from rumbling subway noise, with traffic and sirens bleeding into the mix. Some groups traveled up to the State University of New York in Purchase, whose performing arts center allowed large orchestras a quiet recording space, albeit inconvenient to Manhattan. The only other possibility was Manhattan Center at 311 West 34th Street, built by Oscar Hammerstein in 1906 as the Manhattan Opera House. The ornate Grand Ballroom on the seventh floor, which was used in 1926 by Warner Brothers and Bell Labs to record the New York Philharmonic playing the first soundtrack for a commercially released film, *Don Juan,* was heavily booked by the Philharmonic and the Met because it was surrounded by interior walls and therefore removed from traffic, airplane, and subway noise.

Saxophonist Branford Marsalis slipped inside the studio to listen. He and Terence Blanchard, the jazz trumpeter who composed the film's music, would record the film's jazz tracks separately. Two copyists scribbled intently in the RCA booth, where Terence conferred with Spike Lee. Studio musicians almost never see the music until moments before they must record it, so sight-reading skills and ability to deal with pressure are important. This gig was no exception.

I gave the tuning note, and Terence climbed the podium. An assistant finished handing out the hand-copied manuscript of "Malcolm's Letter." Everyone donned headphones, and Terence began conducting.

Recording "La Rosa Y El Sauce" at St. Peter's Episcopal Church on trumpeter Jon Faddis's Grammy-nominated album, Remembrances, *in 1998. Musicians, left to right: Bill Easley, Blair Tindall, Jon Faddis, John Clark (behind Faddis), Jim Pugh, Lawrence Feldman, George Young, Paquito D'Rivera, Roger Rosenberg. (Alan Nahigian)*

Lyrical violins began the cue, trading the melody off to me, then to a solo English horn. Violins reentered, weaving in a second theme, while the French horn soared above. The music ebbed, grew, and finished three minutes later in a transcendent wash of strings. Not only did this score support the story line, it was deep, rich, melancholy, and expertly crafted.

Recording commercial music in this studio, we were used to playing inaudible long tones dubbed "footballs" for hairpins (<>) marking their dynamics. Maybe I had expanded my narrow definition of "real music" beyond the classical genre, but Blanchard's score was a pleasure to play.

Next, the copyists passed out "Going to Mecca," which wove Eastern harmonies through themes from the first tune. As the cues went on, Terence's elegant score embraced Stravinsky, Brahms, and Mozart, using the jazz musician's harmonic fluency.

269

On the last day, Terence dismissed everyone except me. He'd written the final cue while I lunched on Korean barbecue at Woo Lae Oak. Alone with Spike Lee watching the clock, my belly rumbled from lunch, ruining the take. On take two, the parking garage elevator abutting Studio A roared to life, a problem that had plagued recordings in this studio from the time it was built. On take three, I finally played a perfect solo, as the dying image of Denzel Washington's character flickered across the monitor.

I felt sad leaving RCA Studios, knowing I would probably never return here. Recording the soundtrack had been fulfilling, and I had wished the project would never end. Jobs like this were few and far between— and rapidly becoming scarcer.

The musicians' union, for all its victories in gaining better pay and recognition for its members, had historically fallen short when it came to capitalizing on technological evolution. From the invention of audio recordings, musicians had regarded canned music as a threatening replacement for their services as live performers.

In 1928, some 22,000 musicians playing for silent movies had lost their jobs. "Talkies," the union argued, constituted an "anticultural" force. In 1938, Muzak was labeled a "musical robot" for replacing cabaret performers. By 1942, AFM president James Petrillo declared an all-out ban on recording, arguing that radio station orchestras were being displaced by canned music. Newspapers called Petrillo the "musical Hitler" when small radio stations that couldn't afford to pay orchestras failed as a result of the ban, choking vital communication during World War II.

The Justice Department filed an unsuccessful antitrust suit against the American Federation of Musicians, making it the first labor union investigated by Congress. The 1942 recording ban lasted until 1944, resurfacing again in 1948 for nearly a year, until musicians at last accepted the fact that recorded music would be a permanent part of their professional lives.

During the 1950s, the musicians' union found benefits to recording music by negotiating reuse and royalty payments on recordings and film soundtracks, with television recording following in 1960. Payment for reuse of theatrical films on television and video sales was enacted in 1972.

Recording became problematic again in 1979, when Local 802's president attacked "musical rapists" who secretly recorded the Philharmonic's live performances. Digital technology exploded two years later, when Sony and Philips introduced their first CD players, the technology mushrooming into computer audio applications in studios and Broadway pits.

By the mid-1980s, a computer protocol called musical instrument digital interface (MIDI) enabled composers to create full orchestral arrangements from their electronic keyboard. Since the synthesizers using MIDI contained sound "samples" from acoustic instruments, composers could manipulate the data with musical "word processors," cutting and pasting representations of sound waves and replacing an entire orchestra with one $3,000 computer.

Drummers had already lost significant studio work to the drum machine by the 1980s. Ten years later, the issue became virtual orchestras— a computerized tool that could replace entire bands with a synthesizer and a single musician. Picket lines erupted, nearly putting one nonprofit opera company out of business.

The 1980s launched not only a digital age but also a time of corporate mergers. Bertelsmann bought RCA in 1986, and Sony acquired CBS Masterworks in 1989. Warner Classics gobbled up Erato, Teldec, Finlandia, and Nonesuch. Polygram Classics included Deutsche Grammophon, Philips, and London. The classical labels had never been profitable, but they gave the record company that owned them a little cachet. Virgin and Warner-Elektra optimistically started new classical music labels, and chain record stores remodeled to add huge classical departments.

Compact disc sales skyrocketed as classical fans replaced their favorite records with more durable, cleaner-sounding CDs. After the hoopla of compact discs faded, classical recording's market share plummeted from a 7 percent high in 1987 to 2.8 percent eleven years later.[2] Despite individual successes (over 3 million copies of the *Three Tenors* CD sold since its release in 1996), pop sales dwarfed classical discs. Alanis Morissette's "Jagged Little Pill" sold almost 30 million worldwide. In one 1996 week when the Three Tenors were hottest, the operatic trio sold only 2,000 copies.

New recordings became prohibitively expensive, with American union rates driving the cost of symphonic recording some 60 percent higher than in London. Recording executives railed at domestic orchestras and took their business to the Europeans, who were considered to be more sensitive to changes in the recording market.

Movie companies also sidestepped union expenses like scales and residual payments by recording films abroad, or with one of the few orchestras not covered by a contract with the musicians' union. The musicians received payment for the dates but nothing for broadcast and video—a payment that had once exceeded six figures annually for some players.

Pure classics nose-dived, and executives tried revving up the classical recording industry for a younger demographic. Crossover artists, who wove classical music with jazz, New Age, and world music, were courted. Blind heartthrob Andrea Bocelli and teen songbird Charlotte Church sold millions.

Record companies began looking for pop marketing strategies, which usually meant easy-listening compilations or trendy young soloists. Beginning with Nigel Kennedy's funky interpretation of Vivaldi's *Four Seasons*, creative musical and personal statements broke free of stuffy classical music decorum, sometimes with embarrassing results. During his live appearances, Kennedy, a Jimi Hendrix devotee, bounded onstage to make a fashion statement:

He appeared wearing wrinkled parachute pants hiked up to reveal mismatched socks and shoes of a sickly greenish hue. From the midriff up was . . . a shabby, sleeveless jacket covering a sloppy pirate's shirt tied with a sash. The hair was as usual: strange tufts rising over an almost-shaved skull, as if borrowed from some sorry overcoiffed dog whose breed hails from remote mountainous regions of central Asia.

—*Atlanta Constitution*, 2000[3]

Using sex to sell music was the next logical step; it had worked before. During the nineteenth century, Verdi and Donizetti wrote scantily clad dancers into their operas, Composer and pianist Franz Liszt was the rock star of the mid-1880s, parading his luxuriant mane, flamboyant suit, and Hungarian sword onstage. His groupies rushed backstage, collecting discarded gloves, hankies, even broken piano strings. It was possible, by inspecting the moisture on the audience seats after a concert, to tell which chairs had been occupied by women.

Modern record companies began using blatantly suggestive photos of women soloists on the covers of their classical music recordings. RCA started with cellist Ofra Harnoy, using the Israeli musician's attractive photo to sell records rather than playing up her notable accomplishments. Then came Nadja Salerno-Sonnenberg—classical music's Courtney Love —followed by Singaporean sexpot fiddler Vanessa-Mae Nicholson frolicking in a wet T-shirt with a white violin. The string quartet Bond jumped on board, earning the nickname "Spice Girls with Strings." Next came the sister act Ahn Trio and Lara St. John, who was photographed wearing only a violin.

Midori, Hilary Hahn, and Sarah Chang led a mostly Asian trend of pubescent female fiddlers. "It did not take a Freudian analyst to detect something suspect in a line of teenies being paraded before a concert audience—and particularly a record-buying public—that was overwhelmingly male and middle-aged," observed Norman Lebrecht, author of *Who Killed Classical Music?*[4]

A real *Playboy* Playmate, busty blond Finnish fiddler Linda Lampenius, known by her stage name of Linda Brava, recorded an EMI album of light recital fare. It received a scathing review in the *American Record Guide*. The Mediaeval Baebes—a twelve-woman group composed of an ex-stripper, two fire-eaters, a witch, and former members of the rock group Miranda Sex Garden—staked their claim with Virgin Records. RCA Victor didn't even need a sexy soloist, choosing instead to recycle old recordings into anthologies that promised instant libido, with their three-album Love Notes series: *Shacking Up to Chopin*, *Bedroom Bliss with Beethoven*, and *Making Out to Mozart*.

The babe angle was an easy sell. Newcomers to classical music who were interested in buying CDs faced racks of album covers featuring white men in black tuxedos. It wasn't surprising that buyers were attracted to photos of pretty women posing much like familiar artists on pop CDs.

Journalists, however, censured modern talents who dressed as provocatively as blue-jeaned Tchaikovsky Competition medalist Eugene Fodor or violinist Anne-Sophie Mutter, who always appeared in one of her trademark strapless Dior gowns. The writers' theses leave the reader and potential classical music fan wondering why they would want to spend time and money experiencing an art form that is described to them as lacking in emotion.

"For God's sake, let's put some uncompromising physical ugliness back into classical music, so we all start listening again instead of looking, before it's too late," wrote London's *Evening Standard*. "Classical music has never struck me as an accompaniment to anything else and certainly not to amour toujours. In real life, music-making and love-making aren't synonymous, as they often are on-screen," said the *Cleveland Plain Dealer*. "There may be kids out there who lost their virginity during Brahms's D Minor Piano Concerto, but they don't want to tell the story and you don't want to hear it," wrote Alex Ross of *The New Yorker*.

The *New Yorker* quote, written by a journalist I admire, was both amusing and sad. I had passionately lost my virginity at sixteen while a Brahms string quintet record was playing. I couldn't imagine what created this invisible barrier between listener and performer, a boundary that cheated new audiences of the sensory thrill of classical music.

A receptionist pointed to the Hit Factory's main elevator, which was made accessible to studio musicians only after the caged freight lift we were once required to use plunged four floors in 1994. Several musicians reported bruises, cuts, muscle pain, and recurring nightmares after the accident, which happened following a session to record the film *It Could Happen to You*.

I'd been here a month ago to perform the film score to *Twilight*, which starred Susan Sarandon and Paul Newman. Elmer Bernstein, the elder statesman of movie soundtracks, had conducted his own music. Starting out as a Juilliard-trained concert pianist in 1939, Bernstein studied composition with luminaries Roger Sessions and Stefan Wolpe, scoring such films as *The Ten Commandments, To Kill a Mockingbird, Ghostbusters,* and *The Age of Innocence.* Winner of an Oscar, he'd also won an Emmy and two Golden Globe Awards after nearly a half century of film composing.

Watching his video monitor, Bernstein timed the music perfectly with the movie scenes, just like film recording before click tracks were used by musicians to synchronize their performance with the video.

After *Twilight,* it was surprising to be hired so soon for *Snake Eyes.* The elevator opened on a crowd of musicians, dressed far better than usual, at the only film date some had been called for in years. The room buzzed with false hope that two dates a few months apart meant a recording renaissance.

A tall violinist in her forties flirted with the new contractor, her neckline dipping low over what little bosom she had. Talking importantly into his cell phone, a violist intermittently gulped coffee from a blue cup printed with a white Acropolis. He looked the part of busy musician, nailing down another three-hour $250 recording date. Beyond the recording booth's window, seven or eight men in suits chatted on leather sofas. They were producers, film execs, maybe an actor. A gofer refreshed their basket of finger sandwiches, fruit, and cheeses, while a producer stood over the sound board, watching a video of the film.

They looked prosperous, but the studio air on our side of the double glass hummed with the musicians' desperation and the unspoken hope that sessions like this one would become a regular occurrence once again. An Asian man I'd never seen—the film score's composer—tapped the stand and introduced Brian DePalma. The director looked humble before sixty musicians but quickly retreated back to the booth.

As I watched the violinists' bows going up and down in unison, reflected against glass beyond which sat the film's production team, I was struck by the contrast between the two groups of people. In the booth sat men who made careers out of trying a new idea, succeeding or failing and then trying another. On my side of the business, musicians returned to the same kinds of gigs, playing someone else's music and earning a per-service wage. As the bows went up and down I was reminded of a scene in *Ben Hur* in which galley slaves rowed without much idea of where they were headed.

There was something more personal bothering me, though. So far I hadn't had any physical problems that affected my playing, like violinists did when they suffered from tendonitis, or flutists with shoulder problems. Now I was trying to ignore the sensation that my front tooth was coming loose. I'd knocked it out in a 1977 car accident, and when the dentists replaced it in its socket they told me it would last about twenty years. It was now 1998.

Music of the Heart

IT WAS A scene straight from *Little Shop of Horrors*. My dentist straddled the chair, wielding a fierce set of tongs. He braced one foot against the chair and tugged at my front tooth. Bone creaked against bone while Bach's *Brandenburg* Concerto no. 1 tinkled away in the background. In 1985—Bach's tricentennial—I'd played the piece twenty-one times, with eight different groups, on three continents. Always in the third oboe chair, I'd come to despise the exposed low C ending the slow movement.

"Unh!" grunted the doctor as he produced my tooth, whose rotted roots resembled filigree.

The infections had set in a few years after the 1977 car accident. My old dentist—part of a fraternity catering to musicians by advertising in the union paper—found nothing. I imagined him trading tips with the accountant famous for representing musicians at tax audits he'd caused through incompetence.

A dental implant would come only after eighteen months of bone grafts and gum surgeries. In the meantime, I'd wear a "flipper"—an appliance like an orthodontic retainer but with a dummy tooth instead of wire—glued to the roof of my mouth each night with Poli Grip. Playing the oboe would present much more of a challenge. Nearly forty, lonely and single, and now with my teeth starting to fall out, I hated the oboe, and yet I had no other skills.

My problems paled next to Sam's. When I stopped by his apartment a month ago, he must have weighed only about 110 pounds. His transplanted heart was wearing out. He stayed home to rest and wait for a second transplant, a rarity since patients waiting for a first transplant often took priority. Like a pregnant woman, Sam had a bag packed and ready for a hospital stay, and during rare performances he clipped a beeper to his tux pants. The instant a heart was available for transplant, Sam would literally stop the music and get to the operating room.

I hadn't seen much of him in the three years since Itzhak's party. I still felt like a fool for helping him through the last surgery, time I could have spent in school taking care of my own needs. Nearly sixty-two, Sam suddenly looked older than his years, as if his body had finally worn out for good. Even so, I saw defiance and fight in his face. When I left, he walked me to his apartment door and air-kissed me.

"Love you," he called down the hall, his voice breaking.

Sam was clearly dying. Everything around me was dying too. The business was shrinking. The building was disintegrating. Betty looked older and sadder every time I saw her, and Sydney had moved in with Frank, her CEO boyfriend. I wasn't sure if it was depression or exhaustion, but no one could penetrate her fog. I would turn thirty-nine soon, having lived for over two decades in the Allendale. *Les Miz* had run eleven years already. It would probably close before long. Whatever it took, I would not turn forty in this dump of a building, I told myself. I filled a tumbler of jug wine, as I had begun to do almost every afternoon, and found my Johnson O'Connor aptitude test in the filing cabinet.

Public relations. International business. Teaching. Music. Advertising. Journalism. The last word popped out as if it were in bold print. I had been noticing my aptitudes in the year since I had the Johnson O'Connor evaluation. Sydney had once complimented my ability to communicate. My mother had given me a journal when we lived in Austria in 1967 and had been encouraging me to write ever since. Why hadn't I seen it before? There was a positive side to the life I'd led, fascinating tales to tell about people and places and a desire to make a tangible social contribution. Didn't Columbia have the top journalism school? My neighbor from 1978, Billy Lichtenstein, had graduated from there, and I knew the program only took nine months. I could change my life by this time next year. Enrolling at a real university would minimize my two useless music conservatory degrees and, at the same time, immerse me in the world outside classical music.

I poured the wine down the kitchen sink, suddenly disgusted by the dishes I'd allowed to pile up. It was October, and I didn't have time to waste. I wanted to learn about journalism schools right away and apply in time for their deadlines. The elevator was taking forever, so I ran down six flights to the lobby.

Outside, Betty was once again helping her married lover into a cab, his head trembling as she slid his cane in beside him. I turned my head away to pass them, trying to separate myself physically from the Allendale and everything it represented. My purposeful steps felt odd after so much inertia, almost as if I'd awakened after a long hibernation. I walked briskly toward the Olympia Theater, past Cannon's pub and Amir's Falafel to Columbia's gates.

Stopping inside Columbia's journalism building, I picked up an application and a catalog. In the university bookstore, I bought a college guide that evaluated journalism schools. I couldn't wait to get to Les Miz that night and start reading the materials.

It was only a month before application deadlines. I chose programs at two of the top three schools, Columbia and the University of Missouri. I picked the University of Wisconsin as a safety fall-back school. Stanford University was on my list because of its small size, ten students and five professors, two of them Pulitzer winners; one of them was a journalist whose work I had long admired. I had visited my parents at Stanford in 1979, when my dad was on sabbatical at the university's Center for Advanced Study in the Behavioral Sciences, and loved the area, so dramatically different from New York City. I followed through with the Stanford application, even though I could never afford the journalism program's $24,000 tuition. At least at Columbia I could continue working on Broadway to pay my way through school.

Next, I attended to the other application requirements. I took the Graduate Record Examination, something I never could have completed three years before when I lacked math skills. I labored over a personal statement, the first essay I had written in sixteen years. Next I made a lunch date with my old oboe teacher, Joe Robinson, to ask him for a letter of recommendation. He stood me up. He forgot the second appointment as well, taking his BMW for an oil change instead and showing up ninety minutes later, after a phone call to his home. Sitting across from him that afternoon at Shun Lee West, I decided instead to ask Carl Schiebler, the Philharmonic's personnel manager, for the letter.

My efforts and energy still felt hollow and unrealistic. Journalism schools probably wouldn't take me seriously, but I had to try.

Two months later, I received a slim envelope from Stanford. The mailbox slammed shut, its broken lock bouncing against the wall. Thin envelopes always contained rejection letters.

In my apartment, I tossed out the recital notice, the catalogs, and the Stanford letter. I poured myself an early afternoon wine and started scrubbing the pan from last night's nachos. I couldn't stop thinking about the letter.

Oh, what the hell. I had to face the truth. Brushing coffee grounds off the Stanford envelope, I ripped it open. Inside was a single sheet with only a couple of typed paragraphs. I took a long draft of wine, unfolded the letter, and braced myself.

You have been accepted to the graduate program in journalism at Stanford University.

I'd heard about hallucinations in the late stages of alcoholism, but didn't they usually involve spiders? I read on.

We are pleased to award you a full tuition fellowship in the amount of $24,000.

Later, I received acceptances from Columbia and Wisconsin, and another full fellowship at the University of Missouri. Columbia was most students' first choice, but I feared my age and strange background would cause me to get lost in a crowd of young competitive reporters. I picked Stanford, my dream school.

Since I had never written anything, I decided to try to get published. Wouldn't my solo travels through Japan after a New York Pops tour make a perfect travel essay for *The New York Times*? I stopped mentioning my project to other musicians and the few writers I knew, because every-one said it was impossible to land that column, especially for a neophyte like me.

It was a long shot, but so was journalism school. However paralyzed Sydney was in her own life, she said she knew I could do it. Maybe she was living vicariously through my dreams. Sam believed in me too and asked one of his reporter friends to help me contact the *Times* travel editor.

Sue called, saying Sam was slipping toward death after his second trans-plant. He was losing his resolve and wanted me to come see him. "He said the difference between the first transplant and this time is that you're not here now," Sue said. So he does admit I was there for him when no one else was, I thought, scolding myself for my selfishness. This time I hadn't been to see him even once. Carlie, a member of Sam's net-work and heir to the Thom McAn shoestore fortune, had even offered me money to spend time with him. I didn't take it.

The first time I went to Columbia Presbyterian after Sue's call, Sam had been alert, even though his body was obviously ravaged. As I walked into the room, his mood changed from defeat to optimism. I told him that my travel essay on Japanese bathhouses would be pub-lished in the Sunday *Times* in a few weeks, probably helped along be-cause his reporter friend had made sure my manuscript had gotten to the travel desk.

"I'm so glad I could finally do something for you, honey," he said earnestly. I said that the travel piece had opened the door for an assign-ment from *The Wall Street Journal*, which would appear four days after the *Times* essay. It was quite a debut week for a beginning journalist.

We listened to Mahler's Fifth on Sam's Walkman, which was hooked to miniature speakers. Sam had closed his eyes and swooned, then turned his hands over and over, skeletal fingers bloated with growths and bruises. "My playing days are over," he said, wilting back into his defeated mood. I thought back on all those musicians at Itzhak's party. Where were they?

Sam looked about eighty pounds, curled in a helpless wad. I sat on the bed like I did after the first surgery, to prop him up. We sat there, slumped together in silence for several minutes. I rubbed his hair in the way he used to like. At last Sam spoke softly.

"I know you never forgave me, and I don't expect you to," he said of Itzhak's party. I didn't say anything but let the quiet settle around us. I was still angry, mostly at myself for my lack of forgiveness. "Everyone's forgotten me," Sam said. We both knew that, on many counts, he was right. For the most self-serving of Sam's crowd, a dying man was useless as a business connection. However, I could tell that some people had visited. One of his students, who had taken over my former role as nurse-maid, had brought an electronic keyboard, which sat in the corner. I saw cards from Sam's daughter and the violinist Jaime Laredo.

I stroked his arm softly, trying to soothe without hurting his sensitive body. With my free hand I searched the CDs on the table and slipped one of his favorite pieces, Schubert's "An die Musik," into the Walkman. Bryn Terfel's velvety baritone filled the room:

O sublime art,
In how many gray hours
When wild tumult of life ensnared me
Have you kindled my heart to warm love?

"Turn it off!" Sam said tensely. I hesitated. Sam's pupils glowed, possessed.

"*Now!*"

Sam rolled his head toward the bridge he remembered crossing in 1947 on the way to his first childhood surgery. The sight of it wasn't as comforting as it once was. It almost mocked him, as he knew it would remain long after he was gone. We sat in silence for a few minutes while he calmed down.

"Brian asked about you," I said at last, thinking this news would cheer him. Brian was a pianist Sam had championed. He'd recommended him to accompany my debut recital and also to take over during Sam's illness, at Sam's chamber music festival and his Juilliard teaching studio. Earlier, he had mentioned that Brian hadn't visited him.

Samuel Sanders in the 1990s. (Christian Steiner. Courtesy of the Juilliard School archives.)

"You stay away from Brian, he's *evil!*" Sam rasped, eyes ablaze. A nurse entered the room to adjust a catheter leading to Sam's urine reservoir under the bed.

"No! Get out of here! I don't want you here!" he spat at the nurse, pulling at the tubes and punching blindly. I slid off the bed. "Please, please, *please* can I just have a little water?" Sam wasn't allowed any liquids. The nurse, looking frightened, quickly retreated.

"Cunt!"

Sam scrabbled at my wrist with skeletal fingers. "The doctors," he whispered, his eyes imploring, "are doing experiments on me. Do something." Sam and his enormous hospital bill were now an investment for the hospital. I saw his point, however deliriously it was conveyed.

Sam had called me here, apparently as a last resort to reverse his decline. I felt as helpless as I had the day I found him catatonic and alone after the first transplant. I was trying to wrestle my anger into compassion. I held a grudge against a dying man. I wasn't proud of myself; it was just wrong, and I struggled to change my attitude.

"It would mean everything to me if you recovered," I said, wondering if I sounded insincere. I took a deep breath and made sure to speak more emphatically. I could see in Sam's fiery eyes that he realized many of the people he'd considered friends had used him. "Everybody loves you. Can't you try hard—?"

"Why," interrupted Sam, "would you want a man like me?" He stared at me intensely and with the innocence of a child. It had been thirteen years since we'd been lovers. The years of unspoken words between us had created outsized hurt. I had lived alone with a feeling of betrayal and disrespect. All this time Sam had been wounded by my rejection of him as a lover, yet he put on a friendly face.

I remembered seeing a pad in Sam's apartment one day. He had scrawled *Am I ugly?* on it in his looping script. Sam had gone through life secretly feeling like a freak. We had both affected each other more than we knew, and now it was too late to make it right. Was he reading my mind?

He looked down suddenly and spoke quietly. "I don't know where I stand with anyone except Sophie," Sam said of his daughter. He moved his head as close to me as he could, as if he wanted to tell me a secret. "Sue is crazy," whispered Sam.

So this was all that remained of his distinguished career, that one old friend was offered money to stand by his deathbed.

"Everyone's forgotten me," he whispered again. I said no, it was summer and everyone was away, playing at festivals. In the twenty-four-hour glare of hospital lights, life was suddenly revealed as ugly, and all the Mahler in the world couldn't gild the truth.

By the time I got to the hospital a couple of days later, it was dusk. The George Washington Bridge twinkled in the distance behind Sam's wires and monitors. Pings and gurgles echoed through the cardiac intensive care unit, and a dozen patients lay in their cubicles around a central desk.

Flat on his back now, Sam looked like a cadaver. His lips curled back to expose blood-caked teeth behind a crop of whiskers. Tubes sprouted from his chest. His ankles were swollen to the size of my thigh and his shoulder blades stuck out like wings. An aide came by and emptied his bag of urine. He'd contracted hepatitis C from a blood transfusion. The only thing working in him was someone else's heart.

He'd had a massive seizure, the nurse said. Right before it happened, he said the pain was off the charts, so Sue went to get him morphine. She'd already arranged the cremation.

I left New York in the morning to play the opera *Barber of Seville* near Tanglewood, which Sam's friend Joel was conducting. The musicians were housed in a ski resort for the week, where I worked on my *Wall Street Journal* piece. In the daytime my apartment mates, Pauline and Sarah, gave me input on the story, which concerned the first post-bankruptcy concert of the Hudson Valley Philharmonic. Late at night I set up the fax machine and printer I'd brought along. I sent the story to one of my future Stanford professors, who had said he'd advise me before I sent the final version to the *Journal*. As it turned out, his help was essential because I knew nothing of the most basic newspaper rules of style. The sunny condo felt like a halfway house to a better life.

When I checked my answering machine by remote on Saturday morning, my recital manager, Lee Walter from East Hampton, had left a message. Lee was also Sam's publicity agent and had become something of a friend to him. "He's gone," said Lee, leaving a message about sitting shiva at Sam's brother Martin's home on Sunday. I knew Joel would go. I knew Brian and everyone at Itzhak's party would be there. I decided to stay at the ski resort. I had said goodbye.

When I returned to New York I tried saying farewell to Sydney, too, before leaving for California. I couldn't get her attention. Her schedule was crammed, and she spent her one night off, every Sunday, at a weekly dinner with friends of Frank's that she didn't like. I was sad when she missed the bon voyage party that one of my friends had arranged so beautifully. I had a sense I wouldn't see her again unless I dropped by her new home in the Village.

Sydney was consumed by helping Frank plan his co-op's renovation. She showed me the plans for their kitchen, and the Sub-Zero and Miele appliances that would make it a showplace. It would be a far cry from the Allendale, I agreed. Sydney's opulent surroundings contrasted with her mood, which was more negative, downcast, and uncommunicative than I'd ever seen her. She took me down the spiral staircase to an area that was designated as her own private space for practicing.

The basement, which had been gutted, overflowed with Sydney's boxes. Piles of faded Sarah Arizona sweaters bought at sample sales for $18 were toppling onto more boxes. I saw where she'd dug through a box of silk scarves in enough colors to match her collection of outfits. In the bathroom, hundreds of hotel shampoo bottles spilled from baskets and shelves, and her papers, bank statements, and bills lay in towering piles on every surface. There was no place to stand. She mentioned that her diamond ring, the one her bassoonist boyfriend of the 1980s had given her, was missing. "Workmen in the house, you know," she said. She couldn't pinpoint the day her ring disappeared, or her huge Nordic Track either. Months ago, maybe.

I was growing more alarmed. This should be a happy time in Sydney's life, especially since she had escaped the Allendale for such a beautiful home. Her eyes were rheumy. She rarely spoke an entire sentence. As we walked to a café, she stumbled along looking at the pavement, one of her shoe soles flopping unglued, and she dangled an expensive ceramic tile nonchalantly from her fingers. It was a choice for Frank's renovation that she wanted to show me over lunch.

We sat down in the café near Seventh Avenue, ordering Caesar salads and the ubiquitous bottle of wine. I wondered if I should say something.

"Are you certain you want to live together?" I asked at last. She had her own money, some $115,000 ten years ago and probably much more now. She had spent little, outside of hair and skin care and clothing. Her current yearly income nearly reached $100,000, which was enough to rent or buy something decent.

"But where . . . would I *go?*" she said. I knew how she felt. We had both felt trapped inside the Allendale, which was nothing if not a symbol for the entire music business on which we were dependent. With such cheap rent, it would be crazy to leave. We'd be crazy to leave the music business too, since outsiders viewed our lives as so glamorous.

In that moment, I gave up on Sydney; we were splitting off in different directions. I knew my path would lead to growth and more personal fulfillment. I hoped Sydney's path would too, but I feared she would remain as miserable as ever. I made small talk until we finished eating and asked for the check.

"Look, I gotta go," I said to Sydney, crumpling a twenty on the table next to the forgotten tile lying there. I headed out the door to get home and finish packing for my move. I looked back as the waitress topped off Sydney's glass. She sipped her wine, holding herself just so. She jutted her chin and shook her beautiful hair, staring mysteriously into the distance. I still could not see what was there.

A few weeks had passed since late June, when I shoved my resignation from the show into Rieling's hand. He suddenly turned sweet, offering me a nine-month leave. I turned it down.

I was leaving an $82,000 salary, health insurance, pension contributions, and a flexible schedule for a year of school with little income and a future of low-paying journalism work. I felt weightless. My colleagues' responses varied. Some couldn't believe I'd quit the security of a long-running show. Others were incredulous that I was willing to leave New York. Others drew me aside to ask how I "got out."

Ironically, my final night in New York was spent playing principal oboe at the New York City Opera, sight-reading Mozart's *Don Giovanni* in performance because the regular oboist, my long-ago lover Randy, had called in sick at the last minute. Since I hadn't ever played the opera and didn't have a chance to attend the rehearsals, the pressure was extreme. For once I had a terrific reed. The music came out of me naturally and expressively, and all the other woodwind players responded. It was a passionate elegy for the death of my musical career.

A violinist approached me afterward in the State Theater's locker room. "That was some of the most beautiful playing I've ever heard," he said. I thanked him and turned to pick up my oboe bag. Musicians were always complimenting one another in order to schmooze, and I was tempted to tell him I'd be of no use to him after tonight. He lingered. "No, really, I mean it," he insisted, making certain that I understood he was sincere. "All these years. Why didn't we know you played so well?"

I could have told him that my romantic disasters with oboists had shut me out of the best gigs early on or relegated me to second chair. I could have pointed out that no one claimed the limelight for long anyway. I might have confessed that I preferred the financial security of Broadway, that from depression I sometimes drank too much and no longer practiced enough. Five years ago I would have felt intense anxiety over his compliment, feeling that this one concert was a positive turning point for my musical career; that's what Sydney would have said. But I knew that the night had just been a lovely isolated gift, one perfect plum from a tree that bore little fruit. I thanked the violinist warmly and took the 1 train home.

The night would be long. I had to finish packing before the movers came in the morning to load the Ryder truck I'd rented. I planned to drive myself to North Carolina, back to the house on Burlage Circle where my parents had brought me home as an infant in 1960. I'd spend three weeks with them before driving to California. They were seventy-eight years old now, and I hadn't seen them for more than a few days at a time in twenty-five years.

I could faintly hear a violinist downstairs playing scales with a practice mute clamped on her violin bridge to muffle the sound. It was 2 A.M. The sound of a car alarm's siren suddenly boomed in the emptied bedroom. I looked across West End to the darkened window where I once watched the couple having sex. The mother and her two high school sons must be sleeping. The father had disappeared last year; I guessed they had divorced. I turned back to my closet and removed an armload of clothes.

Thinking again about the violinist's compliment, I folded up the sequined gowns I'd worn to play the occasional solo concerts. My future was unknown but would satisfy me in small ways during every hour of the day, as a child's fairy-princess fantasy could not. I tucked the midnight-blue chiffon of the magic dress from my debut recital inside the cardboard box and taped it securely shut.

Encore
The Lark Ascending

As I DROVE west to California, memories of New York quickly faded. I traveled through states I'd never visited, stopping to hike in the Grand Canyon and watch the sunset turn its walls a flaming orange. Listening to conversations of the other tourists admiring the view, I was struck by the irrelevance of classical music to these people's rich and varied lives. How could I have allowed such an insular incestuous business to rule me for a quarter century? Renewed, I felt like a pioneer driving on across the Mojave, up Highway 5, and finally to Stanford University, which lies thirty miles south of San Francisco.

After a few days on campus, I relaxed and stopped wondering when someone would discover me to be an imposter. Unlike the music business, there was room here in the real world for everyone to learn, work, and enjoy life. Starved for natural beauty after years in the noisy city, I soaked up the Stanford environment. A lemon tree and purple trumpet flowers grew outside my dormitory window. It was so quiet I could hear crickets in the evening, and the air was clean and cool. I ran six miles every morning in the Stanford hills before the sun rose on another day of blue skies. I was in heaven. I was also scared to death.

My brain moved slowly from years of boozy nights in the Broadway pits. I was the oldest journalism student at Stanford by thirteen years. I had no experience arguing points in class or organizing complex ideas. I wasn't used to speaking at all; I had been blowing into an oboe for thirty years. Other students in my Internet journalism class easily published the Web site that was a required assignment, but I could barely type. I didn't even know how to turn on a computer and spent hundreds on high-tech tutors. With so much to do and learn, my interest in drinking quickly disappeared along with my chronic boredom.

Working a local newspaper internship at the *Palo Alto Weekly* for $15 a week humbled me. I entered police statistics into an ancient computer, attended my first city council meeting, and navigated local politics. I wrote stories about solar energy, dot-com start-ups, philanthropy, cycling activists, and Silicon Valley real estate. My subjects included an eighty-year-old librarian who grew psychotropic cacti, the dedicatee of *One Flew Over the Cuckoo's Nest,* and an old hippie named Perusha who got me stoned at the commune Joan Baez had started in 1969.

The work was compelling, but I felt lonely. Although the age difference between me and my classmates didn't bother me, the cultural divide did. I felt like a nineteenth-century cartoon character with my classical music background; I couldn't follow the impassioned discussions carried on by students who were starting their own dot-coms from dorm rooms.

One day, though, the San Francisco Symphony called me to substitute. When I walked onto the Davies Symphony Hall stage, I knew at least one third of the musicians, and the standard rehearsal protocol was comforting. I began a schizophrenic life, driving between classes, my reporting internship, and the various Bay Area performing groups that paid for my living expenses.

I turned forty in the dorm, three thousand miles from the Allendale. I celebrated the milestone with my 1979 Allendale roommate Kathleen Reynolds, who now played principal flute with the part-time Santa Rosa Symphony and taught elementary school in the daytime. We shared dinner at Chez Panisse in Berkeley.

I had worked hard, and now things were going well. My masters thesis and photographs about a Vietnamese newspaper were accepted for publication in Harvard's *Nieman Reports*. I landed a $2,500 feature assignment for *Sierra* magazine. The *San Francisco Examiner* offered me a staff business reporter job, so I scheduled my classes on one marathon weekday and worked the other four. At age forty, I had my first office job ever.

At school, my magazine-class professor asked us to write about a situation that affected us emotionally. When I read my story of Sam's death aloud in class, there was a long silence. "You have to write a book," the professor urged at last, describing my portrayal of the classical music business as "devastating." I waved off his suggestion, afraid to alienate people in the only business where I was sure I could earn a full-time living. Like many classical musicians, I still didn't believe I could be good enough at anything else to be paid for it. People had always acted as if music was my only real talent.

After graduation I used savings from my Broadway salary to buy my first home, a sunny Oakland condominium whose balcony overlooked a swimming pool. I still clung to music jobs, since newspaper journalism didn't pay very well, and drove between Bay Area orchestras in a routine jokingly called the "Freeway Philharmonic." I left the *Examiner* for an art critic's job at a suburban newspaper, and also taught journalism at Stanford and oboe at the University of California-Berkeley. I thought more seriously about a book but was not yet ready to let go of my old life.

At one concert with the San Francisco Contemporary Music Players, I performed a solo piece by the Mexican composer Mario Lavista that was accompanied by eight crystal water glasses. Between the glasses' eerie ringing sounds, some dramatic stage lighting, and the unusual oboe multiphonic chords (producing more than one note simultaneously on a wind instrument by using alternate fingerings), I felt an unusual electricity from the audience.

Something strange was happening with my music-making, although I couldn't put my finger on it. I loved my new writing life, which included reviewing art exhibitions and driving up the California coast to cover tidepools and nature walks for *Sierra*. At the same time, I was starting to look forward to playing the oboe as well, since I didn't *have* to be a musician anymore. I was finding journalism positions through want ads and employment interviews; unlike music, there were plenty of jobs where sleeping with the boss was definitely not a prerequisite. On the other hand, landing the scarce and competitive music work still required a humiliating degree of self-abnegation. It would take a reminder from my former life to make me see the difference clearly and to recognize my own evolution and new self-esteem as well.

While I was playing a production of *South Pacific* with Robert Goulet at the Golden Gate Theater, Boston Pops conductor Keith Lockhart called to ask me out for drinks late the same night, as we had done before in New York. Keith was a familiar link to my old ways of thinking. After wine in the Huntington Hotel's dark-paneled bar, we went upstairs to his room and had sex. I felt empty.

Keith then invited me for a weekend in Salt Lake City, where he was music director of the Utah Symphony. Without thinking carefully, I accepted. The night before my departure he called to cancel because his wife was suddenly visiting him there in order to get pregnant. We discussed the situation, including the sex act, in a series of e-mails. Keith did not offer to reimburse me for my nonrefundable plane fare but did so after I asked him to: a check drawn on a North Carolina account he shared with his mother. I was relieved not to be going to Utah, since I'd recognized my mistake. I came to California to leave these self-destructive behavior patterns behind. What was I doing?

I got nothing out of that night with Keith. I no longer wanted to participate in these tawdry scenarios; I now craved a value-driven life, centered around my own accomplishments. My California years enabled me to view the music business with detachment, and the evening provided me with a final turning point.

It was time to write the book. Almost as soon as I decided, I was offered a Broadway show job in New York, where it would be easier to negotiate a literary agent and publisher. I sold my condo and drove back to New York.

I reentered New York's freelance music world in November of 2002, three years after I'd left. I was forty-two. The *Man of La Mancha* production at the Martin Beck Theater included a pleasant group of musicians assembled by its music director, Bob Billig, whom I knew from *Les Miz* and *Miss Saigon*. I also resumed playing City Center's *Encores!* series and subbing in the New York City Ballet.

Sitting in the ballet pit next to Randy, I felt none of the love for him of our summer relationship fifteen years earlier. Now he had three children and a devoted wife. Yet for some reason Randy wrote out a sixteen-page account of the long-ago love affair between us—that he had never publicly acknowledged—and gave it to me. The torrid story was scribbled on the back of a photocopied *Trio Sonata* by Jan Dismas Zelenka. I tucked it in my oboe bag and listened to the ballet orchestra's performance.

Randy's colleagues were understandably bored after playing *The Nutcracker* forty-five times every December for decades. Fiddlers sawed away vacantly. During one long rest, an ancient bassoonist belched expressively, the sound rippling audibly into the audience. One flutist propped the *Daily Racing Form* on his stand and began playing the perky "Dance of the Mirlitons," possibly for the two-thousandth time in his career. A wind player who disliked him leaned forward and whispered in rhythm, "Take-a-silver-flute-and-then, shoveitupyourass!"

Walking to the subway after the performance, I saw Juilliard students lounging by the conservatory's entrance across Lincoln Center's plaza. Many of them would never find work in music, nor would they be qualified for many other jobs. Unless they had the wherewithal to earn and pay for a second college degree, they would settle for menial retail or office jobs or a dead-end job that required only brief professional training. Except for the occasional star soloist, the luckiest would land a position somewhere like the ballet pit I'd just left. Those who won full-time orchestra positions would worry whether their jobs might disappear. The percentage of orchestras reporting deficits had risen steadily from 37 percent in 1998 to 73 percent in 2003. Only one American orchestra negotiated a salary increase in 2003, with the rest reporting freezes or pay cuts. Some musicians would still be able to earn at least sporadic income on Broadway, since the 2003 theater contract put a moratorium on reducing orchestra size for another ten years.

Music had not become the glamorous and elite profession of Cold War–era fantasy but an overpopulated, stagnant, and low-paying business. Many of its practitioners were highly intelligent and motivated, but they had ended up in careers that barely supported them and offered few opportunities for growth or creativity. Ironically, these players would perform little of the public service that classical music is expected to provide. They would instead demand handouts and contributions for their survival, without asking the big questions: "Why is classical music essential, and do I really enjoy it?"

A field trip to the Allendale should become part of the required conservatory curriculum. The Allendale building, a metaphor for the classical music business, looks worse than ever. The missing water tower roof was never replaced, and the water tank finally failed, gushing into four floors of apartments and unleashing a swarm of cockroaches whose century-old nests had been disturbed. Inside, the elevators creak ominously. On my last visit, my old mailbox was labeled KIM, and its lock was still broken. On the street level, the building's exterior planters were still barren, and a few more cardboard squares patched the basement windows. The ivy had grown long enough to reach the fourth floor, and Jules still stood guard at the door.

However, the building pulsed with sounds of musicians practicing, as it had for decades. I could hear Bobby White's distinctive tenor, probably demonstrating phrasing for one of his students from Manhattan School. The string quartet that rehearsed on the ground floor was practicing Beethoven's *Grosse Fuge*, and an unfamiliar flutist was playing long tones. The plaid curtains in Sam's old apartment had been removed and a cello case now stood inside the window. I ran into a former actress and massage therapist who had lived there thirty years. She was turning forty-nine and had finally found a secretarial job with health benefits. Another tenant told me that Brunhilde had "renovated" certain apartments with cheap appliances and now charged over $2,000 for them. She said that when the tenant moved out, the appliances appeared on the street to be replaced with new "renovations" and higher rent for the next occupants.

After waiting thirty years, Betty married her opera-singer boyfriend after his wife died. They live in the Allendale, spending part of the winter in his Florida apartment. Betty quit her ballet job and now pushes his wheelchair up the Allendale's single step into the lobby. I saw Joan on the street with a new matted dog. A few old tenants trudged by, absorbed in their troubles with their eyes downcast, and did not look up to recognize me.

Sydney left the Allendale in 1998 to move in with her CEO boyfriend. She and I met at the Cottage restaurant before the show, where the waitress recognized us and immediately brought a half-liter of cheap wine, pouring it to the brim in our two glasses. I lifted the wine to my mouth, but it smelled so nasty I set it down again. Sydney took a sip and sighed. She still looked beautiful; she took good care of her hair and skin and worked out at Equinox. I talked enthusiastically of my book and other writing projects. Sydney was supportive, offering to be my editor. The waitress replaced the empty wine carafe with a new one. By the time our usual steamed chicken and broccoli arrived, Sydney's voice began slurring into complaints about the show and the paranoia of competing musicians' motives. "It's so awful," she choroused, reverting to the duet we had performed together for so many years. I was singing an entirely new song, however, and had grown out of our friendship.

Other pieces of my past looked equally absurd in the rearview mirror. I remembered the holidays when I had stayed in New York to "further my career" and play jobs during those busy times. One Christmas, I had sat all alone in my apartment and opened the presents my mother had carefully shipped to me. That evening I had Christmas dinner by myself at the Brew N' Burger across the street from the Broadway Theatre, thought of my parents and brother sitting cozily in our North Carolina living room, and then went inside the theater to spend Christmas night performing *Les Miserables*.

My education now looked like a farce as well. Critics of the North Carolina School of the Arts were becoming more vocal as the school approached its fortieth anniversary in 2005 with only a $17.5 million endowment. Nearly half the government-supported institution's students came from outside North Carolina, and few of its artsy alumni earned enough income to donate to the school. "If they could show me what the benefit is to the state and the average person, I might have a different attitude," said state representative Cary Allred in 2003, declaring the school's existence unjustified.

As NCSA chancellor Wade Hobgood explained in a newspaper interview, "There's that automatic assumption that we have strange things happening here." He was right. In 2004, North Carolina auditors determined that a school administrator had diverted nearly $1 million in foundation money for country club memberships, a Cadillac Escalade, and a down payment on a million-dollar condominium. The scandal was compared to Enron and predicted to represent just the tip of the iceberg.

The two male dance teachers whom my 1970s classmates had dubbed Crotch and Groin had been forced to resign in 1995, after a former student sued the school, alleging the pair had seduced him. My high school lover, the flute instructor twenty-seven years my senior, had retired. He married one of his three daughters' former childhood playmates and sired another child at age seventy. There were sad stories about NCSA's star students. Patrick Bissell had become a star with American Ballet Theater and then died of a drug overdose in 1987. José, my violin-smashing first boyfriend, was struggling in Kansas City to complete his first bachelor's degree at age fifty-two. He was majoring in math.

I started writing about classical music for *The New York Times*, first with an op-ed piece during the Broadway strike. The essay was well received. Before long I spoke to a *Times* editor and gave him a list of story ideas. He chose an article about the exorbitant salaries of "nonprofit" orchestra executives and conductors that ran as the cover story of the Arts & Leisure section.

Some of the pay packages are huge, many of them at orchestras that have run deficits for years. At the New York Philharmonic, conductor Lorin Maazel earned $2.3 million for fourteen weeks of work. Executive director Zarin Mehta got a $600,000 salary plus $150,000 in benefits, despite overseeing the orchestra during a year that included a botched move from Lincoln Center to Carnegie Hall and three canceled tours. Soloists also command huge salaries, with Itzhak Perlman said to charge $65,000 per night and Yo-Yo Ma, $80,000. The large sums not only challenge the budgets of these so-called charitable organizations but also destroy morale within the ranks of musicians who earn a fraction of their bosses' pay.

Communicating with the orchestras sometimes proves difficult. As organizations granted tax-exempt status by the Internal Revenue Service, orchestras are obliged to release the salaries of their highest-paid employees and contractors. Almost without exception, they refuse to provide financial information any more recent than the year-old tax documents available online. This was particularly frustrating in the case of the Boston Symphony, which had just hired Metropolitan Opera music director James Levine as its conductor. Levine's salary had not yet showed up on Boston Symphony forms. At his other job, the Metropolitan Opera, the salary was concealed in tax documents that listed two independent contractors—whose payments totaled $2.2 million—"Phramus" and "Dry Fly," one or both of whom could have been Levine.

A disturbing picture emerges. Conductors and executives are regarded as a class of workers whose superior skills entitle them to demand astronomical salaries from nonprofit organizations that are already in debt. As the oxymoronic concept of such classical music "stars" grows, the musicians themselves begin to appear peripheral to the organizations, or even the music interpretation. One midwestern conductor I spoke to said that board members don't respect the musicians because they are willing to work for such meager wages and benefits. (The conductor himself earned a salary exceeding $130,000 for his season of under twenty weeks.)

Sadly, many arts organizations like orchestras, opera and ballet companies, and performing arts centers are failing to fulfill their missions because they are not functioning as charities providing a public service. The people most likely to benefit from these "nonprofit" groups are a handful of star performers and administrators, as well as wealthy donors who receive a tax deduction for their financial contributions to organizations that, themselves, pay no taxes. Many lower- and middle-class citizens interested in attending cannot afford ticket prices, which have risen sharply in an attempt to cover escalating costs.

I discovered huge salary discrepancies among orchestras of similar budget size. In presenting five weekends of concerts, Connecticut's Stamford Symphony spent a total of $847,000 on expenses ranging from musician salaries, advertising, and fund-raising, yet paid executive director Barbara Soroca $105,000, a salary that was 12 percent of the orchestra's total expenses. A few miles away, the Greenwich Symphony also put on a similar season of five weekends of concerts but spent only $465,000. Its president, Mary Radcliffe, took no compensation at all.

The New York Philharmonic was particularly elusive. Its public re-lations director did not return my calls for two weeks. He spent our two brief phone conversations discussing "the media" instead of providing information that might have tempered an unflattering portrait of the or-chestra and its administration.

The salary story piece ran in *The New York Times* on July 4, 2004. The responses I received were almost all positive, although many were transparent; musicians who hadn't acknowledged me for years now wanted me to help them with their own publicity. Could I place an article about their chamber group in *The New York Times*? Did I have friends who could write up their summer festivals? Their voices were filled with desperation.

I received two negative messages. The first came from a prominent musician whose salary of over $350,000 was revealed in the story. He complained that I'd let "the world" know he was underpaid, because he suspected one of his competitors earned slightly more. The second message came from a symphony representative who said I'd miscalcu-lated the percentage increase of their president's raise. As it turned out, the executive had calculated the percentage equation backward, basing it on the salary amount that included the raise instead of the pre-raise salary. That phone call ended quickly.

As I continued learning about nonprofit organizations, I began to see a pattern. Major health research centers, museums, performing arts groups, and university endowments pay disproportionate executive com-pensation compared to other types of public organizations. In many cases the nonprofit structure has become a new scheme for members of the middle class to earn big money by declaring unique knowledge of arts or other specific fields, claims that much of the public is too intimidated to question or challenge.

The musicians, however, were relieved to have the information out in the open after my *Times* article appeared. Through a delegate to the ICSOM convention, I heard that my story opened up the topic of con-ductors' and administrators' salaries for the first time in contract talks. I felt I had at last done something constructive for classical music. The uproar over the story subsided over the next month, and I began working on a second *Times* article about drugs used for stage fright, with several more ideas in the works.

There *are* positive signs in the orchestral business. Some organizations are either shifting their priorities or downsizing. The two major West Coast orchestras, for example, are leading something of a revolution. Under the artistic direction of Michael Tilson Thomas, the San Francisco Symphony has been drawing record audiences with its intelligent contemporary music programs. The futuristic Disney Hall in Los Angeles, designed by Frank Gehry, has become an icon of that city's cultural renaissance. At its center is the Los Angeles Philharmonic, which under the guidance of managing director Deborah Borda and music director Esa-Pekka Salonen has achieved both financial stability and musical relevance, with accessible concert formats at both Disney Hall and the Hollywood Bowl.

A trend has also emerged for larger orchestras to experiment with hiring several regular conductors instead of relying on a single absentee music director. The New York Philharmonic will play not only under its music director Lorin Maazel, but also with David Robertson, Adam Gilbert, and Ricardo Muti. The Atlanta Symphony employs two conductors, Robert Spano and Donald Runnicles, and the Pittsburgh Symphony added a trio of conductors who will trade off concerts. This experiment may provide a more consistent musical identity for the orchestras or it may become a colossal expense, as not one but three music directors demand enormous salaries.

It will take years for orchestras to reconcile the needs of musicians with those of their listeners. One major orchestra's executive said that his job revolved around finding ways to meet the musicians' full-time employment demands rather than serving the audience. Another asked plaintively why the musicians were so belligerent during contract negotiations. Although the top ten orchestras are not likely to shorten their seasons, smaller orchestras are already cutting both season length and orchestra size. In doing so, they put the needs of their communities first.

Symphonies that have gone bankrupt and reorganized with smaller expectations and shorter seasons include those in Oakland, California; Denver and Colorado Springs, Colorado; and Birmingham, Alabama, and they are thriving as part-time orchestras with schedules in proportion to their region's population. Those sticking with the old full-time model are unlikely to succeed. Yet for some musicians, an orchestra is an all-or-nothing proposition, a local expense that their adopted communities are required to bankroll whether they like it or not. "We're not going to be the poster child for making per-service orchestras out of full-time bands," said one unemployed woodwind player in the former Savannah Symphony, which went out of business in 2003 under a crushing debt.

Musicians are finally beginning to understand that the way they have done business is no longer working. When four of the "big five" orchestras came up for contract negotiation simultaneously in the fall of 2004, Philadelphia, Chicago, and Cleveland were rumored to be considering strikes. At first, musicians of the Philadelphia Orchestra would not budge on issues like eliminating the thirteenth viola chair, complaining that such an action would compromise their artistic integrity. However, as contracts expired and talks continued for weeks, all three orchestras finally settled. This time, musicians agreed to reducing orchestra size (and the collective cost of full-time benefits) through attrition, higher healthcare premiums, and more flexible scheduling that will allow performances to break free of formal concert formats.

The classical music business is experiencing a kind of market correction, as groups reduce the number of formal concerts they produce and provide, instead, more intimate and convenient performances within their communities. Perhaps classical music could learn from the diamond companies, which have transformed a relatively common mineral into something precious by limiting its abundance in the marketplace.

Good music, accessibly presented, is not a hard sell. On a morning television show in early 2004, I saw the beautiful soprano Renee Fleming performing on the air with her pianist, dressed in a simple pants outfit with a casual, contemporary hairstyle and little jewelry. She looked nothing like the stereotypical opera diva. The camera angle showed pedestrians in the background, gathering on the sidewalk outside the broadcast studio's windows as Fleming began singing her aria. Almost immediately, the listeners' faces softened. The crowd grew larger and everyone watched her intently, as if the world around them had disappeared.

I imagine most of these people thought they didn't like classical music, yet they were mesmerized by Fleming's simple performance.

The same listeners might not have enjoyed a typical concert setting so much, forced to sit for two hours or more and absorb sounds that tell no story. For that matter, I have always disliked attending concerts myself. I recently went to a New Jersey Symphony concert in order to hear a friend play a concerto with the group. Even in the wealthy New York area community of Bergen County, the audience was sparse, and almost everyone was over fifty. I watched sour-faced musicians drift onstage, some of them in wrinkled outfits. In between pieces, stagehands took forever to reset the stage, yet the auditorium lights were left dark so that we could not even read our programs in the interim. I left at intermission, wondering why the people around me had paid to attend such a boring event.

As I worked on this book, I played shows at night and wrote during the day in my new condo perched atop the New Jersey Palisades. From its windows, Manhattan looks like a surreal film backdrop rather than the inescapable prison I had considered the city to be only five years before. Across the Hudson River I can just glimpse the tip of the Allendale's water tower, although it is hard to spot among grander rooftops, which in turn are dwarfed by the city's shiny new skyscrapers.

I am forty-four now. My life has paralleled America's so-called culture boom, an unprecedented era of interest in and support for culture that began in the sixties. The boom went bust in many ways as the arts community developed in a vacuum over four decades. Outdated rhetoric charging that the arts are a "necessity" sounds hollow at a time when so many Americans are hungry, homeless, unemployed, and without decent health care. Ironically, some of them are performers and artists. Culture can improve the spirit in many ways, but only for those who can afford the time and money to attend performances or become involved in making art themselves.

Classical music has built a fortress that alienates audiences and has priced itself out of reach of the casual listener. Many of its performers are miserable, as revealed by mediocre performances that further repel the ticket-buying public. No one has ended up a winner, except for a handful of multimillionaire musical superstars and six-figure arts administrators, many of whom are unqualified to earn nearly this salary in any other business. In music, however, there are few gatekeepers.

Why are so many young people still planning to become professional classical musicians? Why is musicianship regarded so highly that young people are encouraged to train exclusively for a career in an industry that is clearly failing? A little girl wearing pink hair bows and playing a quarter-size violin is adorable. A sixty-year-old fiddler who can't afford health insurance, has no retirement account or savings, and is virtually unemployable is not. Music schools, teachers, parents, and students need to ask themselves hard questions about the true value of their craft and how it might best serve their interests, the future of its students, and the community around them.

A young person who dreamily "wants to go to Juilliard" or "be a concert pianist" should research the reality of these statements. Seek out a variety of professional musicians: soloists, teachers, and orchestral, theatrical, and freelance musicians. Tag along for an afternoon or evening. See where they live. Ask what their days are really like and how they pay their living expenses. Ask if they like what they do and why. Most important, ask yourself if you are willing to sacrifice hours to tedious practice and nights, weekends, and holidays to playing concerts at times friends and relatives are socializing and relaxing with one another. How do you feel about long periods of substandard pay, lack of health insurance, and possible unemployment? Do you love music, or are you just hooked by the attention your performances bring? Somebody else is paying the bills now, but that won't always be the case. If you truly have a passion for classical music, by all means pursue your dreams. You are one of the lucky ones.

Parents of talented children should ask plenty of questions. Is your child receiving a scholarship to music school because he or she is a budding Heifetz or because the school is desperate to recruit new students to fill its empty classrooms? Perhaps the music student could gain a more valuable education by applying to a liberal arts college that needs musicians to fill its orchestra. Is your child receiving an adequate general education? Is he or she genuinely enjoying the music? It is possible to receive both quality music training and a well-rounded academic education by enrolling at a conservatory that is part of a larger university, like those at Indiana University and Oberlin College.

It is essential to learn what really goes on during the child's private lessons, which take place one-on-one behind closed doors. When else have you handed your child over to a stranger, unsupervised? Many of my friends have been confronted with sexual misconduct, sometimes extreme, in this private setting with a primary teacher who can exercise enormous influence in their lives. The music business is largely populated by generous and ethical teachers. Unfortunately, like any other field it also shelters sexual predators of varying degrees who abuse their positions of power. I was surprised when not one of my Stanford professors would allow a closed door during private conferences with me. Music schools should be no different, perhaps requiring that a window remain uncovered in the door of every teaching studio.

Audiences need to ask their local symphony, during the next "emergency" fund drive, how much the executives, conductors, and soloists are making. Look up the 990 forms yourself at www.guidestar.org. You will find the salaries on page four, page seven, or in the list of directors at the end of the document. How much is the group spending on fund-raising and marketing? What is the orchestra doing to cut costs? How large is the staff and how many weeks does each employee work? If the concerts are not selling out, why aren't they producing fewer performances of higher quality instead? Go to a concert even if you don't "know" music and then speak your mind. It's your money. It's your symphony.

The local orchestra is a community resource, subsidized by taxpayers. Symphonies are classified as public charities, just like food banks, public hospitals, libraries, and museums. They do not pay taxes. They are funded by a system of incentives that give donors tax breaks on their contributions. By the nature of this IRS-granted status, orchestras are expected to provide a public service, and taxpayers have every right to question their expenditures, even if they don't know Mozart from Moby.

Arguments over a perceived decline in interest of classical music have become too noisy to let the beauty of a fine performance speak for itself.

Music is a language anyone in the world can understand, even without a background in the arts. What's more, classical music *isn't* on the decline; audiences have actually increased slightly over the last twenty years. It's just that they're bombarded with an absurdly large increase in the number of performances that enable the glut of full-time musicians, arts administrators, and consultants who resulted from the culture boom's now-stalled momentum to make a living.

The role of classical music in American society has changed since 1960. In the thirties, forties, and fifties, music had been a part of everyday life for Americans, many of whom played instruments or sang together as amateurs. Today, classical music has become peripheral and irrelevant to mainstream life. It is regarded as an incomprehensible art that must be performed perfectly or not at all. Even in recent years, the number of American instrumentalists has dropped markedly. In 1992, some 7.8 million Americans played instruments, but that number shrank to 3.7 million—less than half—by 2002, according to the National Endowment for the Arts.

Today, amateur musicians are conservatory-trained professionals who cannot find work. Typically, their lives are the reverse of those of the 1950s amateurs—highly trained in their hobby but uneducated in whatever becomes their money-making career. Instead of earning a college degree in a field that will support them adequately and playing music in their spare time, they have spent their college years refining the musical talent that will become only a pastime. They are unprepared for professions or day jobs to support them financially and may flounder through life doing nonmusical work that does not use the high levels of ambition and intelligence many gifted musicians possess. True amateur musicians lose out as well, reporting that they have a hard time finding playing opportunities, now that community orchestras and chamber music groups are filled with conservatory graduates.

I'm one of those part-time musicians now. When I do play music, it is a joy. The reality of performing full-time wasn't the fantasy I'd imagined as a little girl. What offers me a meaningful life today are the infinite possibilities in our modern world, of which music is only one. Thousands of people have been influenced by the *Sierra* magazine articles I've written about environmental conservation. Many more are reading my *New York Times* stories about classical music, which I hope will open a window to new listeners.

Sitting in my condo this clear night in November, Manhattan looks more beautiful than ever. The Empire State Building is lit up in autumn colors of orange and burgundy. I had always loved fall because of its promise of new beginnings, until every autumn became hopeless and repetitive. This year, though, I am renewed and confident. Now I have the knowledge and the voice to make every autumn new and better. In the end, I didn't need a magic dress at all.

Acknowledgments

I AM GRATEFUL to the many people who shared their memories, expertise, and support to this story. Lisa Monheit's copyediting and reading were indispensable. Other friends include Robert White, Robert Sylvester, Margo Garrett, Kathy Canfield, Christopher Soderlund, Noelle Tretick Gosling, Kristin Quigley-Brye, William J. Baumol, Margaret Steele, Clifford Tretick, Geoffrey Wall, David Sherman, Patty Drury, Elisabeth Gilaspy, Kevin Beavers, Lisa Carey, Ellen Slezak, Erin Flanagan, Jerry Pasewicz, Michael Avedon, and Joan Petrokofsky. Many thanks also to Kathryn Shattuck, Jorge Perez, Barry Lopez, and Paddy Woodworth for reading my manuscript or proposal.

A special thanks goes to Martin Sanders, who took the time to share memories of his beloved brother, Samuel.

Research was aided by John Shepard of the New York Public Library for the Performing Arts, Patrice Slattery of the North Carolina School of the Arts, Jane Gottlieb and Jeni Dahmus of the Juilliard School archives, and the North Carolina Collection at the University of North Carolina in Chapel Hill. From the American Federation of Musicians, Bill Dennison, William Moriarity, Florence Nelson, and Eric Beers provided unique information and documents. Others lending essential perspective include Joseph Polisi, Nick Webster, and Henry Fogel. Conversations with authors Norman Lebrecht and Alice Goldfarb Marquis, and composer and journalist Greg Sandow provided valuable context.

This book would never have been possible without the superior journalism training I received through a full fellowship at Stanford University. I thank professors William Woo, James Risser, Larry Bensky, and

Ted Glasser, as well as my former *San Francisco Examiner* editor Steven Zuckerman and *Sierra* magazine editor Paul Rauber, for their literary guidance.

The woodwind section in the 2002 Broadway production of *Man of La Mancha*—flutist Kathleen Nester, clarinetist Lino Gomez, and bassoonist Braden Toan—encouraged me as I edited in the Al Hirschfeld Theater's orchestra pit. A residency at the MacDowell Colony in Peterborough, New Hampshire, and another at the Kimmel Harding Nelson Center for the Arts in Nebraska City, Nebraska, gave me the time and space to write. Thanks also to Kathy Puzey, Julie Blake Fisher, and the Book Clinic of Nebraska City.

My agent, James Fitzgerald, promoted me like a rock 'n' roll star, while Grove/Atlantic president Morgan Entrekin saw high opera in my backstage tale. Brando Skyhorse was the most thoughtful editor imaginable, transforming not only this manuscript but my ideas and writing as well. Thanks also to Kevin Goering of Coudert Brothers, who provided legal counsel.

I found courage to enter my "jungle" through the support of Dale Maharidge, from the book's inception in his Stanford magazine writing class to its delivery four years later. I also thank my brother, Bruce McGarrity Tindall, and most of all my parents, George and Blossom Tindall, for their constant love and confidence in me. I offer this book as a gift on their fifty-ninth wedding anniversary, with the promise of a bright future chapter that they have made possible.

Notes

Chapter Two

1. Alice Goldfarb Marquis, *Art Lessons: Learning from the Rise and Fall of Public Arts Funding.* New York: Basic Books, 1995: 26.

Chapter Four

1. Alvin Toffler, *The Culture Consumers: Art and Affluence in America.* Baltimore: Penguin, 1965: 21–22.

2. Joseph Wesley Zeigler, *Arts in Crisis: The National Endowment for the Arts Versus America.* Chicago: Chicago Review Press, 1994: 2.

3. John Kreidler, "Leverage Lost: The Non-Profit Arts in the Post-Ford Era." *In Motion,* February 16, 1996. < http: /www.inmotionmagazine.com/lost .html>

4. Lawrence Levine, *Highbrow/Lowbrow.* Cambridge, MA: Harvard University Press: 26–28.

5. Ibid: 90–97.

6. Paul DiMaggio, *Nonprofit Enterprise in the Arts.* New York: Oxford University Press: 46.

7. Marquis: 2.

8. Lawrence Levine: 128–29.

9. DiMaggio: 115.

10. Marquis: 6.

11. Marquis: 25.

12. Toffler: 38.

13. Marquis: 25.

14. Marquis: 28.

15. The Rockefeller Brothers Fund, *The Performing Arts: Problems and Prospects: The Rockefeller Panel Report on the Future of Theatre, Dance, and Music in America*: 11–12.

16. Paul Goldberger, "West Side Fixer-Upper." *The New Yorker*, July 7, 2003.

17. Edgar B. Young, "Lincoln Center Aids Ancient Spa: Purchasing Travertine from Quarries Outside Rome." *New York Times*, August 27, 1963: 33.

18. Marquis: 41–48.

19. Harold Taubman, "Lincoln Center Reorganizing in Crisis." *New York Times*, January 14, 1969: 34.

20. Harold Taubman, Lincoln Center Ends Its Capital Fund Drive." *New York Times*, July 2, 1969: 34.

21. Harold Taubman, "Lincoln Center Reorganizing in Crisis." *New York Times*, January 14, 1969: 34.

22. Zeigler: 6.

23. "WPA Music and Theatre Projects in Danger." *Allegro*, May 1938: 6.

24. Marquis: 101–102.

25. W. McNeil Lowry, editor. *The Arts & Public Policy in the United States*. Englewood Cliffs, NJ: Prentice-Hall, 1984: 52–53.

26. Marquis: 61.

27. Marquis: 92–93.

28. Marquis: 92–94.

29. Marquis: 66–68.

Chapter Five

1. James Bovard, "Suburban Guerrilla." *The American Spectator*, September 1994.

2. Alice Goldfarb Marquis, *Art Lessons: Learning from the Rise and Fall of Public Arts Funding*. New York: Basic Books, 1995: 15.

3. Judith Kogan, *Nothing but the Best*. New York: Random House: 223.

Chapter Seven

1. Donal Henahan, "Women Are Breaking the Symphonic Barriers." *New York Times*, January 23, 1983.

2. Ibid.

Chapter Eight

1. Will Crutchfield, "Why Today's Orchestras Are Adrift." *New York Times*, December 22, 1985: Sec. 2 p. 1.

Chapter Nine

1. "Violinist Arrested on Drug Charges." *New York Times*, April 6, 1983.
2. "Cleveland Opera Performer Found Dead." *Associated Press*, December 1, 1998.
3. Walter Price, "The Rehabilitation of Eugene Fodor." *New York Times*, December 31, 1989.
4. Michael McLeod, "Juilliard Graduate, Master Cellist, Crack Addict, Prostitute." *Sun-Sentinel*, August 15, 1993.

Chapter Eleven

1. Judith Miller, "As Patrons Age, Future of Arts Is Uncertain." *New York Times*, February 12, 1996.
2. Thor Eckert, Jr., "Supporting the Arts Helps Shine Up the Corporate Image." *Christian Science Monitor*, November 6, 1984.

Chapter Twelve

1. John Kreidler, "Leverage Lost: The Non-Profit Arts in the Post-Ford Era." *In Motion*, February 16, 1996. <http://www.inmotionmagazine.com/lost.html>
2. Howard Taubman, "The Philharmonic—What's Wrong With It and Why." *New York Times*, April 29, 1956: 139.
3. Alice Goldfarb Marquis, *Art Lessons: Learning from the Rise and Fall of Public Arts Funding*. New York: Basic Books 1995: 144.
4. Joseph Wesley Zeigler, *Arts in Crisis: The National Endowment for the Arts Versus America*. Chicago: Chicago Review Press, 1994: 58.
5. Donal Henahan, "Dip in Concert Audiences Troubles Impresarios." *New York Times*, December 21, 1968.
6. Marquis: 145.
7. Ibid.
8. Ibid.
9. Waldemar A. Nielsen, "Where Have All the Arts Patrons Gone?" *New York Times*, October 26, 1980: Sec. 2 p. 1.
10. Marquis: 172.
11. "Portrait of the 1980s." *New York Times*, December 24, 1989.
12. Zeigler: 65.
13. William H. Honan, "Arts Dollars Pinched as Never Before." *New York Times*, May 28, 1989: Sec. 2 p. 1.

14. "Corporate Giving to the Arts Dipped 18% in 3 Years." *The Chronicle of Philanthropy*, January 12, 1993.
15. Donal Henahan, "Our Orchestras Are Splintering." *New York Times*, September 13, 1987: Sec. 2 p. 35.
16. David Finkel, "Classical Survival." *Washington Post*, December 1, 1991.
17. Zeigler: 153.
18. Alan Flippen, "Fiscal Woes Silence Renowned Buffalo Orchestra." *Associated Press*, September 21, 1990.

Chapter Thirteen

1. Peter Goodman, "Today's Classical Music, The Financial Blues." *Newsday*, November 13, 1990.

Chapter Fifteen

1. Bernard Rosenberg and Ernest Harburg, *The Broadway Musical*. New York: New York University Press, 1993.
2. Ibid.
3. Frank Rich, "Miss Saigon Arrives, from the Old School," *New York Times*, April 12, 1991.

Chapter Sixteen

1. Greg Sandow, "Behind the Tuxedo Curtain." *Village Voice*, September 17, 1996.
2. Samuel Lipman, "The Culture of Classical Music Today." *The New Criterion*, September 1991.
3. Paul R. Judy, "Life and Work in Symphony Orchestras: An Interview with J. Richard Hackman." *Harmony*, April 1996: 8.
4. Scott Duncan, "Strikes Ultimately May Stop the Music." *Orange County Register*, December 22, 1996.
5. Allan Ulrich, "The Day the Music Died." *San Francisco Examiner*, January 12, 1997.

Chapter Nineteen

1. Nicole Edwards, "Orchestra Suit Settled," *Poughkeepsie Journal*, June 16, 2001.

Chapter Twenty

1. Ellen Winner and Lois Hetland, *The Arts and Academic Achievement: What the Evidence Shows*. Los Angeles: The Getty Center, 2001.

2. George Seltzer, *Music Matters: The Performer and the American Federation of Musicians*. Metuchen, NJ: The Scarecrow Press, 1989: 225.

3. Bachelors', masters', and doctors' degrees conferred by degree-granting institutions, 2001. National Bureau of Education Statistics. <http://nces.ed.gov/programs/digest/d02/tables/dt255.asp>

4. John Kreidler, "Leverage Lost: The Non-Profit Arts in the Post-Ford Era." *In Motion*, February 16, 1996. <http://www.inmotionmagazine.com/lost4.html>

Chapter Twenty-One

1. Peter Goodman, "A Heavy Blow to NY's Recording World." *Newsday*, December 9, 1993.

2. Bradley Bambargar, "Career-Building in a Post-Recording World," MusicalAmerica.com, 2001. <www.musicalamerica.com/features2001/careers.htm>

3. Susan Elliott, "Fun Facts About Violinist Kennedy." *Atlanta Constitution*, April 2, 2000.

4. Norman Lebrecht, *"Who Killed Classical Music?"*: 287.

Bibliography

Banner, Leslie, and Douglas C. Zinn, ed. *A Passionate Preference: The Story of the North Carolina School of the Arts.* Ashboro, NC: Down Home Press, 1987.

DiMaggio, Paul J. *Nonprofit Enterprise in the Arts: Studies in Mission & Constraint.* New York: Oxford University Press, 1986.

Grout, Donald Jay. *A History of Western Music.* New York: W. W. Norton, 1973.

Howitt, Basil. *Love Lives of the Great Composers.* Toronto: Sound and Vision Publishing, 1995.

Kogan, Judith. *Nothing But the Best: The Struggle for Protection at the Juilliard School.* New York: Random House, 1989.

Kreidler, John. "Leverage Lost: The Non-Profit Arts in the Post-Ford Era." *In Motion,* February 16, 1996. < http://www.inmotionmagazine.com/lost.html>

Kusinitz, Marc. *The Encyclopedia of Psychoactive Drugs: Drugs & the Arts.* New York: Chelsea House Publishers, 1987.

Lebrecht, Norman. *The Maestro Myth: Great Conductors in Pursuit of Power.* New York: Citadel Press, 2001.

Lebrecht, Norman. *Who Killed Classical Music? Maestros, Managers, and Corporate Politics.* Secaucus, NJ: Birch Lane Press, 1998.

Levine, Faye. *The Culture Barons: An Analysis of Power and Money in the Arts.* New York: Thomas Y. Crowell, 1976.

Levine, Lawrence W. *Highbrow/Lowbrow: The Emergence of Cultural Hierarchy in America.* Cambridge: Harvard University Press, 1990.

Lipman, Samuel. *Arguing for Music: Arguing for Culture.* Boston: David R. Godine Publisher, 1990.

Lowry, W. McNeil, ed. *The Arts & Public Policy in the United States.* Englewood Cliffs, NJ: Prentice-Hall, 1984.

Marquis, Alice Goldfarb. *Art Lessons: Learning from the Rise and Fall of Public Arts Funding.* New York: Basic Books, 1995.

The Performing Arts: Problems and Prospects: The Rockefeller Panel Report on the Future of Theatre, Dance, and Music in America. New York: Rockefeller Brothers Fund, 1965.

Rosenberg, Bernard, and Ernest Harburg. *The Broadway Musical.* New York: New York University Press, 1993.

Seltzer, George. *Music Matters: The Performer and the American Federation of Musicians.* Metuchen, NJ: The Scarecrow Press, 1989.

Toffler, Alvin. *The Culture Consumers: Art and Affluence in America.* Baltimore: Penguin, 1965.

Zeigler, Joseph Wesley. *Arts in Crisis: The National Endowment for the Arts Versus America.* Chicago: Chicago Review Press, 1994.